101 916 603 7

SHEFFIELD HALLAM UNIVERSITY
LEARNING CENTRE
WITHDRAWN FROM STOCK

Developing Web A

D1434987

ONE WEEK L

Developing Web Applications

Ralph Moseley

Middlesex University

John Wiley & Sons, Ltd

Copyright © 2007   John Wiley & Sons Ltd, The Atrium, Southern Gate, Chichester,
                      West Sussex PO19 8SQ, England

                      Telephone (+44) 1243 779777

Email (for orders and customer service enquiries): cs-books@wiley.co.uk
Visit our Home Page on www.wiley.com

All Rights Reserved. No part of this publication may be reproduced, stored in a retrieval system or transmitted in
any form or by any means, electronic, mechanical, photocopying, recording, scanning or otherwise, except under
the terms of the Copyright, Designs and Patents Act 1988 or under the terms of a licence issued by the Copyright
Licensing Agency Ltd, 90 Tottenham Court Road, London W1T 4LP, UK, without the permission in writing of
the Publisher. Requests to the Publisher should be addressed to the Permissions Department, John Wiley & Sons
Ltd, The Atrium, Southern Gate, Chichester, West Sussex PO19 8SQ, England, or emailed to
permreq@wiley.co.uk, or faxed to (+44) 1243 770620.

Designations used by companies to distinguish their products are often claimed as trademarks. All brand names and
product names used in this book are trade names, service marks, trademarks or registered trademarks of their
respective owners. The Publisher is not associated with any product or vendor mentioned in this book.

This publication is designed to provide accurate and authoritative information in regard to the subject matter
covered. It is sold on the understanding that the Publisher is not engaged in rendering professional services. If
professional advice or other expert assistance is required, the services of a competent professional should be sought.

Other Wiley Editorial Offices

John Wiley & Sons Inc., 111 River Street, Hoboken, NJ 07030, USA

Jossey-Bass, 989 Market Street, San Francisco, CA 94103-1741, USA

Wiley-VCH Verlag GmbH, Boschstr. 12, D-69469 Weinheim, Germany

John Wiley & Sons Australia Ltd, 42 McDougall Street, Milton, Queensland 4064, Australia

John Wiley & Sons (Asia) Pte Ltd, 2 Clementi Loop #02-01, Jin Xing Distripark, Singapore 129809

John Wiley & Sons Canada Ltd, 6045 Freemont Blvd, Mississauga, ONT, L5R 4J3, Canada

Wiley also publishes its books in a variety of electronic formats. Some content that appears
in print may not be available in electronic books.

Library of Congress Cataloging-in-Publication Data:

Moseley, Ralph.
   Developing Web applications/Ralph Moseley.
      p. cm.
   Includes bibliographical references and index.
   ISBN-13: 978-0-470-01719-7 (pbk. : alk. paper)
   ISBN-10: 0-470-01719-8 (pbk. : alk. paper)
   Web site development. 2. Application software–Development. 3. Web programming. I. Title.
   TK5105.888.M684 2006
   006.7'6–dc22

                                                                        2006017996

British Library Cataloguing in Publication Data

A catalogue record for this book is available from the British Library

ISBN-13: 978-0-470-01719-7 (PB)
ISBN-10: 0-470-01719-8 (PB)

Typeset in 10/12 Bembo by Laserwords Private Limited,
Printed and bound in Great Britain by Bell & Bain, Glasg
This book is printed on acid-free paper responsibly manu
in which at least two trees are planted for each one used f

Contents

CHAPTER 1: **THE WAY THE WEB WORKS**   **1**

A basic introduction to how the WWW works within the context of the Internet with supporting protocols and applications.

CHAPTER 2: **THE CLIENT SIDE: HTML** 23

This chapter starts to look at the client side and static Web page development using HTML. You will learn how to develop simple Web pages and formatting, together with tables, images and frames.

CHAPTER 3: **FROM HTML TO XHTML**

Here we continue the exploration of HTML into XHTML. You will learn about the various standards that have been developed for HTML. More advanced HTML will also be studied, and the ability to control search engines, cache refresh and meta information.

CHAPTER 4: **GETTING SOME STYLE: CSS**   **75**

In this chapter you will learn how to present and control the format of Web pages using CSS. This includes the ability to precisely control the positioning and attributes of content while maintaining the structure of the document itself.

CHAPTER 5: **JAVASCRIPT: INTRODUCTION TO CLIENT SIDE SCRIPTING**   **107**

This chapter will prepare you for developing with this popular scripting language, showing you the syntax and possibilities of use. The aims here are to show you how it is placed within a page, variables, strings, arrays and loops. Program flow is also discussed and how conditional operators and commands are used.

In this chapter you will learn about using objects in JavaScript, both the built-in types and creating your own. You will also learn about the Document Object Model (DOM), which allows HTML documents to be manipulated and accessed. Forms and ways of validating information submitted are explored here too.

The aim of this chapter is to bring dynamic aspects of site design together. You will learn about animation, caching, event driven scripting and browser compatibility. It's in this chapter you will also find out more about compatibility and the need to provide alternatives for different browsers.

CHAPTER 8: XML: EXTENSIBLE MARKUP LANGUAGE 167

In this chapter you will learn about the basics of XML and how it can be used to store information away from the mechanism of processing or formatting of such data. You will learn how to build simple XML files, and be able to manipulate and refer to them.

CHAPTER 9: XML, XSL AND XSLT: TRANSFORMING XML 183

The aim of this chapter is to learn about and explore the possibilities of using XML as the starting point for data to be transformed into other target formats using XSLT. Style sheets are used and linked to documents. It is shown here that it is possible to process XML with a browser or a programing language on the client side.

CHAPTER 10: WEB SERVICES, FEEDS AND BLOGS   197

Here you will learn about three important areas of Web activity: how it is possible to create language- and platform-independent services that utilize common Web protocols and XML; how information can be disseminated automatically to interested people; and finally, the phenomenon of the blog!

CHAPTER 11: **THE SERVER SIDE** **213**

This chapter aims to give you your first contact with the server side and introduces you to the server; the various possible packages and platforms; how to set up and the options involved; testing your server; logging users and dealing with dynamic IPs.

CHAPTER 12: **PHP 1: STARTING TO SCRIPT ON THE SERVER SIDE** **231**

This chapter gives a basic introduction to PHP and dynamic programing on the server side. You will learn how to develop simple PHP, how to structure your programs and embed script within HTML.

CHAPTER 13: **PHP 2: ARRAYS, FUNCTIONS AND FORMS**   **251**

Here, you learn how to further manipulate data within PHP and in the process get to grips with new functions, loop structures and the verification of data input through forms. Simple arrays to dynamic structures are discussed, along with the ability to manipulate strings through special functions. Attention is particularly given to how to enlist specific features of PHP when processing data and how these can be used to add security.

CHAPTER 14: **MORE ADVANCED PHP**   **273**

The aim here is to provide a glimpse of the further possibilities within PHP, including cookies, sessions, objects and more advanced file handling.

CHAPTER 15: **NETWORK AND WEB SECURITY**   **297**

The aim of this chapter is to make you aware of threats to online security that you and your users must guard against. The most common forms of attack are studied, such as viruses and worms, cross site scripting, email problems, Trojan horses, phishing and many other mechanisms. Possible solutions are also looked into, including firewalls and anti-virus software.

CHAPTER 16: **DATABASES**   **315**

The aim of this chapter is to help you understand databases so that they can easily be utilized in your Web applications and sites. The basic idea of the database is explored, together with how well it can be linked in with server side scripting. All the basic functions are studied, together with how these can be communicated directly to the database server.

CHAPTER 17: **ALTERNATIVE SCRIPTING LANGUAGES** 339

The aim of this chapter is to have a look at the various technologies available for developing Web applications. This can be useful to familiarize you with legacy code that may be met while maintaining older applications and Web sites.

CHAPTER 18: **FUTURE: GAINING A PERSPECTIVE** 357

This chapter's main focus is to acquaint the reader with the leading edge of Internet and Web technology, to give some idea of the currently active research areas and inspire interest for future study.

Preface

INTRODUCTION

This book is the product of teaching undergraduate Web development courses but it equally applies to anyone who wants to learn how to construct Web sites and applications.

It concentrates on passing on the appropriate knowledge and techniques clearly and accurately while encouraging the reader to engage in activities to broaden their interests. Each subject area is built up carefully, making sure it is relevant and supported by information from industry and independent of any specific platform. An example of this is the importance of stressing security concepts and technologies right from the beginning of work with servers. A progression is made from basic Web page construction, to dynamic client side scripting and finally full-blown server side development.

Any one of the book's subject areas can be looked at in much more depth, in fact whole books can found on any one of these subjects! What is attempted here is to provide an essential overview that locks the various subject areas together and gives guidance on where to take your studies further. The choice of the areas to focus on has been informed by actual application development, study, teaching and industry concerns. The book attempts to grasp what makes the subject such an interesting one to many people and leads them to their own discoveries.

There is much reference material and clear examples, which are not hidden beneath gimmicky language or frustrating non-essential asides. The basic aim of a chapter is set out at the beginning, along with a more extended introduction. Each subject section ends with the main *checkpoints* being highlighted for revision to help grasp the main thrust and direction of the topic. Sections also contain *test yourself* parts, which engage the reader in activities relevant to that particular part or subject area. A chapter also ends with a quiz, which is composed of questions to extend knowledge and activities encouraging a wider appreciation of specific relevant points.

Each chapter also has a subject-specific glossary, as it is important to break down all those key words, phrases and abbreviations that are embedded in this subject! A larger glossary is included at the back of the book for quick access at any time. A chapter also contains useful Web addresses, providing links to information and software hubs. These help as extension activity starting points, further reference or by giving an entirely new viewpoint on an area.

Any included examples have been kept brief to emphasize single points and do not include massive amounts of comments, simply because they are expanded upon in the surrounding text. Students should be encouraged to make their own scripts as clear, commented and structured in layout as possible!

FEATURES

This book draws on several key principles:

- Keep it simple and clear, don't try and do too much all at once, particularly in examples.
- The subject area is interesting; don't forget to include what makes it so!
- Start at the beginning; what do you really need to know?
- Make it easy to use as a reference as well as a tutorial.
- Where an area becomes more involved than the scope of the book can do justice to, provide pointers to further information and study.
- Sections include test yourself questions to check if important points are grasped.
- Include chapter questions to provoke further interest, as well as to test ability.
- Add checkpoints to summarize sections and chapters.
- Include resource boxes, which include pointers to software or information, much of which is free to use or access.
- Include end of chapter subject-related glossary and end of book glossary.

ADDITIONAL MATERIALS

Code examples, links and other up-to-date supporting information will be placed on the Web at:

http://ralph-moseley.co.uk/devwebapp

TRADEMARKS

ActiveX, JScript, Internet Explorer, Visual Basic, Visual C++, Visual C#, Microsoft, MS-DOS and Windows, Windows XP, Windows 2000, Windows NT are registered trademarks of Microsoft Corporation.

Apache is a registered trademark of the Apache Software Corporation.

Unix is a registered trademark of The Open Group.

Dreamweaver is a registered trademark of Macromedia Inc.

Apple and Macintosh are registered trademarks of Apple Computers Inc.

Java, JavaScript and Java-based marks are trademarks or registered trademarks of Sun Microsystems, inc.

Linux is a registered trademark of Linus Torvalds.

Netscape is a trademark of the Netscape Communications Corporation.

All other trademarks, registered trademarks and service marks are the property of their respective owners.

ACKNOWLEDGMENTS

Writing any book is demanding and I believe computer books are particularly attention seeking! It's important to realize that a book is born from your own experience of contact with the subject and the people who teach it. So, quite rightly, I should acknowledge the teachers in my past and the colleagues who I work with at Middlesex University, London, for their encouragement and professionalism. In particular, the Computer and Multimedia Technology group and the PGCHE course have provided inspiration.

I should also say a big thanks to the students who actually were *subjected* to the material in this book, much of which is drawn from my lectures and laboratory sessions. What works and what doesn't is always pointed out by their sharp inquiring minds!

A book like this is very time consuming, so I should say a big thanks to Amanda for being forgiving enough to allow me the space to pursue its ends! Not to mention a critical teacher's eye when it counted.

Thanks must also go to the Cats for their purr-fect guidance and random interjections at the keyboard. Pooka, your prawns are in the post. Suki, please stop talking.

Ralph Moseley

1

THE WAY THE WEB WORKS

A basic introduction to how the WWW works within the context of the Internet with supporting protocols and applications.

This first chapter aims at equipping you with a thorough grounding in what you need to know to start developing applications and pages for the Web.

To begin with there is a brief history lesson on how the Internet and in particular the World Wide Web (WWW) was developed, which explains how various aspects of the technology such as hypertext came about. As time went on, more applications were found that could be handled by the Internet, each one of these slowly becoming standardized in the way they went about communicating across the Web until there were many protocols available for different tasks. The more important protocols are explored here.

To develop applications you need to be able to interact with a server that will show your Web pages and run your applications. To communicate with this machine you need a way of uploading and talking to it. This is shown here along with some issues you may meet along the way.

One of the most important tools you will be using while developing will be the Web browser so some of its useful features, to both a user and developer, are explained. This is approached in a generic way and therefore should be equally applicable to your favorite browser.

1.1 HISTORY

First of all, let's start with a bit of history – how did it all begin and why? As long as information has been collected and stored there has been a need for duplication and, with that, a means for communicating it to other places. This was true when the first books and other documents were being written throughout history. When computers came on the scene it became important that information could be stored and transferred between machines so other people could access the information and maybe add to it.

Computers were initially linked together to store information in universities, defense organizations and government departments. As they did not all have a common standard to communicate by, information could not be passed between dissimilar systems. A university may have had a department where scientists could share their work and papers but it would become a problem to connect to someone else's system and transfer documents or data.

Possibly the biggest driving factor to develop interoperability between systems was the needs of the US Department of Defense. They required a communications architecture for command and control that was reliable, universal and in some way self-healing. The idea here was that if a certain center, or node, was lost in the network (for example by enemy attack) then information would not be disrupted but would find its way around it to its intended destination. In the late 1960s, the Defense Advanced Research Projects Agency (DARPA) worked with both industry and universities, starting a network to test various ideas out in this line. The network was known as ARPANET and was used to develop protocols and techniques that are now used on the Internet.

The standards that were developed in that period were passed on in the 1980s to the US Department of Defense's Defense Communications Agency. The agency became their guardian until finally, with the establishment of a more widely used Internet in the 1990s, they were passed on to the Internet Architecture Board (IAB), an independent organization.

1.1.1 The WWW

The WWW is part of the history of the Internet. Its inventor, Tim Berners-Lee, in 1980 was investigating how computers could store information with random links. In 1989, while working at the European Particle Physics Laboratory, he proposed the idea of a global hypertext space in which any network-accessible information could be referred to by a single 'Universal Document Identifier'. In 1990 this idea was expanded with a program called 'WorlDwidEWeb', a point and click hypertext editor running on a NeXT computer; further developments led to the browser and Web server. Several specifications were developed here including URIs, HyperText Markup Language (HTML) and HyperText Transfer Protocol (HTTP) and were in fact published on the first server to promote wide adoption and discussion.

Over the years 1991 to 1994 the load on the first Web server info.cern.ch increased by a factor of ten every year. A selection of browsers was developed for different types of computer. Initially academia and then industry started taking notice. Under pressure to define future direction, Tim Berners-Lee formed the World Wide Web Consortium (W3C) in 1994, which acted as a neutral forum where companies and organizations could go to discuss and agree on new common computer protocols.

1.2 THE INTERNET AND THE WWW

The Internet works by defining an address for each resource attached to it. In the case of attached computers and some devices, this is the Internet Protocol (IP) address. Without some form of address, no link could be formed between computers, resources or systems. An example of an IP address is 158.162.131.236. The numbers break down to a country, to a specific domain, right down to a machine itself.

Ordinarily, of course, we don't use numbers to find resources and machines – we use a name like mycomputer.co.uk. The name actually will have an associated number but when a name is entered, say, into a Web browser, the computer will use a special system called the Domain Name System (DNS) to look up the associated number which it will then use to get in contact with the desired server. Figure 1-1 shows the basic idea behind IP addressing for one particular network. In this diagram a group of computers are connected to a Local Area Network (LAN), each having a local IP address. These are connected to a gateway or router, which in turn is linked to an Internet Service Provider (ISP), usually with some type of modem. The ISP allows access to the Internet, DNS lookup services and email. The ISP also allocates an IP address for the network, which in turn can be utilized to resolve to individual machines using techniques such as Network Address Translation (NAT).

The discussion behind how the actual communication takes place deserves a book or course of its own but the basics will be described here. Any communication that occurs on the Internet uses the TCP/IP (Transport Control Protocol/Internet Protocol) suite. This is a set of communication protocols, or conventions, for dialogue between computers and devices. These protocols implement a stack, each layer of which solves problems relating to the transmission of data, as well providing service to higher layers than itself. Higher layers are logically closer to the user, dealing with more abstract data and rely on the lower layers to provide the means in which they can be physically manipulated.

Table 1-1 shows the Operating Systems Interconnection (OSI) reference model, which is a layered abstract description for describing communications and computer network protocols. It is roughly adhered to in the computing and networking industry and is often simplified to produce a model for the Internet as shown in Table 1-2. Note here that the session and presentation layers have been absorbed into the application layer.

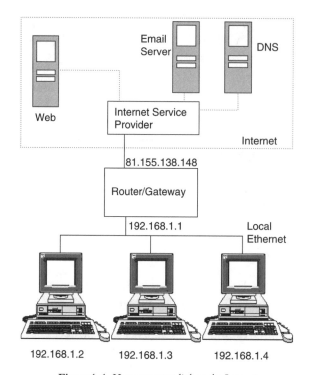

Figure 1-1 *How computers link to the Internet*

Level	Stack layer	Protocol
7	Application	HTTP, SMTP, SNMP, FTP, Telnet, SSH, Scp, NFS, RTSP
6	Presentation	XDR, ASN.1, SMB, AFP
5	Session	TLS, SSH, RPC, NetBIOS, ASP
4	Transport	TCP, UDP, RTP, SCTP, SPX, ATP
3	Network	IP, ICMP, IGMP, X.25, CLNP, ARP, RARP, BGP, OSPF, RIP, IPX, DDP
2	Data Link	Ethernet, Token Ring, PPP, HDLC, Frame Relay, ISDN, ATM, 802.11 Wi-Fi, FDDI
1	Physical	Electrical, radio, laser

Table 1-1 *OSI model*

OSI level	Stack layer	Protocol
7	Application	HTTP, SMTP, SNMP, FTP, Telnet, SSH, Scp, DNS
4	Transport	TCP, UDP, RTP, SCTP, SPX, ATP
3	Network	IP, ICMP, IGMP, X.25, CLNP, ARP, RARP, BGP, OSPF, RIP, IPX, DDP
2	Data Link	Ethernet, Token Ring, PPP, HDLC, Frame Relay, ISDN, ATM, 802.11 Wi-Fi, FDDI
1	Physical	Electrical, radio, laser

Table 1-2 *Internet layered model*

Where the OSI model was theoretical and produced at an earlier stage in the evolution of networks, the Internet model, as shown in Table 1-2, was produced as a practical solution to the engineering problems involved.

The *physical layer* deals with the physical characteristics of communication such as conventions about the medium used for communication (e.g. wires, fiber optic or radio links). Other related details such as connectors, channels, modulation, signal strengths, level synchronization, timing and distances involved are also included here.

The *data link layer* specifies how packets of information are transported over the physical layer, such as how it is framed or set out with special start and stop bit patterns. The *network layer* is concerned with how the packets are transferred over and between networks.

Protocols at the *transport layer* can deal with solving problems like reliability; that is, whether or not the data reached the location it was intended to and ensuring that data arrives in the correct order. Transport protocols within the TCP/IP suite also determine which application any given data is intended for. TCP is one such protocol that exists here and is said to be reliable and connection oriented. UDP (User Datagram Protocol) also exists at this level and has some interesting characteristics. For example, because it is usually used for streaming video or audio it is a 'best effort' or 'unreliable' protocol in that it does not verify that packets reach their destination; rather its concern is that they arrive on time.

Finally, the *application layer* is the layer that programs use to interface with in order to communicate across a network with other programs. Data is passed from the program in an application format and encoded into a standard protocol. Some programs are considered to run in this layer, with their associated protocols. Once the data from an application has been encoded into a standard application layer protocol it is then passed down to the next layer of the OSI model.

Checkpoint!

We now know:
- ■ there was an initial need for information exchange between systems
- ■ information exchange was the catalyst for developing networks
- ■ networks require common conventions for dialogue (protocols)
- ■ each resource in a network needs a unique identifier (IP address)
- ■ an IP address can be associated with a name using DNS
- ■ a stack of protocols exist, providing services and communication between the various levels in a system.

1.3 PROTOCOLS AND PROGRAMS

To enable communications to occur between parties, there are a few aspects that have to be considered:

- where the communication takes place (usually a specific *port*, a kind of interface for communication over a network)
- how it takes place
- the rules and conventions involved.

For the Internet, there are many ways of communicating between machines and devices, depending on what is actually required. Often there are many ways to do the same thing, which is important because the particular context that a device is in may limit what resources are available to it.

A specific task usually requires a particular form of communication. Here we look at a few contexts in which we may wish to transfer information between systems and the mechanisms available for the task.

1.3.1 Files

If you want a file to go from one machine to another, how would you do it? You could, for example, simply email it and pick up the email on the other machine. There may be problems with this – what if there was no email client or the file was simply too big? What other possibilities are there? You could use a disk or memory of some kind. Another way could be to use File Transfer Protocol (FTP) to load it either directly on the machine, or to a server, so it can be downloaded on to the target machine later. Let's say you want to transfer a file called myIndex.doc; a typical session may run like this:

```
>ftp mysuperserver.co.uk
Connected to mysuperserver.co.uk.
220 FTP Server ready.
Name (mysuperserver.co.uk:ralphmoseley): ralph101
331 Password required for ralph101.
Password:
230 User ralph101 logged in.
Remote system type is UNIX.
Using binary mode to transfer files.
ftp>put myIndex.doc
```

The file will then be transferred. Notice that different files require either binary or ASCII (American Standard Code for Information Interchange, pronounced *ass-key*, a character set) modes, text-based files need to be sent using ASCII. Graphic files, such as JPEG or GIF, and word processor formats, such as MS Word doc, require binary.

When you are logged in you have a range of commands available, mainly based on UNIX commands, such as those shown in Table 1-3.

As you can see, there are lots of commands but there are some that are used more than others:

- ftp – start an ftp session
- ls – list files
- get – download a file from the server
- put – upload a file to the server
- mkdir – make a directory on the server
- cd – change to a new directory on the server
- close – close the connection
- open – open a new connection
- bin – binary mode transfer
- asc – ASCII text mode transfer.

These provide an adequate capability to allow a user to get their files from or upload them to a server. When developing Web pages or applications, there is a need for a cycle of local editing and updating of the files on the server. This can be done with an FTP connection; some editors even include the ability to transfer files online!

!	Features	mls	Proxy	size
$	fget	mlsd	put	sndbuf
account	form	mlst	pwd	status
append	ftp	mode	quit	struct
ascii	gate	modtime	quote	sunique
bell	get	more	rate	system
binary	glob	mput	rcvbuf	tenex
bye	hash	msend	recv	throttle
case	help	newer	reget	trace
cd	idle	nlist	remopts	type
cdup	image	nmap	rename	umask
chmod	lcd	ntrans	reset	unset
close	less	open	restart	usage
cr	lpage	page	rhelp	user
debug	lpwd	passive	rmdir	verbose
delete	ls	pdir	rstatus	xferbuf
dir	macdef	pls	runique	?
disconnect	mdelete	pmlsd	send	
edit	mdir	preserve	sendport	
epsv4	mget	sendport	set	
exit	mkdir	progress	site	
		prompt		

Table 1-3 *FTP command set*

Test Yourself!

- Access a command line window and try connecting to an FTP site using the commands mentioned above – ls, put, get . . .

1.3.2 Problems with FTP

There are some possible problems when using FTP that you should be aware of. Most machines connected to the Internet have some kind of firewall in place to stop intrusion. A firewall can be part of your operating system, a piece of software you install or included on a piece of hardware on your network. A firewall may be set up to stop access either outward bound or inward toward your computer, on any of the available ports. This includes the FTP port 21. So, if your computer is having connection problems it's worth checking this; it is usually possible to allow communication on specific ports while others are blocked.

It must also be remembered that normal FTP on port 21 is not very secure and it is possible to intercept and view data that is sent, as well as any passwords. This is because information is sent as clear text without any form of encryption. If the data is sensitive or personal, other methods exist for transfer of information.

Lastly, if you use FTP to transfer files for your Web site, don't forget that any newly uploaded pages may take a while to appear to a browser due to factors such as local caching (a store to help speed up regularly viewed pages) on individual machines and servers.

Checkpoint!

We now know how to:

■ **open an FTP connection to another machine**
■ **do various operations such as listing the files on the remote server**
■ **get single and multiple files from the server**
■ **put single and multiple files on the server**
■ **close the FTP connection**
■ **be aware of problems concerning FTP such as security and firewalls.**

1.3.3 Email

Email existed as long ago as 1965 on time-shared user mainframes and pre-dates the Internet itself. The use was extended to work on networks between many computers. Modern email works by a user writing their message using a mail client (or Mail User Agent, MUA); this program then uses Simple Mail Transfer Protocol (SMTP) to send the message to the local mail transfer agent (MTA), which usually exists on the user's ISP. The MTA then deciphers the email address of the recipient (who the email is to!), which takes the form of myname@myaddress, where myname is the local part and myaddress is the domain name. The MTA uses the DNS to find the appropriate mail exchange server accepting messages for that domain. Once the mail server is found, the message is sent on using SMTP, and from there it is placed using the local name (myname) to find the correct mail box.

To pick up the mail, a user's client retrieves it from the mail box via his MUA, probably using Post Office Protocol (POP3).

1.3.4 Instant Messaging

It's possible to use an Instant Messaging (IM) service to talk to a friend on another computer, so how does this work? The problem here is that the protocols and programs in use are fairly, at this point in time, non-standard in the sense that each has its own approach. One of the more popular is Internet Relay Chat (IRC), which is designed for group communication in channels (group areas where people meet) but also allows one to one communication. IRC is an open protocol that uses TCP and if desired, Secure Sockets Layer (SSL). Users connect with a client application (of which there are many, for each type of operating system), which links to a IRC server. The actual protocol is plain text; that is, it is quite possible to link to an IRC server with Telnet. However, it is easier to use a client as some character encoding can cause problems and the client makes it considerably easier with built-in commands, for example.

An interesting development on IRC were bots, automated clients that perform some duty or service, such as exercising operator privileges (controlling channels and acting, if abuse is detected). There are also bots that perform the opposite to annoy users by sending out unwanted messages to them!

1.3.5 Remote Machine Access

If you need to access a machine from a distance, to maybe run a program or retrieve some data, there are a few ways to do this. One way is through Telnet, which allows you to open a connection to a remote machine and issue commands as if you were actually sat at that machine. It is important to understand that the other end of the connection must be a process (or daemon) that will act as a server. Telnet uses port 23 and is largely now considered a security risk due to vulnerabilities that have manifested themselves over the years. This comes from the degree of flexibility allowed by the Telnet program and also from weaknesses within the protocol. Telnet does not encrypt any communication, so passwords are open to eavesdropping, which can be done fairly easily. It is also possible to hijack (or, take over) a Telnet session due to the lack of authentication between the parties, so it's impossible to know whether parties are who they pertain to be. A better means of remote access is to use SSH (Secure Shell), which is, like Telnet, both a program and a protocol. A typical SSH session runs like this (user typing in bold):

```
Raptor-Computer:~ ralphmoseley$ ssh ralph@192.168.1.4
Password:[type password]
Last login: Sat Mar 12 18:50:54 2005 from 192.168.1.2
Copyright (c) 1980, 1983, 1986, 1988, 1990, 1991, 1993, 1994
The Regents of the University of California.  All rights
                reserved.

FreeBSD 4.10-RELEASE (GENERIC) #0: Tue May 25 22:47:12 GMT 2004
```

```
Welcome to FreeBSD!

aphid# ls
.cshrc    .login          .rnd            server.csr
.history .mysql_history  mbox            server.key
.klogin  .profile        server.crt
aphid# logout
Connection to 192.168.1.4 closed.
```

1.3.6 Web Pages

The main protocol used for communication between a browser and a Web server is HTTP. This protocol was designed to enable documents to be transferred but can be used with other types of data too. For Web documents the HTTP protocol works by sending commands over a TCP connection.

To understand how information gets passed from machine to machine we need to know how such systems can connect to each other. Generally, the main model used for the Web is client–server.

The first stage is the user typing a URL in the browser address window.

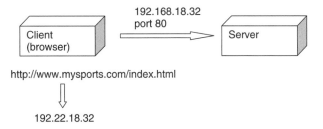

In the next stage the URL is converted to an IP address, which is then used to make a connection to the server at that location via port 80, the one used for HTTP and the Web.

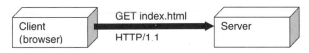

Once the connection is established, the client application extracts the file name that is required from the URL and sends the request down the established connection. When received, the server looks up the request.

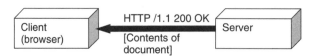

http://www.mysports.com/index.html

If all is well the HTTP message is sent saying that the page was found, followed by the page itself. When the page has been sent the connection is dropped.

The following HTTP command may originate from a browser to request a Web page from a server:

```
GET /index.html HTTP/1.0
```

This command, which is a text-based command, as above, has several fields:

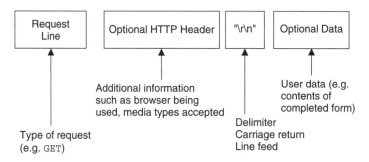

In fact, it is quite easy to pretend to be a Web browser! Using a Telnet program it is possible to connect to a Web server and ask for the initial page, usually index.html or index.htm. The session may run something like this:

```
$ telnet aphid.dynalias.net 80
Trying 81.155.138.148...
Connected to 81.155.138.148.
Escape character is '^]'.
GET /index.html HTTP/1.0

HTTP/1.1 200 OK
Date: Fri, 04 Mar 2005 20:02:01 GMT
Server: Apache/1.3.29 (Unix) PHP/4.3.6 mod_ssl/2.8.16
          OpenSSL/0.9.7d
```

```
Last-Modified: Mon, 06 Sep 2004 12:43:33 GMT
ETag: "4c9003-a71-413c5b75"
Accept-Ranges: bytes
Content-Length: 2673
Connection: close
Content-Type: text/html

<!DOCTYPE HTML PUBLIC "-//W3C//DTD HTML 3.2 Final//EN">
<HTML>
<!--Web page here -->
</HTML>
Connection closed by foreign host.
```

The initial command opens the connection to the server. The first thing the computer does is translate the name of the server to an IP address by using DNS. It then can link to the server and form a temporary connection for requests. Once established, commands can be written just as a browser does. Here there is a request for a Web page, index.html, using protocol HTTP 1.0. The server then responds by saying the command was understood, followed by some other identification data and then by the Web page itself. Finally, the connection is closed as the request has been dealt with.

Lots of things can go wrong when asking for a Web page in this way! You may write the command in carefully but the page doesn't exist, in which case you will receive an error code back instead of a Web page. Some of the more common ones are:
- 404 = Not found
- 401 = Unauthorized
- 500 = Internal server error
- 501 = Not implemented.

There are quite a few more too, such as errors involving redirection services. A browser will also send other information along with the request, identifying its various properties and capabilities but not the user.

Test Yourself!

- Using a command line window as above, type the telnet command to talk to a Web server on port 80 e.g.:

  telnet www.yahoo.com 80

  GET /index.html HTTP/1.1 [press enter twice]
  If you type this correctly you could get a few responses:

> The correct page
> A redirection page
> Can't find it page
>
> All will be in HTML, as you would expect! The connection will then close (it's not a persistent connection, remember).
> You also try this with some terminal programs such as PuTTY.

1.4 SECURE CONNECTIONS

Most of the protocols that have been looked at are not secure; they use plain text to transfer data and could be viewed or tampered with at some stage. There are some protocols that make it more secure to send and receive data, which include special versions of FTP as SFTP/FTPS and HTTP as HTTPS. Other ways of actually executing and logging into a machine exist too, similar to Telnet. These include SSH and various virtual networking tools that allow a user to create a secure tunnel through to the host machine, almost as if the connection were local. Table 1-4 shows the various protocols, associated ports (which can be changed) and whether security is available with that particular communication mode.

SSH allows communications to take place in a secure manner over port 22, with encryption, minimizing the risk of interception or tampering. The SSH program is similar to Telnet in that it allows a user to log in and execute commands on a remote computer. It is usually included with UNIX (and its variants) as a program. A server process/daemon usually also exists to accept incoming requests. Other operating systems have similar programs available that are freeware or shareware, such as WinSCP.

To transfer files in a similar way to FTP there exists a version that uses a secure method of communication, SFTP. It is important to note that there are several protocols with this name: the one referred to here is Secure (Shell) File Transfer Protocol (another one is Simple File Transfer Protocol). SFTP can refer to the protocol or the application program involved, depending on the context it is used in. It is not simply an FTP connection run through a secure shell but a completely new protocol.

Yet another version of FTP exists as FTPS, which utilizes Secure Sockets Layer (SSL)/ Transport Layer Security (TLS) to secure any connections made.

For shopping, banking and financial transactions on the Web another protocol was called for, besides the insecure and easy to intercept HTTP. This is HTTPS and it provides authentication and encryption for electronic commerce by encrypting communications using a version of SSL or TLS. You will know when you encounter it as the URL is `https://`

Communication	Application	Protocol	Port	Security
Web page	Browser	HTTP	80	—
Web page	Browser	HTTPS	443	Secure
Files[Binary/Text]	FTP	FTP	21	—
Files[Binary/Text]	SFTP	SFTP	22	Secure
Files[Binary/Text]	FTP	FTPS	990	Secure
Commands	Telnet	Telnet	23	—
Commands	SSH	SSH	22	Secure
Instant Messaging	IRC	IRC	194	Not usually secure

Table 1-4 *Transfer of various media and appropriate attributes*

rather than `http://`. HTTPS provides a measure of security while the data, such as credit card details, is in transit to the server. However, once at the server and possibly stored in a database, the data may still be open to attack prior to any further transmission to a credit card processor, for example.

Checkpoint!

We now know:

- **the importance of using the correct level of security required by a situation**
- **the choices available to provide a secure alternative**
- **SFTP and FTPS can be used in place of FTP**
- **SSH can be used in place of Telnet**
- **the SSH TCP port is 22.**

1.5 APPLICATIONS AND DEVELOPMENT TOOLS

For example, you can use FTP from a console window in Windows or a UNIX-based system and it will allow you a basic level of ability to move, copy or manipulate files. It is also possible to use a far more complex program that enhances capabilities in some sense. This may all be presented in a graphical manner rather than text driven so, for example, you can drag and drop files from a local folder into the remote server. In the case of FTP it can be useful to have the ability to transfer groups of files and directories without typing, as it also allows a better interface with your working environment.

There are lots of resources on the Web for developers, some of which are freeware, shareware or proprietary. The resources you can find cover most things you will ever need; from fully featured Integrated Development Environments (IDEs), through to simple editors and graphic tools. What will you need to start developing applications? To some extent it depends on whether you take a minimalist approach or whether you prefer environments and tools that automate tasks for you.

You can make do with a simple text editor that probably already exists on your computer, your browser and an FTP client if you want to upload your files to a server. You can get editors that are specific to the languages you are using or download plug-ins to assist you. These exist for HTML, JavaScript, PHP, Perl and most other Web languages. There are syntax checkers, program coloring aids and even editors with built-in mini-servers to test code.

Development environments and editors will also automate tasks such as uploading pages via FTP or the batch conversion of files from one type to another.

All these various tools can be bought (as you usually would) from shops or online. There are also freeware or shareware versions where you pay a small fee or nothing at all. You may encounter the term open source while looking for suitable software, these are projects that are freely available to the general public and are usually ongoing, developed and supported by a volunteer community. The code behind such projects is usually available to view and alter. End users have the right to change such code and redistribute the software. Open source licenses may have some restrictions applied though, such as the requirement to preserve an author's name and copyright statement in the code.

Freeware can be distributed under a different kind of license where, although the code isn't available to view or alter, you do not pay a charge for it. It may possibly have a restriction such that it may not be sold on or used by government agencies or armed forces.

Shareware is usually software that is distributed ahead of payment, which is set to some point in the future so you have time to try it out.

Resources!

■ Open up your browser and, using a search engine, have a look around for various types of utility that may help you. You have various choices for types of license for software:

• freeware is free to use and download

> - shareware to try and then pay later
> - off-the-shelf to buy.
> ■ You may find FTP utilities and more secure software that use SFTP or FTPS.
> ■ Freeware examples include: WinSCP, PuTTY ...
> ■ There are also lots of editors available for every kind of language and platform you are developing on.
> ■ You may need tools later to convert files, such as graphics, between different formats.

1.6 THE WEB BROWSER

Possibly one of the main tools you will be using while developing Web applications is the Web browser. This connects, as we have seen, over the Internet to a Web server that answers requests from selections of hypertext documents. The HTTP protocol is used in this dialog. Pages are located through the use of URLs – Uniform Resource Locators – which usually begin with `http://`, although most browsers will also support `ftp` and `https`.

Most browsers share common features in that they will display graphics and support many media features. However, this doesn't have to always be the case; there are browsers that allow the Web to be visited using text only, which is very fast.

The format of incoming Web pages is HTML which is interpreted by the browser and displayed as the instructions describe. In addition to HTML most browsers support other types of file such as JPEG, GIF and PNG. More can be supported using plug-ins – units of software that can be added into the browser.

There have always been problems with standards and issues over compatibility, ever since browsers came about on various machines and platforms. When a new browser was made available there were things it did slightly differently, which led to that difference making a required change in HTML. In this way there was an evolution of the language over time, which allowed new browser features to be used, such as displaying images, changing colors or fonts. This led to several strands of the language developing and it therefore being non-standard. Standards were introduced to bring about the ability for pages to look the same no matter what browser they were loaded into. There are now many modern browsers that will work within the standard versions of HTML and XHTML (Extensible HyperText Markup Language).

Browsers have expanded their capabilities beyond simple HTML rendering and often have support for IRC, newsgroups and email.

1.6.1 **Choices**

So, if you are going to develop applications, or even just Web pages, which browser do you choose? The best way to answer this is to ask yourself what you need and, probably more importantly, what your visitors are going to be using.

You could develop using a browser that you find you are comfortable with, then check on a few popular browsers. What features do browsers generally have? Obviously, their main function is to show text and graphics and possibly other media. Other features exist though that you should try and familiarize yourself with. For example, you should know that browsers can also open local files, usually under 'files' on the menu. A useful function of most browsers is the ability to look at a Web page's source code, which is usually under 'view' on the file menu. This can be useful when developing HTML, JavaScript or even to just check that the page you expect to load is the one displayed.

Most browsers include a section in 'preferences' or 'tools' where you can customize to some extent or set up special options. It's possible, for example, on most to set your home page (the place where the browser initially will go to, or visit when you click on the home button).

Browsers also use a cache, a local memory area, to speed up the loading of regularly visited pages. This is done by simply storing a copy in the client computer, which it will show when the page is requested again. You can usually adjust the size of this buffer, along with some other options such as how often a page in the cache is updated. Another option is to clear the cache, a very useful function at times! For example, if you are developing Web pages, what happens if a page you are working on gets cached? It may not update when you refresh (ask it to reload) the current page view. You could turn caching off or put a cache size of 0. As well as these methods there are ways of turning off caching through the Web pages themselves, which we will look at later.

Another set of options in your preferences on a browser relate to cookies. Cookies are small pieces of information that identify you to an application when you (re)visit the site. This may be to set up preferences so that when you do visit again, it knows what you like and will change the screen and greet you. This is not generally taken as foolproof for security; you will usually be asked for a password to verify if it is appropriate. For various reasons you may not want to be identified or have your habits tracked, so you can usually switch off the acceptance of cookies or set it so you're asked when one is presented.

Other options relate to the auto-filling of forms – do you want your details automatically added when a site gives you a form to fill out? Another useful option allows you to select where files that you want to download (such as MP3 or programs) will go.

Both cached pages and cookies can be cleared from memory, either individually or all together.

Test Yourself!

- Explore the various options of your favorite browser.
- How big is the cache?
- How do you clear all cookies and the cache?
- How do you stop cookies being accepted?
- Change the home page.
- Where do files go to that you download, the desktop or . . .?
- Load a page from a Web site, or one of your own, and look at the source code through the browser – is it what you expect?

Checkpoint!

We now know:

- ■ a browser contains quite a few interesting features beyond simple site visiting and viewing
- ■ a home page can be changed and set to whatever you want
- ■ a cookie is a small piece of information usually to identify a visitor the next time a site is visited
- ■ a cache is a memory area, or buffer, that is used to store Web pages that are frequently visited
- ■ how to change and view where downloaded files go.

1.7 CHAPTER SUMMARY

- ■ The Internet was developed as the need to communicate information between remote locations became evident.
- ■ The WWW is a large subset of the Internet and was developed as a way of connecting information that could be universally accessed.
- ■ The main model for communication on the WWW is client–server based.
- ■ HTTP was developed as a protocol to work for document transfer and is essentially request/response in nature.
- ■ Other protocols exist for different uses, such as the transfer of files between machines.
- ■ Many useful command line and applications exist that utilize the various protocols to help with file transfer and remote access.

■ Some problems do exist with certain protocols, which can be overcome.
■ Security should always be considered when transferring or accessing information over the Internet.

Chapter Quiz

• See if you can find out a little more about the origins of the Internet by using search engines such as Google. You can also use the useful Web addresses at the end of this chapter.

• Other models of communication exist than just client–server as in the case of using a browser. Can you think of any software you use that may use a different kind of approach?

• Is the computer you use for development protected by a firewall and, if so, how is it configured to allow various communications through the ports, such as FTP?

Key Words and Phrases

FTP File Transfer Protocol, a standard for transferring files between computers

FTPS File Transfer Protocol over SSL, another version of FTP running over SSL/TLS for security

HTML HyperText Markup Language

HTTP HyperText Transfer Protocol, the main method of transferring information on the WWW, using a request/response mechanism

Internet When written with a capital 'I', this refers to the publicly available system of interconnected networks that communicate standardized protocols such as IP

IP Internet Protocol, one of the main protocols used on the Internet

Port An interface for communicating with a computer program over a network

Protocol A standard, or set of rules and conventions that enables communication between two systems. A protocol can exist in hardware terms as well as software

SFTP Secure Shell (SSH) File Transfer Protocol, a more secure protocol for transfer of files

SMTP Simple Mail Transfer Protocol, the standard text-based method for transferring email

SSH Secure Shell, both a protocol and a command line program for connecting to remote computers

SSL Secure Sockets Layer, a secure protocol with encryption

TCP Transmission Control Protocol, a connection-oriented protocol with reliability, working at the transport layer level

TLS Transport Layer Security, the successor to SSL with few differences between SSL 3.0 and TLS 1.0

UDP User Datagram Protocol, a fairly minimal message-oriented transport layer protocol, providing no guarantee for message delivery

URI Uniform Resource Indicator, an Internet protocol element that consists of a string of characters that indicate a name or address referring to a resource

URL Uniform Resource Locator, a standardized address for some resource on the Internet or elsewhere; it is a type of URI

WWW Refers to the World Wide Web, an information space and large subset of the Internet, where items (known as resources) are accessible via links

Useful Web Addresses

```
http://www.w3.org/
http://www.isoc.org/internet/history/
http://en.wikipedia.org/wiki/Internet
```

2

THE CLIENT SIDE: HTML

This chapter starts to look at the client side and static Web page development using HTML.

You will learn how to develop simple Web pages and formatting, together with tables, images and frames.

Showing the basics of client side, static Web page development using HTML, this chapter describes how to manipulate output with styles, emphasis and fonts. It explores how to embed images into your Web pages along with hyperlinks, which are of prime importance to how the Web works.

This chapter covers the development cycle of producing your Web sites and applications right from the beginning:

- HTML tags, attributes and document structure
- adding emphasis, styles and fonts
- using color
- commenting and readability of HTML
- pre-formatted text
- hyperlinks
- definition, ordered and unordered lists
- tables
- images
- simple forms
- Web site structure.

2.1 INTRODUCTION

A Web site is generally composed of individual pages that are linked together, each of these relating to a different aspect of your site, such as news, links and biography. It is possible to try other ways of breaking your site down but at this stage it is best to consider it in terms of pages.

To begin with you don't even need a server to put your pages on; you can just develop on your own computer and view any pages you make with your Web browser.

2.2 THE DEVELOPMENT PROCESS

When developing there is a cycle that takes place, which generally matches the usual cycle within software development: design, write code, test. For Web development it's probably closer to: study the requirements, design, write the HTML (or script), upload, test and go through it again.

2.2.1 Requirements

It's important to make sure you understand what you are being asked to do before you start! This can be seen from the point of view of both graphic design and functionality. The best idea is to make at least some sketches at the start to play with ideas, then see if you can work out which pages should link to each other.

2.2.2 Design

The design stage tries to provide a solution to match the requirements. It should also take into account what is possible with the various technologies that are available. Sometimes hand coding, although more precise, can simply not be fast enough to meet a deadline! In these cases you may be able to get help from applications such as Dreamweaver. Web sites can require a large amount of work with art and graphics packages as well as code tools.

2.2.3 Write Code

This is the point where you start writing your HTML. Hand coding is slow but precise and usually easier to follow. Generated script and HTML from an application can sometimes also be non-standard!

2.2.4 Test

After spending some time working on your masterpiece you will want to see what it looks like. If you develop using an editor, then the next stage will be to point your browser at the page. If you work with an IDE (Integrated Development Environment), then it's possible that it will show you what a page looks like simply by clicking a button! If your browser is already on the page you can press refresh for it to reload.

2.2.5 Upload

When you are happy with your page you will want to upload for public viewing!

2.2.6 Re-Iterate

The next stage isn't so much a stage, as an instruction to do the above again until you've got it right and it works without bugs.

Checkpoint!

We now know:
- ■ **to develop we need an editor, a browser and if we want to upload to a server then we also need an FTP client**
- ■ **there is a cycle involved in the process of developing Web pages and applications. This involves designing and thinking about the requirements, writing the HTML, uploading (or simply viewing locally), then viewing with the browser which may simply mean hitting the refresh button if it is already pointing at the site or page**
- ■ **the cycle starts again with any changes we want to make after viewing.**

2.3 BASIC HTML

HTML can be considered as the main language of the Web in some respects. All browsers understand it and because of its simplicity it's generally not taxing for the computers involved. Here we look at initially developing static pages; that is, ones that do not change depending on user input or interaction.

The main aim of HTML is to format a Web page hopefully in the same way for every browser, although it doesn't always work out that way in practice.

2.3.1 Loading Pages with the Browser

A page can be loaded into a browser in a couple of ways: by writing in a URL in the address bar or by going to the menu and clicking on 'file' then 'open' if it's a local file.

If you point your browser at a directory on a Web site it will try and find a series of files beginning with `index.html`, then usually `index.htm`, `index.shtml`, `index.php` and so on. Generally when you are browsing it's best to write in an address ending in a directory with a trailing forward slash otherwise the browser thinks it is a file and tries to load it, before correcting itself. Don't add the forward slash to URLs ending in a real file though!

2.3.2 A Page on the Web

How do we start? Generally if you point a Web browser at a document it will do its best to read it. For example, if you use 'open' on the file menu of your browser and enter the name of a local file called `hello.txt` containing some simple text:

```
Hello there!
```

It will actually read and display it.

2.3.3 HTML Document Structure

To make a 'real' Web page we need to add some elements and rename the file to either htm or html. Open a new blank file in your editor and write some code in:

```
<html>
        A little bit of hypertext
</html>
```

Anything written in triangular brackets is known as a tag and is part of the markup language. So, in this small page we have a number of tags but what do they mean? The first thing to look at is the `<html>` tag, which simply identifies this as HTML. Notice here that the first line and the last line are both `<html>` tags except the last one contains a slash, meaning that this one is a closing tag and matches the tag at the top. Most HTML follows this convention, although there are several tags that don't and you can get away with just the one tag, as an instruction. Also notice that the HTML tags are in lowercase. Although HTML tags are not case sensitive, the World Wide Web Consortium (W3C) suggests the use of lowercase tags in their HTML 4 recommendation.

The `<html>` tag identifies a section of HTML code, opening with the `<html>` and closing with `</html>`. Everything between these is the code itself. Here we find a simple text message, which is output straight to the browser screen:

```
<html>
        <head>
                <title>
```

```
                        The amazing art of Web programming
                </title>
        </head>
        <body>
                a little bit of hypertext
        </body>
</html>
```

Our next, more properly formed HTML Web page extends the first, adding a title to the page and dividing the document up into head and body sections. The body section contains the main document while the head contains details such as the title as shown here. All full HTML documents should follow this structure and include a body and head.

An HTML element then begins with a start tag and ends with a closing tag:

```
<title> The amazing art of Web programming </title>
```

In our simple Web page, there is also the tag, **<body>**. This identifies the next part between **<body>** and **</body>** as the main section. This contains the code for the Web page document.

2.4 FORMATTING AND FONTS

If we want to add more lines into the body section as text to output we can add them with our editor:

```
<body>
        a little bit of hypertext<br>
        makes the world go round<br>
        and <i>around</i><br>
</body>
```

This body section contains several new tags. The **
** or break tag makes output start on the next line down at the beginning of a new line. Notice how this tag is self-contained in that it does not need a closing tag. If the lines were formatted in the HTML document in some other way, would it matter? Like:

```
<body>
        a little bit of hypertext<br>makes the world go round<br>
        and <i>around</i><br>
</body>
```

The answer to this is no, because formatting is only taken from the tags themselves not the layout of your document. It is still a good idea though to lay out your HTML in a readable manner so you can understand it easily should there be a problem that you need to find. It's quite a good idea to lay it out in a structured way, following indentations that relate to the structure, as is done in the programs here.

Some programs will generate code, allowing you to design your Web page at a 'top level' more like a graphic designer, or simply output your text document, capturing its styles and formatting as well as any images that are embedded. These usually produce almost unreadable and copious quantities of code that are hard to follow and nearly impossible to correct, change or debug by hand.

Another way of adding breaks is to define paragraphs with the `<p>` tag. This can be used on its own, like the `<br>` tag or with a closing `</p>` at the end of the paragraph. The `<p>` tag places a blank line before the line it is on.

To break sections of a page the tag `<hr>` can be used; this creates a line or horizontal rule. Like `<br>` it does not require an ending tag.

Test Yourself!

- Try writing a Web page in an editor.
- Add line breaks and suitable formatting.
- Save it with an HTML extension.
- Start up a browser and open it with the 'file' command on the menu.
- Is it what you expected? If not go back to the editor, alter it and try again!

2.4.1 Using Types of Emphasis

The previous HTML code used the `<i>` tag; any words enclosed by the `<i>` and `</i>` will be made italic. There are many ways of emphasizing or altering the text you output, as is shown in Table 2-1.

2.4.2 Pre-Formatted Text

A useful formatting element is `<pre>`...`</pre>`, which enables you to embed text that is already formatted so you don't have to put break tags in, for example:

```
<pre>
 This is already set out in the way I want it
 It has some advantages and is quick
 You don't have to add line breaks but
 It hasn't proportional spacing and is in courier font...!
</pre>
```

Tag	Format
`<i>...</i>`	Italic
`<b>...</b>`	Bold
`<tt>...</tt>`	Typewriter effect
`<em>...</em>`	Emphasis
`<blink>...</blink>`	Blinking
`<sup>...</sup>`	Superscript
`<sub>...</sub>`	Subscript

Table 2-1 *Adding emphasis*

The text is output in courier font which is not proportional spacing, i.e. all characters take up the same space. This allows you to position text with white space (the space character) if you like, which makes it a little easier to format. Other tags can still be embedded inside to help with formatting headings, font sizes and aligning.

2.4.3 Font Sizes

You may also want to change the size of your text. There are a few ways of doing this too. You can use the `<font>` tag or the `<h...>` tags. As you can see from Table 2-2 the `<h...>` tags don't just control the size but some degree of emphasis for headings.

Font size	Heading	Point size
7	–	36 pt
6	`<h1>`	24 pt
5	`<h2>`	18 pt
	`<h3>`	12 pt
4	`<h4>`	12 pt bold
3	body text	12 pt plain
	`<h5>`	10 pt
	`<h6>`	7 pt
2	–	9 pt

Table 2-2 *Font comparison*

The size of your text can also be changed with the `<font size=...>` tag and associated end tag `</font>` with the font size running from 2 to 7. The ending font tag will make the font revert to the previous font used.

You can align your text to `left`, `right` or `center` by combining one of the above tags with the align markup:

```
<html>
    <head>
        <title>
            the amazing art of Web programming
        </title>
    </head>
    <body>
        <p align="center">a little bit of hypertext<br>
        makes the world go round<br>
        and <i>around</i><br></p>
    </body>
</html>
```

This will make all the text be centered in the current document until the ending paragraph tag, `</p>` is met. The align tag is added as an option to the main function. You can also put these optional align statements into heading tags `<h...>`.

```
<html>
    <head>
        <title>
            the amazing art of Web programming
        </title>
    </head>
    <body>
        <h1 align="center">hypertext alignment</h1>
        <p align="center">a little bit of hypertext<br>
        makes the world go round<br>
        and <i>around</i><br></p>
        <p align="left">to the left... </p>
        <p align="right">... and to the right</p>
    </body>
</html>
```

Test Yourself!

- Write another Web page, utilizing font changes, page breaks, horizontal rules and alignment of text.

- Write a Web page using the `<pre>` element. Experiment with layout, compare with using HTML formatting tags to do the same thing.

2.5 COMMENTING CODE

When the HTML code starts building up and looking complicated it's probably time to add commenting. You can do this using `<!-- ... -->`:

```
<!-- This is a complex part of my Web page, it adds a border and
                     several types of font -->
```

Later on, when you have forgotten what you have done in a Web document this can help you understand quickly the various sections of your nicely structured HTML. It's also good from the point of view of other people understanding it who may take over the responsibility of maintaining a Web site, after you have gone.

2.6 COLOR

Adding color (the right color, that is!) to a Web site is an important part of both the design and coding.

The two main basic parts to add color through HTML are the background of the browser display and the text. You can use:

```
<body bgcolor = value text = value>
```

which will set both within the body section of the document. If you want to just change the color of the text it's possible to use:

```
<font color = value>
```

which is similar to the optional `size` attribute that can be added. The actual values involved are based on a red, green, blue (RGB) scheme, usually entered as hexadecimal numbers. Hexadecimal is the number system that runs from 0 to 9, then through the letters A–F, as shown in Table 2-3.

If you want to convert from hex to decimal, multiply the first digit (in the case of a two digit number) by 16 and add the last number to it. For example, if we have the hexadecimal number A2 then we multiply 'A' (which is 10) by 16 and add in 2. So in this case A2 hex = 162 in base 10.

Base 10	0	1	2	3	4	5	6	7	8	9	10	11	12	13	14	15	16	17	18	19
Hex		0	1	2	3	4	5	6	7	8	9	A	B	C	D	E	F	10	11	12	13

Table 2-3 Number base conversion

With two digits the maximum number that can be represented in hexadecimal is FF, or 255.

To set a color value for HTML you supply six digits, representing the RGB color proportions you want; a guideline is shown in Table 2-4. The value then is actually composed of three numbers, each of two digits. So, the following would set the color to red for the background:

```
<body bgcolor="#800000">
```

whereas:

```
<body text="#ffff00">
```

will set the main document's text to yellow.

R	G	B	Color produced
00	00	00	Black
FF	00	00	Bright red
00	FF	00	Bright green
00	00	FF	Bright blue
80	00	00	Dark red
00	80	00	Dark green
00	00	80	Dark blue
FF	FF	00	Bright yellow
80	80	00	Brown
FF	00	FF	Magenta
80	00	80	Indigo
00	80	80	Turquoise
80	80	80	Grey
FF	FF	FF	White

Table 2-4 Some example colors with codes

In theory, any color you want can be made from the red, green, blue palette by combining different amounts of the colors in the right proportions.

Test Yourself!

- Try out using colors; can you make each letter of a word a new color, giving a rainbow effect?

2.7 HYPERLINKS

Hyperlinks are one of the strongest aspects of why the Web came about in the first place – creating the ability to associate information between resources. The way to form a link is fairly simple:

```
<a href = "http://www.someWebpage.com">the text link</a>
```

The actual hyperlink tag is `<a href...>`, the Web address in quotes is where it goes if clicked on and the text afterwards is what is printed on the screen to select. Finally, the link ends with a closing tag. The `href` stands for Hypertext REFerence, the `a` stands for anchor because the link can't be used alone; it must have either an image or text to anchor to. The link formed is a URL, which can be any of the usual kinds, including FTP.

Sometimes it's useful for a selected link to open in a new browser window rather than using the current one. To do this the `target` attribute is used:

```
<a href="http://www.someWebpage.com" target="_blank">the text
            link</a>
```

Links can also be made to places within an already loaded page. This is done by creating an anchor point to the place you may want to jump to and a corresponding link:

```
<html>
    <a name="thetop">introduction</a><br>
    this could be a long document!<br><br><br><br>
    <hr>
    this may be some way down the page.<br><br>
    complete with a link to
    <a href="#thetop">back to the top</a>
</html>
```

The `<a name="...">` creates the anchor point for the link to jump to, while the `<a href="#...">` is the link. It's also possible to form a link from another page to an anchored point. For example, if the page above was called `leaparound.html` then the link:

```
<a href="leaparound.html#thetop">
```

would point the browser at the anchored point on that page.

It's possible to reference sub-directories under the current working directory by using links such as:

```
<a href="images/seaside.jpg">my day out</a>
```

If you are in a sub-directory and want to link into a file above that, then use the two dots:

```
<a href="../mypage.html">up to that other page</a>
```

Checkpoint!

We now know:
- the basics of making a Web page and displaying it with the browser
- the structure of a Web document
- how to output text and add emphasis
- how to control text font size
- the basis behind using color
- how to add commenting to make HTML easier to understand
- how to create hyperlinks to other documents and places within the same document.

2.8 LISTS

A useful ability in HTML is to form quick, concise lists, which can be numbered or just bulleted.

2.8.1 Unordered Lists

A simple bulleted list can be made with the ... tags. For example:

```
<html>
    <head>
        <title>
            the amazing art of Web programming
        </title>
    </head>
```

```
        <body>
            <ul>
                <li>Life of Pi
                <li>Sophie's World
                <li>Jonathan Strange and Mr Norrell
                <li>The Sandman Endless Nights
            </ul>
        </body>
    </html>
```

will produce a list of book titles that is bulleted with round points. The actual character used can be changed and set to square, disc (default) or circle. To do this, simply give the option to the <ul> tag:

```
<ul type="square">
```

2.8.2 Ordered Lists

It's also possible to have ordered lists using <ol>...</ol>:

```
<ol>
    <li>Life of Pi
    <li>Sophie's World
    <li>Jonathan Strange and Mr Norrell
    <li>The Sandman Endless Nights
<ol>
```

Again, there are options available. In this case it is possible to have different numbering rather than the default 1, 2, 3, 4 . . .:

```
<ol type= i>
```

where the various types are:

- i   Roman numerals i, ii, iii, iv
- I   Roman capitals I, II, III, IV
- a   Lowercase letters a, b, c
- A   Capital letters A, B, C.

2.8.3 Nested Lists

You can also nest one list within another, so you could make an unordered list inside a numbered one, or vice versa:

```
<html>
```

```
<h2>To Do List</h2>
<ol>
    <li>clear out garage
    <li>prepare report
    <li>write email to Ray
    <li>go shopping
        <ul>
            <li>tomatoes
            <li>pasta sauce
            <li>vegetarian cheese
            <li>long spaghetti
            </ul>
    <li>repair fence
</ol>
</html>
```

In this example, we have first an ordered list, then switch to yet another list under go shopping in which there is a list of items to buy. Once that ends the old list is resumed. You can also change the font of one list, or change the emphasis to make it stand out.

2.8.4 Definition Lists

There is also another kind of list that is used for lists of terms and definitions but could be used anywhere you want sets of sub-headings followed by text:

```
<html>

    <dl>
        <dt>Hawthorn Shield bug
        <dd>Beetle which mainly lives on hawthorn bushes
        <dt>Minstrel bug
        <dd>A black and red striped beetle
        <dt>Green Shield bug
        <dd>Large beetle common in UK gardens
    </dl>
</html>
```

2.9 TABLES

Often we need to show data in tabular form; that is, an area that is split into columns and rows to show associations, for example. In HTML this is fairly easy to achieve and requires only a few tags.

2.9.1 Table Structure

A table starts with a `<table>` tag and ends with `</table>`. Each row begins with `<tr>` and ends with `</tr>`; between lie the columns defined with table definition tags `<td>` ... `</td>`:

```
<html>
    <table>
        <tr>
            <td>column item 1</td>
            <td>column item 2</td>
        </tr>
        <tr>
            <td>another item</td>
            <td>and another</td>
        </tr>
    </table>
</html>
```

You may want to group your data with associated headings, for example:

```
<html>
    <table border>
        <tr>
            <td><b>Egyptian</b></td>
            <td>Osiris, Isis, Horus, Thoth, Ptah, Hathor </td>
        </tr>
        <tr>
            <td><b>Norse</b></td>
            <td>Odin, Frigg, Thor, Loki, Freya</td>
        </tr>
        <tr>
            <td><b>Greek</b></td>
            <td>Zeus, Apollo, Persephone, Hermes, Hera</td>
        </tr>
        <tr>
            <td><b>Roman</b></td>
            <td>Jupiter, Luna, Mars, Mercury, Diana</td>
        </tr>

    </table>
</html>
```

As you can see from this example the table now has a drawn border on all sides and the columns and rows. This is defined by using the border option inside the table tag to increase the width of the border shown; for example, `border=n` where n is the thickness in pixels.

2.9.2 Table Headers

It's also possible to create a table with properly defined headers:

```
<html>
    <table border>
        <tr>
                <th></th>
                <th>Green Park</th>
                <th>Oxford Circus</th>
                <th>Euston</th>
                <th>Finsbury Park</th>
        </tr>
         <tr>
                <th>Tube</th>
                <td>5mins</td>
                <td>8mins</td>
                <td>10mins</td>
                <td>13mins</td>
        </tr>
        <tr>
                <th>Bus</th>
                <td>12mins</td>
                <td>14mins</td>
                <td>18mins</td>
                <td>20mins</td>
        </tr>

    </table>
</html>
```

This table is set out with a necessary blank cell as a spacer for the titles in the columns and rows; the HTML is simply a header with no entry. Figure 2-1 shows this table.

	Green Park	Oxford Circus	Euston	Finsbury Park
Tube	5mins	8mins	10mins	13mins
Bus	12mins	14mins	18mins	20mins

Figure 2-1 *A simple HTML table*

2.9.3 Irregular Tables

The kinds of table mentioned so far are relatively simple and symmetrical but sometimes it's necessary to make irregularly shaped tables:

```
<html>
     <table border>
          <tr>
               <th rowspan=2></th>
               <th colspan=4 rowspan=1>Tube Station</th>
          </tr>
          <tr>
               <th>Green Park</th>
               <th>Oxford Circus</th>
               <th>Euston</th>
               <th>Finsbury Park</th>
          </tr>
          <tr>
               <th>Tube</th>
               <td>5mins</td>
               <td>8mins</td>
               <td>10mins</td>
               <td>13mins</td>
          </tr>
          <tr>
               <th>Bus</th>
               <td>12mins</td>
               <td>14mins</td>
               <td>18mins</td>
               <td>20mins</td>
          </tr>

     </table>
</html>
```

Figure 2-2 shows the table produced.

	TUBE STATION			
	Green Park	Oxford Circus	Euston	Finsbury Park
Tube	5mins	8mins	10mins	13mins
Bus	12mins	14mins	18mins	20mins

Figure 2-2 An irregularly shaped HTML table

This table is irregular because of the added heading within the table. To include this, four columns had to be used and also space added at the start for a block of two rows by two columns. The way this is done is by the optional attributes colspan and rowspan within <th> tags, describing how many columns and rows it should take up. These can be added to <td> tags as well.

Another formatting option within tables is alignment; this is added using `align` for horizontal and `valign` for vertical alignment. For example, it's possible to center code within a cell using this code:

```
<tr>
     <th>Tube</th>
     <td align=center>5mins</td>
     <td align=center>8mins</td>
     <td align=center>10mins</td>
     <td align=center>13mins</td>
</tr>
```

It's important to remember that tables will adjust to fit any window that's open so such alignment is important and you may want to consider using vertical as well as horizontal alignment.

2.9.4 Tables and Page Layout

Tables can also be used to format the layout of an HTML page. You can easily divide the page into sections and fill the different areas with text, which will be held in place by the table. The table can be invisible, without borders so it does not interfere with the design:

```
<html>
<head><title>table style</title>/head>
<body>
<table border="0" width="100%" cellpadding="10">
<tr>
<td width="50%" valign="top">
This is the left column containing some interesting text.
Dividing the text like this is similar to newspaper columns.
</td>
 <td width="50%" valign="top">
This is the right column which contains yet more text.
This simply fills the right side of the page.
</td>
</tr>
</table>
</body>
</html>
```

The attributes used in the table in this case are:

• `Border`, which sets the border width in pixels around the table
• `Width`, which in this case is as a percentage of the screen
• `Cellpadding`, to give the distance in pixels between the inner border and the text.

Another optional attribute is cellspacing, which sets the spacing in pixels between the inner and outer borders.

The data cells within the table are defined by the <td> tag, which also in this case uses width to set the width of the cell as a percentage of the browser window. The valign puts any data at the top, middle or bottom of the cell.

Some complicated layouts can be made using tables to control the placement of items.

Test Yourself!

- Experiment with building tables in HTML by drawing up your weekly schedule or timetable.

2.10 IMAGES

As well as text, HTML can be used to place images within pages. This is done using the <img src="filename"> tag, which, if used on its own, would place the image aligned to the left.

2.10.1 Positioning and Placing Images

```
<html>
<h2>show an image</h2>
<img src="photosnap.gif">
my holidays!
<p>the snow slopes where I went skiing...</p>
</html>
```

This would place the image photosnap.gif on a page with the writing straight after it. The graphic should be in the same directory as the HTML file, or directed to the file using the path.

You can use the option align within the image tag to make any accompanying text wrap around the image at various positions. Usually the text will be placed in line with the bottom of the image. Any long text following an image, if there is enough space, will fit in the remaining space, wrapping on to the lines below. The align options are bottom (default), middle or top.

The image can be set to the middle of the page by using the <img src> tag, wrapped by a <center> tag.

It's often useful to place a border around an image to space out surrounding text. This is done by using the options hspace (setting space left and right) and vspace (setting space above and below the image). The amount you set is in pixels. The border is not marked with lines unless you want it to be, using border=n.

2.10.2 Resizing an Image

Images can be manipulated to set them to the size you want them to be for the layout you are using, so it's possible to increase or decrease their size in the X and Y directions. The size can be set in pixels or as a percentage of the browser display. The fixed method relies on the options height and width within the <img src> tag; for example, if you want to set a size of 100 by 100:

```
<img src="snapone.gif" height=100 width=100>
```

On the other hand a relative variable setting will sometimes be more useful:

```
<img src="snapone.gif" height=50% width=25%>
```

The height in this case will be 50% of the browser height by 25% of the current browser width. Just setting one of these values will make it be applied to both.

Sometimes an image may fail to load for some reason, or image loading may be switched off or not available. You may want your visitor to still know what was on the page and missing; the way to do this is by using the alt option attached to the <img src> tag:

```
<img src "me.jpg" alt="my picture!">
```

2.10.3 Background Images

Sometimes you may want the background filling with an image, and this is done using different markup. Instead an option is added into the <body> tag as:

```
<body background="mypattern.gif">
```

This might be one huge image or it could be a simple picture that can be repeated over the area of the screen, possibly a simple pattern or tile. The rule here is that an image smaller than the window will be tiled (repeated) over the area of the browser screen. Remember, if you want to read text or see other images, then any background image should be fairly simple.

An image may also be used as a link rather than text:

```
<a href="biog.html"><img src="mypic.gif"></a>
```

Checkpoint!

We now know how to:

■ implement different types of list
■ utilize tables to give structure to data and layout
■ embed images and use them as background pictures.

2.11 SIMPLE HTML FORMS

Up until now all the HTML that has been dealt with is one way – as output to the browser – but often there is the need to collect information from the user, such as name, address and other contact details. It may be that if your site is an e-commerce site you want to also collect customers' card or payment details along with their choice of product.

Once the user has filled out a form the information needs processing so, on their own, forms don't do a lot! The processing can be done on the client side, using a language like JavaScript, or on the server side with a language such as PHP.

2.11.1 Making a Form

The main tag to build a form is `<form>`. It has a few optional attributes too. Here is an example of the form element:

```
<form action="processform.php" method="post">
</form>
```

The `action` attribute tells the HTML where to send the collected information, while the `method` attribute describes the way to send it.

2.11.2 Types of Input

The main tag for collecting information from the user is `<input>`. A simple example here could be:

```
Enter your email address<input name="email" size=35>
```

The text is to give a prompt as to what is expected from the user. The tag itself contains a `name` attribute, so that we can refer to the input by a name, and the size of the entry box in characters:

```
<html>
    <form>
        please enter your user name
        <input name="user" type="text" size=30><br>
        favourite color
        <input name="color" type="text" size=14><br>
    </form>
</html>
```

There are quite a few different types of input to choose from:

- `<input type="text"/>` This is the default input type and accepts characters and numbers into a text box. It can also have a `value` attribute attached to it, which will give it an initial value.
- `<input type="password"/>` This is similar to the above text box but anything that is typed cannot be seen; instead an asterisk is printed to cover up the entry. As the name suggests, this is used for password entry.
- `<input type="checkbox"/>` This gives a box that can be toggled between `checked` and `unchecked`. It can initially be set to one or the other with `checked="checked"`.
- `<input type="radio"/>` This is similar to the checkbox but in a group of radio buttons only one can be selected at a time. This can also have an initial checked state on one of the radio buttons.
- `<input type="file"/>` This will give a box to allow you to choose a file similar to when you open or save files usually on your machine. It can be used to select a file on the local machine for upload to a server, for example.
- `<input type="submit"/>` This allows a form to be submitted. When pressed, the information will be passed on for processing, usually to a script mentioned in the `action` attribute option of the form.
- `<input type="image"/>` This will also submit the form when selected and, like the `img` tag, requires the `src` attribute to specify an associated image.
- `<input type="button"/>` This makes a button available.
- `<input type="reset"/>` This will reset the form to its initial state when selected.
- `<input type="hidden"/>` This allows hidden data (not seen by the user) to be passed along with the form.

2.11.3 Text Areas

Sometimes you may want to allow the user space to write comments or a message. For this you probably want a larger space for them to write and the best way to do this is to use `<textarea>`:

```
<hr>you can leave a message for me here:
<textarea name="comments" rows="10" cols="70"
```

```
wrap="wrap">message:</textarea>
```

Again, the text area is given a name so the information typed in can be referred to when it is being processed. The size of the area is defined by two optional attributes rows and cols and the wrap option provides several ways of letting the wrap within the box: off, virtual and physical. The off option stops all wrapping on lines and requires the user to type 'enter' to finish a line. virtual wraps the sentence in the box but sends it as one long string and physical provides full text wrapping, with information being kept as it is seen on the display.

2.11.4 Drop Down Menus

Drop down select boxes are another input method that can be used. This is a simple example:

```
<select>
<option value="selected1">Option 1</option>
<option value="selected2">Option 2</option>
<option value="selected3">Option 3</option>
</select>
```

When an option is selected the value returned is set appropriately to selected1, selected2 or selected3. The text displayed is the Option n string. In a similar way to the check-boxes with the checked option, the select tag allows selected="selected" for a default, initial value.

All form values must have a name attribute otherwise they cannot be processed properly!

Elements can also have a readonly attribute, which stops an element from being changed. This may be to confirm past information with new data added, for example.

Listing 2-1 incorporates the form features that have been explored.

```
<html>
  <head><title>My Form</title></head>
  <form action="processor.php" method="post">
    <fieldset><legend>log in now</legend>
    <b>Please enter your user name</b>
    <input name="user" type="text" size=30><br>
    <b>Your password is </b>
    <input name="pass" type="password" size=10><br><br>
    </fieldset>
    <fieldset><legend>Choices!</legend>
    <b>Favourite color</b>
```

```
        <input name="color" type="text" value="green"
                    size=14><br><br>
     My favourite fruit is:
     <select>
         <option value="selected1">Apple</option>
         <option value="selected2">Banana</option>
         <option value="selected3">Orange</option>
     </select>
     <br><br>
     I live in a:
     <input type="radio" name="accom" value="house"
                    checked="checked"/>House
     <input type="radio" name="accom" value="flat"/>Flat
     <input type="radio" name="accom" value="bedsit"/>Bedsit
     <input type="radio" name="accom"
                    value="caravan"/>Caravan
     <br><br>
     My upload file is:
     <input type="file" name="upload" size=40><br><br>
     </fieldset>
     <fieldset><legend>Leaving?</legend>
     <b>You can leave a message for me here:</b>
     <textarea name="comments" rows=10 cols=70></textarea>
     <br><br>
     <input type="submit" value="Go!">
     <input type="reset" value="Start again"></fieldset>
   </form>
</html>
```

Listing 2-1 *Summarizing simple HTML forms*

The form begins at the <form> tag with the **action** attribute being pointed at the script, which would process the data supplied by the user who fills the form out. The processing, including the method **post**, will be covered in some detail in later sections on JavaScript and PHP. In this page the form is broken into several sections using the **fieldset** element, which basically draws rectangles around the areas (see Figure 2-3). **legend** gives a heading to each input section.

Test Yourself!

- Create a form to collect details of a user such as name, login, address, telephone number. Also, collect details of items they wish to purchase, such as in a book store, along with a final comments box.

- Notice how there are different ways of inputting the same data for choices: you can use selection boxes or radio buttons, whereas some data is better collected through a text box.

```
┌─Log in now──────────────────────────────────────────────────┐
│                                                              │
│  Please enter your user name  [                         ]    │
│  Your password is  [               ]                         │
│                                                              │
├─Choices!─────────────────────────────────────────────────────┤
│                                                              │
│  Favourite colour  [green        ]                           │
│                                                              │
│  My favourite fruit is:  [ Apple  ▲▼ ]                       │
│                                                              │
│  I live in a:  ⊙House  ○Flat  ○Bedsit  ○Caravan              │
│                                                              │
│  My upload file is:  ( Choose File )  no file selected       │
│                                                              │
├─Leaving?─────────────────────────────────────────────────────┤
│                                                              │
│  You can leave a message for me here:                        │
│  ┌────────────────────────────────────────────────────┐     │
│  │                                                    │     │
│  │                                                    │     │
│  │                                                    │     │
│  │                                                    │     │
│  │                                                    │     │
│  └────────────────────────────────────────────────────┘     │
│  ( GO! )  ( START AGAIN )                                    │
└──────────────────────────────────────────────────────────────┘
```

Figure 2-3 *A simple HTML form*

2.12 WEB SITE STRUCTURE

A Web site is a collection of pages associated by hyperlinks, but it should also be broken up into areas for structure, which aids both memory and ordering resources. So, your main site can be broken into several sub-sites. Not only this, but you can separate specific files on their types; for example, graphic files can be kept in their own folder as long as they are referenced properly.

A Web site generally has a root directory, the one which is entered first, then several sub-directories that serve as the sub-sites.

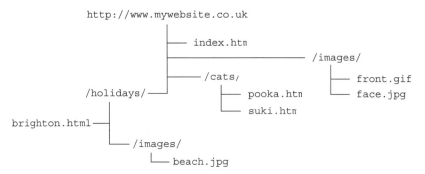

Figure 2-4 *Mapping a Web site*

In Figure 2-4 the main site has a default `index.html` page, which will be picked up by the browser simply by going to `http://www.mywebsite.co.uk`. The `index.html` page uses several images that are collected under an images sub-directory. There are two further sub-sites under the main root directory, namely cats and holidays. What would happen if the browser was pointed to the following?

`http://www.mywebsite.co.uk/cats/`

An error message would come up, as there is no default page such as `index.html`! So, hopefully there would be a link to the two cat pages from the main `index.html` page. This also applies to holidays, which has a single HTML page and a directory for any images.

By breaking the site into directories it makes it a lot easier to find files and also to navigate the actual Web site, which uses the sub-directories as extensions of the main site.

Checkpoint!

We now know:

- the basics of form development using HTML with various types of input
- the importance of structuring your Web site properly and breaking material up into sub-directories on the basis of file type and subject matter.

2.13 CHAPTER SUMMARY

- The Internet and the Web in particular can be seen as having applications and events that occur on two sides: the client side and the server side. The client side is the computer with the browser running on it.

- The development of Web material follows a cycle: requirements capture, design, write code, test, upload, re-iterate.
- A browser will do its best to load a resource it is pointed at, whether it is a text file, image or HTML page.
- Properly developed HTML pages have a defined structure.
- Using HTML a wide range of text and formatting controls exist, including emphasis, fonts, styles, color and layout formatting.
- You should add comments, particularly in complex documents and endeavour to increase readability by adding space and structure.
- Hyperlinks can be added to connect documents and resources. Web links can be made to open in a new browser window, if required.
- Various kinds of list can be created easily and quickly.
- Tables can be used to format data and control the layout of pages.
- Images and graphics can be embedded into pages or used as background pictures to make sites more appealing.
- Forms can be used to gain user interactivity and input of data, which can be processed by scripts. Many types of user input exist as choices for the designer.
- Care should be taken over the structure of a developed Web site. Sub-directories can be used to sort different kinds of file and also to allow a site to be more easily navigated.

Chapter Quiz

- Try and find out the history of the various versions of HTML.
- What are the four kinds of markup elements in HTML?
- Use search engines to find out about the project Semantic Web. What is the role of markup language within it?

Key Words and Phrases

Attribute An optional item added to an HTML element tag, which alters specific features

Client side Refers to operations that are performed by the client in a client–server relationship; in this context, this is the side that has the browser operating

Element An HTML tag is usually comprised of an opening tag consisting of optional parameters/content and a closing tag, which is not always required. An empty element contains no content or end tag but may still have attributes

Emphasis A way of adding a degree of impact to some text, such as making it bold or italic

Font A member of a typeface, a co-ordinated set of character designs usually comprising an alphabet, a set of numerals and punctuation, although it may also contain symbols too

Form A data collection mechanism within HTML that allows the design of various styles of input to suit most types of information

Heading A set of tags that specify font size and emphasis for different levels within a document

Horizontal rule A horizontal line that runs across the page; different types can be selected

Hyperlink A reference to another document or resource

Line break A formatting term that relates to where a sentence or paragraph is dropped to the next line down. In HTML this can occur when a <br> element is used

List An HTML element that allows the simple presentation of lists of information in unordered or ordered (enumerated) forms

Point size A relative measure of the size of a font, which used to have a more concrete meaning

Radio button A type of input mechanism on an HTML form, which usually selects one item from many others

Server side Refers to operations that are performed by the server in the client–server relationship. Typically it is the machine that runs the Web server or other server software

Table An HTML element that allows layout and data to be structured

Tag Part of element in HTML, comprising `<tagname attributes>`; that is, a triangular less than, the tag name and a list of optional attributes. Usually, there is a closing tag such as `</tagname>` but it is not always required

Text area An input area on an HTML form, which can be sized as required

Upload To copy or move files to the server from the client. This is usually done as part of the development cycle of producing a Web site or application

Useful Web Addresses

```
http://www.w3schools.com/html/
http://www.htmlgoodies.com/
http://www.w3.org/MarkUp/Guide/
```

3

FROM HTML TO XHTML

Here we continue the exploration of HTML into XHTML.

You will learn about the various standards that have been developed for HTML. More advanced HTML will also be studied, and the ability to control search engines, cache refresh and meta information.

This chapter charts the rise of XHTML (Extensible HyperText Markup Language) and important standards to correct the failings of early attempts at harmonization between different browsers. It also provides more advanced knowledge of HTML and XHTML:

- the XHTML standard
- syntax and document differences between HTML and XHTML
- the meta tag
- Web page caching, refresh, search engines and expiry
- character encoding and entities
- frames.

It finishes with a more detailed look at the architecture of a Web browser, the way it works and how it deals with input and output along with multimedia.

3.1 MORE HISTORY, MORE STANDARDS

The last chapter introduced you to the practicalities of developing for the Web but before we go much further we need to take another brief look at history to understand where the Web is heading.

The Web was initially conceived as a place where resources were available to all. The idea was that information was linked together and not necessarily in a linear or even hierarchical fashion but that anything on the Web could be accessed from many different pathways and directions. It would not be a static source, like a book for example.

One of the main problems connected with this universality is that although the tools exist, in the form of HTML, to present the information, it is not experienced in the same way by everyone. There are a lot of factors that alter the perception of any resources placed on the Web such as the type of computer, the connection speed and the browser.

So when you develop pages and applications you must take into account these differences, which do alter the experience of the Web. The key here is to create pages so that the greatest number of visitors can view them as closely to the way you designed as possible.

In the past, efforts were made, in the famous 'Browser Wars', to segregate this experience more by creating extensions to HTML that only a specific browser could use. Netscape, in 1994, did just this and although people using their browser could see pages with colored text, images etc., those who didn't use it could not see things in the same way. The extensions created had some impact on the Web surfing community and many went over to using Netscape. Other companies, such as Microsoft, fought back with their own creation in the shape of Internet Explorer, which in turn had its own extensions that only it could recognize.

This continuing fragmentation into groups created problems for those designing pages. A large proportion of their time was taken up trying to develop ways to get around the proprietary tags that had been added to HTML. Multiple versions of the same Web sites had to be created, which had to be loaded according to which browser you were using.

3.1.1 Changes

All this confusion and demarcation of the Web led a lot of designers to believe that standards were the answer. The way this was and still is being achieved is through the World Wide Web Consortium (W3C), directed by the Web's inventor, Tim Berners-Lee. Universality was one of the main aims of the Web and it is this that the W3C tries to maintain while trying to keep pages looking good for everyone. The main contenders, Netscape and Microsoft, are now members, along with other companies that are involved, such as Adobe and Macromedia. The idea is to agree on a standard that everyone can use and that companies do not change.

The proprietary extensions that were developed were standardized while other specifications were removed from HTML. The browser developers were encouraged to support the new official specifications so that any pages written according to them would behave the same no matter what they were viewed on. This became HTML 3.2.

The next step was to develop this specification even further than before. The original idea behind HTML was to be able to create single pages in which content, structure and formatting instructions were present. The W3C thought a far better way of doing this would be to separate the formatting instructions from the content and structure, therefore giving the ability to apply them to the whole site rather than just one page. To do this a large number of formatting instructions were marked for removal in the next version of HTML. The new system for formatting was developed and called Cascading Style Sheets (CSS).

Initially CSS recreated the HTML aspects it was to replace, although slowly it became much better with further specifications. For example, it gained the capability to position elements on a Web page with far greater precision, enabling graphics to be displayed like old HTML but allowing professional layouts to be reproduced in the browser.

However, these improvements did not take away problems with the remaining proprietary extensions and HTML code that was badly written. Browsers did not help in this regard as they allowed a lot of mistakes to pass without any error messages being produced. In the process, this made the browser change the way a page would look. HTML needed some radical changes to become stable enough to develop further features.

The next step was XML (Extensible Markup Language).

3.1.2 XML

XML is a meta-language. It is a language used to describe and define other languages. In essence it looks a lot like HTML – it possesses tags, attributes and values – but you can use it to design your own custom markup language, which can then be used to format your own documents. Using XML it is possible, using tags, to identify data and this then makes the data available for use again. A program can then extract that information and manipulate it along with information from other sources and output the combination, possibly in an entirely different format.

However, XML is nowhere near as lenient as HTML and will not allow the mistakes and general sloppy pages that the latter does. The software that interprets the XML is known as a parser and demands that it is written in a strict way, paying attention to case-sensitivity, special punctuation and other details. The idea that the W3C went along with was to rewrite HTML in XML! This had a bonus in that any code written in the new specification could be understood by all the browsers already available. Another point was that anyone who already had some knowledge of HTML could quickly get used to it, provided they learnt the basic syntax required. Since it is built from XML it gains the same power and flexibility of that language too, providing a stable platform for CSS. The name chosen for this new form of HTML was XHTML.

While HTML and XHTML still co-exist, the likelihood is that XHTML is closer to what the future has in store. There are people who prefer one or the other and some who say that XHTML is the only way to go forward.

There are several types of XHTML, which allows some flexibility:
• *transitional*, which allows the use of deprecated (out of date, superseded) tags
• *frameset*, which allows the use of both deprecated tags and frames
• *strict,* which doesn't allow the use of any types of deprecated tag.

Each of these can be combined with CSS.

A special subset of the XHTML 1.0 specification is also defined as the XHTML Basic 1.0 specification, which contains all the components of XHTML except problematic parts, like frames, which can cause problems for browsers on small devices.

It's advisable to avoid using deprecated tags if you can help it!

Checkpoint!

■ Problems were initially caused in the development of HTML by a lack of standards.
■ Browser makers tended to add proprietary extensions that limited those who could see the sites in the way that was intended.
■ This has been termed the Browser Wars of 1990s.
■ The W3C became the main source for standards that browsers were to follow.
■ The evolution of HTML led to the separation of formatting instructions from content, leading to the development of CSS.
■ HTML was redeveloped as XHTML, using XML, to produce a more strict approach to Web coding.
■ XHTML provides a more stable platform for CSS.
■ Several standards were produced: transitional, which allows the use of deprecated tags; frameset, which allows the use of deprecated tags and frames; and strict, which doesn't allow the use of deprecated tags.

3.2 **THE MOVE TO XHTML**

XHTML and HTML share a common vocabulary but have a slightly different syntax.

Both XHTML and HTML 4 are demanding in the structure you imply on your code. For example, to start a transitional HTML 4 and an XHTML page we begin with a DOCTYPE declaration. This lets browsers and validators know how to judge code and check it appropriately.

For HTML 4:

```
<!DOCTYPE HTML PUBLIC "-//W3C//DTD HTML 4.01 Transitional//EN"
          "http://www.w3.org/TR/html4/loose.dtd">
```

This is followed by the usual <html> tag to begin the actual HTML part of the document.

For XHTML pages, because they are an XML application, a page should begin with an XML declaration:

```
<?xml version="1.0" ?>
```

The question marks say that this is an XML declaration. Be careful with spacing: there must be no space between the opening question mark and the xml, for example. The version should be also written like it is here – with quotes around it.

The XML declaration can also contain the character set encoding as an optional attribute:

```
<?xml version="1.0" encoding="UTF-8" ?>
```

Here the encoding format used is 8-bit Unicode Transformation Format. As you can see, any values being assigned the attribute must be contained in quotes. It's possible to specify foreign language character sets, such as those shown in Table 3-1.

Encoding name	Character set
Shift_JIS	Japanese Kanji
ASMO-449	Arabic Farsi
greek7	Greek Cyrillic
KOI8-R	Russian Cyrillic
Big5	Chinese traditional characters

Table 3-1 *Available character sets*

For XHTML there are several possibilities as far as choice of document type goes, each using *Document Type Definitions (DTDs)*.

For XHTML 1.0 strict the tag would be:

```
<!DOCTYPE html PUBLIC "-//W3C//DTD XHTML 1.0 Strict//EN"
            "http://www.w3.org/TR/xhtml1/DTD/xhtml1-
            strict.dtd:>
```

For XHTML 1.0 transitional it would be:

```
<!DOCTYPE HTML PUBLIC "-//W3C//DTD XHTML 1.00 Transitional//EN"
            "http://www.w3.org/TR/xhtml1/DTD/xhtml1-
            transitional.dtd">
```

For XHTML-Basic 1.0 the tag is:

```
<!DOCTYPE html PUBLIC "-//W3C//DTD XHTML Basic 1.0//EN"
            "http://www.w3.org/TR/xhtml1/DTD/xhtml-
            basic/xhtml-basic10.dtd">
```

For XHTML 1.0 frameset:

```
<!DOCTYPE html PUBLIC "-//W3C//DTD XHTML 1.00 Frameset//EN"
            "http://www.w3.org/TR/xhtml1/DTD/xhtml1-
            frameset.dtd">
```

Like every document in XML, XHTML must have a root element that contains everything else. In this case it is the <html> element, which of course contains all your HTML between the opening and closing tags. The <html> tag may also contain some optional attributes.

One of the attributes is the actual human language being used in the form of a code, as shown in Table 3-2.

It's used like this for English:

```
<html xml:lang="en">

</html>
```

The other important attribute is the declaration of its *namespace*:

```
<html xmlns="http://www.w3.org/1999/xhtml">

</html>
```

This is not a strict requirement as the DTD will supply it if it's not included.

Language	Code	Language	Code
Hindi	hi	Korean	ko
Japanese	ja	Chinese	zh
Russian	ru	Norwegian	no
Swedish	sv	Danish	da
Turkish	tr	Greek	el
Portuguese	pt	Spanish	es
Italian	it	German	de
French	fr	English	en

Table 3-2 Human language codes

3.2.1 Document Structure

The document structure for an XHTML document follows pretty much the format we have been using so far, with the additional parts above included:

```
<!DOCTYPE HTML PUBLIC "-//W3C//DTD XHTML 1.00 Transitional//EN"
          "http://www.w3.org/TR/xhtml1/DTD/xhtml1-
          transitional.dtd">

<html xmlns="http://www.w3.org.org/1999/xhtml">

<head>
     <title>My first XHTML page</title>
</head>

<body>
     <p>What else can you say but... Hello World!</p>
</body>

</html>
```

The main difference here is that the head and body elements are required in XHTML whereas in HTML they are optional.

3.2.2 Some Other Differences

- In XHTML it's important to remember to close tags in those elements that need it. HTML was relatively easy going and it was possible to get away without closing some elements properly. Some elements, such as the line break element <br> in XHTML, must contain a final forward slash: <br/>.

- All XHTML tag and attribute names must be in lowercase and all attribute values must be enclosed in quotes.
- You can nest tags but this must be done correctly without overlapping tags.
- Attributes cannot be abbreviated and should appear fully written out.
- An XHTML document must specify a document title.

The head section may again contain the language attribute as described earlier. It may also contain a profile attribute to be used to specify the URL for a meta data profile for the document.

Checkpoint!

- ■ **HTML and XHTML have similar languages but different syntaxes.**
- ■ **XHTML is less forgiving.**
- ■ **XHTML pages should begin with an XML version tag.**
- ■ **Both HTML 4 and XHTML should have an appropriate DOCTYPE declaration.**
- ■ **XHTML must contain a root element provided by the <html> ... </html> element.**
- ■ **XHTML may also have the language attribute attached to the <html> tag.**
- ■ **A namespace can be provided for XHTML, although the DTD will supply it if it is absent.**
- ■ **Both the head and body elements are required in an XHTML document.**

Test Yourself!

- You can have any page you write checked by a validation service such as the W3C checker at http://validator.w3.org/. This will process any page that it is pointed at and provide a detailed report on any failings! Why not try running some of your new XHTML pages through it and see if you are up to scratch? It will also process and report on HTML 4 too.

3.3 META TAGS

Metadata is information about information or, in this context more specifically, metadata is machine-understandable information about Web resources. It can be included in both

HTML and XHTML to describe the actual document rather than the document's content. Metadata is included in the head section of your page:

```
<html>
 <head>
   <title>Cave Dwelling</title>

   <meta name="author" content="Fred Flintstone"/>
   <meta name="keywords" content="stone age, lifestyles,
                  retro"/>
   <meta name="description" content="living prehistory">
   <meta name="robots" content="index,follow">

   </title>
 </head>
 </html>
```

The meta tags are used to provide information to search engine robots; they pick up the data you give and also control to some extent where they go on your site following links. The sorts of information you can give include a general description of your site together with key words.

There is also an instruction here for search engines to index the page and follow any links. It is possible to stop the page being listed:

```
<meta name="robots" content="noindex"/>
```

Other possibilities are:

```
<meta name="robots" content="index,follow">
<meta name="robots" content="noindex,follow">
<meta name="robots" content="index,nofollow">
<meta name="robots" content="noindex,nofollow">
```

Be sure not to give conflicting or repeating directives!

There is also a meta tag attribute called http-equiv that is used with a content attribute to create meta-functions. These functions can be used, for example, to give an expires date, refresh period or redirection.

In the head section to set an expiration date:

```
<meta name="expires" content="Mon, 20 Jul 2007 16:00:00 GMT"/>
```

This sets the expiry point when a page will be reloaded from the Web site, essentially to ensure a cache (a local store of frequently visited Web sites) is kept up to date. Putting a date of ' 0' will stop the page being cached at all.

Again to force a refresh after a period of time, in the head section:

```
<meta name="refresh" content="50;http://myownpages.co.uk/
                mynewssite.html"/>
```

This will cause the page to be refreshed after 50 seconds and a redirection to occur to the URL specified.

3.3.1 Memory Cache

As we have just seen, Web browsers can cache (store) pages for quick reviewing without having to request them again and re-download the document. Each page has a Time to Live (TTL), the time it is kept in the cache without going back and reloading it. This is usually 30 days, when the browser cache has been cleared or the allotted memory is all used up.

A browser can be stopped from caching a page, if it supports the <meta> element's http-equiv attribute. This forces the browser to ignore the cached page and instead make a request again. To do this the value pragma is assigned to the http-equiv attribute and a no-cache value to the content attribute:

```
<html>
<head>
    <title>no cache example</title>

    <meta http-equiv="pragma" content="no-cache"/>
</head>
</html>
```

A search engine can also cache your page and offer it as an alternative if your site is down or inaccessible for some reason. The only problem here is that it may be very out of date! You can stop a search engine from archiving a page by using:

```
<meta name="robots" content="noarchive"/>
```

Again, this should be placed in the head section.

3.3.2 Formatting with scheme

Another useful meta element attribute is named scheme. This can be used to give a context for data such as date and time, which can use several formats:

```
//Here scheme="USA" implies "MM-DD-YYYY"
<meta scheme="USA" name="date" content="09-21-1966">

//Here scheme="Europe" implies "DD-MM-YYYY"
<meta scheme="Europe" name="date" content="21-09-1966">
```

Test Yourself!

- Write a new Web page (or alter an old one) to incorporate some metadata such as author, description, key words.
- Make the page so it isn't cached by the browser.
- How do we also stop it being cached by the search engine?

3.4 **CHARACTER ENTITIES**

What happens if you want to tell someone about HTML on your Web site? Could you just write the following?

```
<?xml version="1.0"?>
<!DOCTYPE html PUBLIC "-//W3C//DTD XHTML 1.1//EN"
        "http://www.w3.org/TR/xhtml11/DTD/xhtml11.dtd">
<html xmlns="http://www.w3.org/1999/xhtml">
<head>
    <title>tell them about HTML</title>
</head>
<body>

This is how you set up a link:

<a href="www.google.com">Google!</a>

</body>
</html>
```

No, because what you would get is the link to the place itself! How would you get the writing of **href** etc.? The answer is to use character entities to describe what you want printing, then it won't be processed by the browser as HTML. For example, the < (less than) symbol can be replaced by the character entity **<** while the > (greater than) symbol can be replaced by the character entity **>** so, it's possible to replace a great many of the special HTML characters with this special set of entities and therefore display HTML code itself:

```
<?xml version="1.0"?>
<!DOCTYPE html PUBLIC "-//W3C//DTD XHTML 1.1//EN"
        "http://www.w3.org/TR/xhtml11/DTD/xhtml11.dtd">
<html xmlns="http://www.w3.org/1999/xhtml">
<head>
    <title>tell them about HTML</title>
</head>
```

```
<body>

This is how you set up a link:

<a href="www.google.com">Google!</a><br/>

&lt;a href=&quot;www.google.com&quot;>Google!</a>

</body>
</html>
```

Character entities can be useful for inserting symbols that aren't usually available or just for placing spaces around text in your code:

```
<?xml version="1.0"?>
<!DOCTYPE html PUBLIC "-//W3C//DTD XHTML 1.1//EN"
        "http://www.w3.org/TR/xhtml11/DTD/xhtml11.dtd">
<html xmlns="http://www.w3.org/1999/xhtml">
<head>
    <title>tell them about HTML</title>
</head>
<body>

Less than &lt;<br/>
Greater than &gt;<br/>
Ampersand &amp;<br/>
Divide &divide;<br/>
Copyright &copy;<br/>
Registered &reg;<br/>
Quote &quot;<br/><br/>

    over here!

</body>
</html>
```

The complete list of entities is very large. Table 3–3 contains some of the most useful.

Checkpoint!

- ■ Metadata provides information about the document not the content.
- ■ The **<meta>** tag can provide information by these:
  - keywords – a list of keywords for search engines
  - description – a description of the pages content

- robots – information for search engine crawlers
- author – who is the author?
- expires – the date the page expires in the cache
- refresh – force a refresh after a specified time
- `http-equiv` – stop caching using `pragma` value
- scheme – give a local context for items such as dates.
- Character entities provide a way of outputting special characters within HTML pages.

Test Yourself!

- Write a Web page that displays a valid HTML document, including a hyperlink and a list of five items.
- How do you output the trademark and copyright symbols?

Character	Character entity	Description
		Space
&	&amp;	Ampersand
"	&quot;	Quote
<	&lt;	Less than
>	&gt;	Greater than
©	&copy;	Copyright
®	&reg;	Registered
TM	&trade;	Trademark
£	&pound;	Pound
¢	&cent;	Cent
÷	&divide;	Divide

Table 3-3 Useful character entities

3.5 FRAMES AND FRAMESETS

A way of dividing content on your Web site when it starts to get large is to use frames to break information up and partition it. For example, you could place a separate frame down one side of the screen and use it to place navigation aids and links while the main content is in a separate frame to one side.

3.5.1 Rows

To separate the different elements of your content it is possible, for example, to divide the page into rows and to place a new page into each frame:

```
<?xml version="1.0"?>
<!DOCTYPE html PUBLIC "-//W3C//DTD XHTML 1.0 Frameset//EN"
        "http://www.w3.org/TR/xhtml1/DTD/xhtml1-frameset.dtd">
<html xmlns="http://www.w3.org/1999/xhtml">
<head>
    <title>Rows of Frames</title>
</head>
<frameset rows="220,*,60">
<frame name="banner" src="banner.html" scrolling="no"/>
<frame name="main" src="mainpage.html"/>
<frame name="options" src="options.html" scrolling="no"/>
</frameset>
</html>
```

The other pages are simply normal XHTML pages, which are individual files. The first one is options.html:

```
<?xml version="1.0"?>
<!DOCTYPE html PUBLIC "-//W3C//DTD XHTML 1.0 Frameset//EN"
        "http://www.w3.org/TR/xhtml1/DTD/xhtml1-frameset.dtd">
<html xmlns="http://www.w3.org/1999/xhtml">
<head>
    <title>options.html</title>
</head>
<button type="submit" id="abutton" name="abutton"
            value="mybutton1">button 1</button>
<button type="submit" id="bbutton" name="bbutton"
            value="mybutton2">button 2</button>
<button type="submit" id="cbutton" name="cbutton"
            value="mybutton3">button 3</button>
</html>
```

The next is `banner.html`:

```
<?xml version="1.0"?>
<!DOCTYPE html PUBLIC "-//W3C//DTD XHTML 1.0 Frameset//EN"
        "http://www.w3.org/TR/xhtml1/DTD/xhtml1-frameset.dtd">
<html xmlns="http://www.w3.org/1999/xhtml">
<head>
    <title>banner.html</title>
</head>

<img src="banner.jpg">

</html>
```

The last one is `mainpage.html`:

```
<?xml version="1.0"?>
<!DOCTYPE html PUBLIC "-//W3C//DTD XHTML 1.0 Frameset//EN"
        "http://www.w3.org/TR/xhtml1/DTD/xhtml1-frameset.dtd">
<html xmlns="http://www.w3.org/1999/xhtml">
<head>
    <title>mainpage.html</title>
</head>

<body>

This holds the main content!

</body>
</html>
```

The output for this HTML code is shown in Figure 3-1. The main parts to the HTML that describes the frames are the `<frameset>`, `<frame>` and closing tag `</frameset>`. Remember here in XHTML you also have to use the appropriate `<!DOCTYPE>` for framesets. The frameset tag in this case contains an attribute, `rows`, which declares the divisions either in terms of pixel or percentage size. You can, for instance, say you want rows that are two rows of 100 pixels wide with the remainder used for another element of the content by using the asterisk. It is also possible to use more than one asterisk at a time, which will divide the remaining space equally between them. To divide space unequally among such content, add a number to the asterisk, such as 2*, in which case between two, two thirds would go to one and the last third to the other. Another way to describe the frames is by percentages of the area available, using the number followed by the percentage sign.

Figure 3-1 *Basic frames in rows*

The name you give in the <frame> tag allows you to identify it later and target more content at it.

3.5.2 **Alternative Content**

Note that you only give a body section to such a program where you want to support browsers that don't have frame capability. Alternative content is given by adding:

```
<noframes><body>
Alternative content, for those without frame capability.
</body></noframes>
```

3.5.3 **Columns**

To create content that goes across the page in columns rather than in rows, simply change the attribute to cols rather than rows and use the numbers in a similar way:

```
<frameset cols="100,150,*">
```

The columns are divided from left to right so the left-most one above would be 100 pixels, followed by 150 pixels with the remaining area being used for the last. Again the area can be specified as a percentage.

3.5.4 Frames Using Columns and Rows

Frames can divide a page by rows *and* columns too. For example:

```
<?xml version="1.0"?>
<!DOCTYPE html PUBLIC "-//W3C//DTD XHTML 1.0 Frameset//EN"
        "http://www.w3.org/TR/xhtml1/DTD/xhtml1-frameset.dtd">
<html xmlns="http://www.w3.org/1999/xhtml">
<head>
    <title>Rows of Frames</title>
</head>
<frameset frameborder="3" rows="*,*,*" cols="*,*">

<frame name="topleft" src="banner.html"/>
<frame name="topright" src="openingpage.html"/>

<frame name="midleft" src="openingpage.html" scrolling="no"/>
<frame name="midright" src="banner.html"/>

<frame name="botleft" src="banner.html"/>
<frame name="botright" src="buttons.html"/>
</frameset>

</html>
```

This creates a series of frames three rows by two columns, filling out to fit the area available, using the asterisk. Notice in this example, the attribute `frameborder` is used to set the border width – this can also be set to 0 for no border. Another attribute for the frame tag is `scrolling,` which allows the frame to be moved with an added bar. Figure 3-2 shows the frames displayed.

3.5.5 Nesting Frames

Frames can also be nested within each other, to further divide a frame's space:

```
<?xml version="1.0"?>
<!DOCTYPE html PUBLIC "-//W3C//DTD XHTML 1.0 Frameset//EN"
        "http://www.w3.org/TR/xhtml1/DTD/xhtml1-frameset.dtd">
<html xmlns="http://www.w3.org/1999/xhtml">
<head>
```

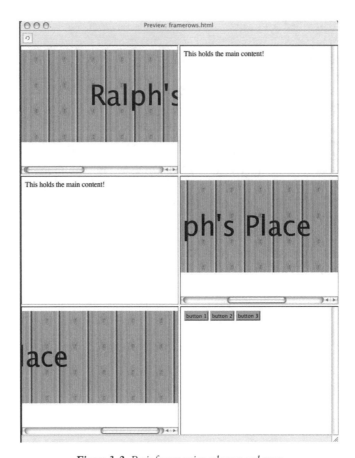

Figure 3-2 *Basic frames using columns and rows*

```
    <title>Rows of Frames</title>
</head>

<frameset cols="20%,80%">

    <frame name="main" src="buttons.html">

    <frameset rows="25%,75%">
        <frame name="top" src="banner.html" scrolling="no"/>
        <frame name="bottom" src="openingpage.html"/>
    </frameset>

</frameset>

</html>
```

Figure 3-3 *Nesting frames*

Figure 3-3 shows how this HTML code divides the screen into useful areas for navigation, main content and banner.

3.5.6 Inline Frames

Content can also be mixed in another way and placed with other graphics and text. To do this, an inline frame can be used:

```
<?xml version="1.0"?>
<!DOCTYPE html PUBLIC "-//W3C//DTD XHTML 1.0 Frameset//EN"
        "http://www.w3.org/TR/xhtml1/DTD/xhtml1-frameset.dtd">
<html xmlns="http://www.w3.org/1999/xhtml">
<head>
    <title>Rows of Frames</title>
</head>
```

```
<h1>An inline frame example</h1>

Inline frames can be used to sit with other types of content
                such as text
and graphics.

<iframe src="banner.html" name="mybanner" width="300"
                height="200" align="right">
This text will appear if the browser can't display the frame
</iframe>
The iframe behaves in some ways like an image in that text will
                tend to flow around it.
Be careful using align as it is deprecated.
</html>
```

This example is shown in Figure 3-4.

The example actually uses a *deprecated* attribute `align`, which means it has been superseded by some other way of achieving the same effect. The `align` attribute can also be used with `image` for the same effect, forcing text to flow around it. The CSS `float` property has now replaced this capability.

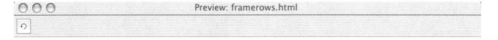

An inline frame example

Inline frames can be used to sit with other types of content such as text and graphics.
The iframe behaves in some ways like an image in that text will tend to flow around it. Be careful using align as it is deprecated.

Figure 3-4 Using an iframe

Checkpoint!

■ Frames are a way of providing layout for pages.

■ Frames can be arranged vertically, horizontally or a mix of the two.

■ Frames can be nested within each other.

■ The parameters for the frame width and height can be stated in pixels, as a percentage or can use the rest of available space using asterisk *, which can also be used to divide the space unequally.

■ Inline frames allow frames to be mixed with other content on a page such as graphics and text.

■ Alternatives should be provided for browsers without the frame capability. The <noframes> element can be used for this.

Test Yourself!

• Draw out a rough design for a Web page using frames.
• Try and incorporate graphics and text that are controlled by a frame layout.
• Implement the design and experiment with the layout; can you get it exactly as you had designed it?
• Now try and embed an inline frame on a page with graphics and text.

3.6 WHAT IS INSIDE A BROWSER?

By now you have had some experience of using a Web browser and probably have done some work with HTML. On the client side probably the most important piece of software connected with the Web is the browser, which we will look at in more detail.

Figure 3-5 shows a conceptual diagram of the internals of a browser. As you can see it has various inputs and outputs with the outside world, or operating system in which it sits, the more important of which are outlined here. The controller acts as the main overseer of operations between the various components, for example it is responsible for collecting input from the user and also managing outgoing requests for the HTTP client to deal with for external communication. HTML and scripts are channeled through to the interpreters as needed and output from these is put through special display drivers. The browser can be extended with plug-in modules, which enhance capabilities such as multimedia, graphics and sound.

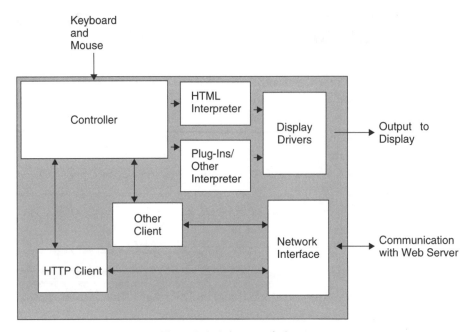

Figure 3-5 *Architecture of a browser*

Checkpoint!

■ **A browser is a complex piece of software.**

■ **It collects input from keyboard and mouse.**

■ **It handles communication with Web servers.**

■ **It interprets HTML and client side scripts.**

■ **It has the capability to be functionally extended via plug-ins.**

Test Yourself!

• Using a search engine find which browsers are currently available.

• What extensions and plug-ins are available for your favorite browser?

3.7 **CHAPTER SUMMARY**

- ■ The initial struggles within the market for dominance of browsers led to the Browser Wars in the 1990s.
- ■ Standards are very important.
- ■ HTML evolved from 3.2 through to the more strict XHTML.
- ■ XML was used to 'rebuild' HTML.
- ■ XHTML has several levels: transitional, frameset and strict.
- ■ XHTML demands a more strict syntax and a more structured document.
- ■ Metadata provides information about the document, not content.
- ■ Metadata can direct how a Web page is dealt with by browsers, servers and search engines.
- ■ Character entities can be used to encode certain characters that HTML uses.
- ■ Frames can be useful to break up the layout of a page.
- ■ Frames can be sized and structured as required.
- ■ Inline frames can be mixed in with other content such as text and graphics.
- ■ Frames can be problematic for some browsers so provide alternative content where possible.
- ■ Some elements and attributes have become deprecated, superseded by new language features and so should generally be avoided.
- ■ A browser is a complex piece of software made of several components including network, display and script interpreter modules that can further be extended by special multimedia plug-ins.

Chapter Quiz

- • Find out a bit more about the origins of XML: which language is it a subset of?
- • What other languages have been developed from XML?
- • Why do some people recommend *not* using frames?

Key Words and Phrases

Browser Wars A name given to the competition between Web browsers for dominance in the marketplace, particularly in the late 1990s

Cache A memory store that can hold frequently requested Web pages

Character entity Certain characters can be encoded as HTML entities, which can take their place. For example '<' can be encoded as <

CSS Cascading Style Sheets, a language used to describe the presentation of a structured document in HTML and XHTML

Deprecated A feature of software or a programing language is said to be deprecated when it is phased out or made obsolete

Driver A software component that provides an interface between different levels in a computer system, usually between software and hardware

DTD Document Type Definition, a declaration in XML that specifies constraints on a document, for example where it is valid XHTML

Frame A feature of HTML that allows layout to be broken into separate areas

Inline frame A frame that can be set out with other text and graphics

Interpreter A software component that analyzes a script and acts on the commands given

Meta tag A meta tag gives information about the page rather than its content

Operating system The system software responsible for management and interaction between applications and hardware

Plug-ins Additional software components that extend a browser's capability

TTL Time To Live, the length of time before a page expires

XHTML Extensible HyperText Markup Language has the same capabilities as HTML in terms of expression but is much more strict in syntax

XML Extensible Markup Language, a general purpose markup language

Useful Web Addresses

http://www.w3schools.com/xhtml/

http://www.w3.org/TR/xhtml1/

http://www.xhtml.org/

4

In this chapter you will learn how to present and control the format of Web pages using CSS. This includes the ability to precisely control the positioning and attributes of content while maintaining the structure of the document itself.

This chapter explains why we need Cascading Style Sheets (CSS) and how it enables the designer to separate presentation and formatting away from content. It looks at the simple structure and syntax used and the basic method that enables the styles created to be linked to pages.

CSS allows you to enhance your Web pages in a way that HTML on its own never could and to keep a logically structured document in the process. Here it is shown how to add background images and colors and to manipulate text and other elements. It is possible to add borders, boxes and alter margins.

In HTML, positioning and layout either occur during the natural flow of the page or by using tables to control the positioning of elements. In CSS, precise control is enabled over where objects are placed either relatively or finely, with absolute pixel precision!

4.1 **THE NEED FOR CSS**

In the early 1990s HTML was largely still concerned with the structural elements of a document. These elements included descriptions of paragraphs, lists, headings and hyperlinks. There was nothing to control layout in the form of tables or frames, for example. The main aim at this point was to have a language that cleanly described the structure rather than the presentation.

Over time, as more browsers such as Mosaic joined the WWW, additions were made to the language to provide features that included more control over displayed text and graphics. There was a demand with the surge of interest that features such as bold and italics control should be added. Marking up a piece of text to be emphasized could mean that it was either made bold or placed in italics, and browsers could determine it one way or the other. What the author created was not always how the reader saw it in the end.

HTML (both 3.2 and 4.0) had large sections given over to presentation aspects such as color, size of text and background. Text was also made to be able to blink through HTML. The amount of HTML in a document given over to this kind of graphical presentation eroded the use of HTML as a structural markup language.

Structural meaning became lost and documents could not be processed in any way beyond providing output in a browser. For example, a speech processor could not rely on the information contained in a document to give it clues about sections or emphasis and there would be no strict rules for early HTML in any case!

If a page has no structure then it becomes difficult to use in several ways:

• Like any poorly structured program in software engineering it makes it hard to follow and therefore difficult to understand what's actually happening. This makes it difficult to update and maintain.
• Search engine indexing becomes more difficult as the lack of structural markup gives a lack of importance to key content.
• Processing by software other than a browser is problematic as there are few hints at specific information.

It soon became obvious, especially to the W3C that this mixing of presentational and structural information could not continue and they began to work on a solution. The basis of this, revealed in 1995, was CSS. This was quickly taken on board and by 1996 had become a full recommendation on a par with HTML.

The initial CSS has been supplemented by a second level, CSS2, which became a full recommendation in 1998. This builds on CSS1, adding extensions without major changes to the actual first specification.

4.2 INTRODUCTION TO CSS

CSS has improved the original messy attempt at controlling presentation within HTML:

- control of text color of any element
- control of background colors
- control of borders around elements
- spacing between elements and borders
- text manipulation and decoration.

Everything that was possible at the height of the HTML presentation days is possible in CSS and more. To give a basic idea of how CSS works and how powerful it is, a simple example is required.

A heading could be given in markup as:

```
<h1>The main heading</h1>
```

If you wanted to add color, emphasis and font control to this using the old way within HTML, there would be a lot of complex layout information to add. With CSS it's possible to do this quite simply by a selector, which in this case is h1, followed by a list of properties and values:

```
h1 { color: red; font: italic 1em Times, serif; text-decoration:
            underline; background: black; }
```

If you wanted to change every h1 tag to a particular set of colors and attributes the old way in HTML, you would have to go through your code and do this individually. CSS allows a particular style to be attached to a selector, which is usually an HTML element.

4.3 BASIC SYNTAX AND STRUCTURE

A CSS document, or section, consists of a list of rules containing a selector and declaration block.

4.3.1 Rules

The basic idea behind the syntax of CSS is simply:

```
selector { property:value; .... }
```

The selector is the identifier of the element, followed by a list of paired property:values enclosed within curly brackets. For example:

```
body { color: yellow }
```

Values that have multiple words must be enclosed within quotes:

```
p {font-family: "sans serif"}
```

If there is more than one property to be set then they are separated by semicolons:

```
p {text-align:center;color:red}
```

It's possible to break these up on to different lines rather than placing them all on one line:

```
p {
text-align:center;
color:red
}
```

which is useful if you have a lot of properties, as it makes them more readable.

As well as attaching quite a few properties to one selector, it is possible to have many selectors. So, to apply a set to h1 and h2:

```
h1, h2 { color: red; font: italic 1em Times, serif;
                text-decoration: underline; background: black; }
```

or to make a whole group of headers red:

```
h1,h2,h3,h4,h5,h6
{
color: red
}
```

4.3.2 Classes

It's possible that sometimes you will need to make several styles for the same HTML element:

```
p.right {text-align: right}
p.left {text-align: left}
```

To actually use this within your HTML document:

```
<p class="right">
This paragraph will be right-aligned.
</p>
<p class="left">
This paragraph will be left-aligned.
</p>
```

You cannot specify more than one class for an HTML element though! A useful technique is to specify a class without its main tag so it can be applied to any other class that the designer wants to use it for:

```
.left { text-align: left }
```

You can then apply this to multiple tags as long as they share the same class:

```
<h1 class="left">
This heading will be left-aligned
</h1>
<p class="left">
This paragraph will also be left-aligned.
</p>
```

4.3.3 ID

Similarly, there is the id selector, which will apply a specific style to an identified element. For example, to declare a style rule with an id:

```
p#bluepara
{
text-align: center;
color: red
}
```

This will create a style rule that will match a paragraph with the id value bluepara. It will match for example:

```
<p id="bluepara">Some interesting thoughts...</p>
```

but not:

```
<h1 id="bluepara">This section...more thoughts</h1>
```

You could match any element with the id of bluepara by using:

```
#bluepara
{
text-align: center;
color: red
}
```

The difference between class and id, although similar, is that class may apply to several parts of a page whereas id applies only to one and it should be *unique*. For example, it would be wrong to do this with the same id:

```
<h2 id="alert">This is an alert!</h2>
<p id="alert">This is an alert!</p>
<h3 id="alert">This is an alert!</h3>
```

4.3.4 Pseudo-Class Selectors

Some selectors can be considered different because of the way the element they belong to works. For example, the anchor that creates a link between documents can have pseudo classes attached to it simply because it is not known at the time of writing the markup what the state will be. It could be visited, not visited or in the process of being selected (clicked upon, or active). To catch these states and say what we want to happen in each, we can use pseudo-class selectors:

```
a:link {color: red}
a:active {color: yellow}
a:visited {color: green}
```

So, a link in this instance would be initially red; when visited it would be green; and in the process of being clicked on it would be yellow. Note here, in the case of pseudo classes, the use of the colon (:) in the rule rather than a dot (.) separator, as used in the usual classes.

There are more pseudo classes; for example:

```
a:hover {font-weight: bold}
```

This will make a link bold when the cursor is above it. However, hover is not constrained to links so it may be possible to have other elements using the same hover. To make it specific to links:

```
a:link:hover {font-weight:bold}
```

Checkpoint!

We now know:

■ the main idea behind CSS is to separate presentation from content

■ CSS controls lots of formatting and layout that used to be part of HTML

■ this method helps structure the document and is block oriented

■ a CSS document, or embedded section, consists of a list of rules

■ elements, or blocks, can be marked up with a name for classes or identifier tags

■ hyperlinks can also have formatting applied to them.

4.4 USING CSS

To use a style sheet, you can either embed the rules in the document you want to apply it to or have a totally separate file.

4.4.1 External Style Sheets

An external file is a good idea when you have a number of pages, or even a complete site, which you need to control in terms of presentation. Obviously this saves a lot of effort as, at one time, you would have needed to alter each page individually. This way you can change the look of the entire site by altering only one file. Each page that uses the style sheet needs to have a link to associate it with the style document:

```
<head>
<link rel="stylesheet" type="text/css"
href="mystyle.css" />
</head>
```

The work is done with the link tag, which needs to be inside the head section.

The actual style document contains lists of rules to apply and has the extension .css. The file can be written with a normal text editor as it contains just plain text. It should not have any HTML elements in it.

Listing 4-1 is an example of an external CSS file. It shows seven CSS rules with multiple properties. Note here the correct syntax of a comment, which is useful for particularly large files where you can annotate the styles as you wish.

```
body {
    background-attachment: fixed;
    background-repeat: repeat;
    background-image: url(images/test.gif);
}
font {
    font-family: Arial, Helvetica, sans-serif;
    font-size: 12px;
    color: #0000FF;
}
.bodytext {
    font-family: Arial, Helvetica, sans-serif;
    font-size: 16px;
    color: #000000;
}
```

```
.pageH {
    font-weight: bold;
}
.bluesubheading{
    font-family: Arial, Helvetica, sans-serif;
    font-size: 14px;
    color: #0000FF;
    text-decoration: underline;
    font-weight: bold;
}
.bluebodytext{
    font-family: Arial, Helvetica, sans-serif;
    color: #0000FF;
}
.subheading {
    font-family: Arial, Helvetica, sans-serif;
    font-size: 18px;
    font-weight: normal;
    text-decoration: underline;
}
```

Listing 4-1 *External CSS file*

4.4.2 **Embedded Style Sheets**

It is also possible to use an internal style sheet; that is style information that is attached to only one document. Here the CSS information is contained within the head section, for example:

```
<head>
<style type="text/css">
hr {color: sienna}
p {margin-left: 20px}
body {background-image: url("images/back40.gif")}
</style>
</head>
```

Any information is given using the style tag followed by the formatting data. One problem here is that when an older browser loads the page, it will ignore the <style> tag then print the CSS information following it on to the browser page! To get around this the best way is to enclose any such code within an HTML comment element:

```
<head>
<style type="text/css">
<!--
hr {color: sienna}
```

```
p {margin-left: 20px}
body {background-image: url("images/back40.gif")}
-->
</style>
</head>
```

New browsers that are processing the CSS information will ignore the comments but older ones will see the comments and not process the information between the start and end of the <style> tag.

Another way of incorporating CSS formatting is to use an inline method; that is, to write the markup into the actual element that requires it:

```
<p style="color: sienna; margin-left: 20px">
This is a paragraph
</p>
```

Although this can be done it does lose some of the advantages of CSS by mixing the content and presentation. It is probably best used when there is a unique occurrence of a style in a site or page.

It's also possible to have several active style schemes, for example an external style sheet and an internal style sheet. In this case the more specific values will be inherited from the internal style sheet.

4.5 BACKGROUND IMAGES, COLORS AND PROPERTIES

Using CSS it is possible to control the color of an element's background, use an image in the background, tile an image (repeat it horizontally or vertically) or place an image at a specific place on a page.

4.5.1 Background Color

To change the background color to yellow, you might place the following in your external CSS file:

```
body {
    background: #F0F8FF;
}
```

or:

```
body {
    background: yellow;
}
```

Remember colors can be set using RGB color codes (hex or decimal) or names. The W3C CSS standard supports only 16 names – aqua, black, blue, fuchsia, gray, green, lime, maroon, navy, olive, purple, red, silver, teal, white and yellow, although most browsers support more (these can be found at `http://www.w3schools.com/css/css_colornames.asp`).

To make sure any text is black you can use:

```
body {
    background: #FFFF20;
    color: #000000;

}
```

To test these out you need an HTML page that links them in:

```
<html xmlns="http://www.w3.org/1999/xhtml">
<head>
    <title>Testing CSS</title>
    <link rel="stylesheet" type/css" href="mycss.css"
                title="green">

</head><body>
How about some color...
</body></html>
```

Notice here that the background property sets all background properties that include `background-color`, `background-image`, `background-repeat`, `back-ground-attachment` and `background-position`. Each of these can be set individually, of course.

4.5.2 Background Images

As well as colored backgrounds, it's possible to set an image as the background. This can be set to repeat over the background or just be placed once:

```
body {
    background: #F4a460;;
    background-image: url("suki.jpg");
    background-repeat: no-repeat;
}
```

The HTML basically stays the same:

```
<html xmlns="http://www.w3.org/1999/xhtml">
<head>
```

```
<title>My Cat Suki</title>
<link rel="stylesheet" type/css" href="mycss.css"
            title="green">

</head><body>
The kitchen cat, Suki!
</body></html>
```

We can see the output from this in Figure 4-1. As you can see there is one image in the background with black writing on top.

Figure 4-1 *Using a background image*

If you want a repeating image in the background, possibly as a pattern for texture, then you just alter `background-repeat` to `repeat` or `repeat-x repeat-y` depending on which direction you want it to repeat in:

```
body {
    background: #F4a460;
    background-image: url("browntile.jpg");
```

```
        background-repeat: repeat;
    }
```

The other thing that you can do is to set an image as fixed when a scroll bar is moved or moves with the rest of the page. To do this, use the background-attachment property, which can be set to scroll or fixed.

The summary of properties is given in Table 4-1.

Property	Description	Values
Background	Sets all background properties in one declaration	as RGB
Background-attachment	Sets whether image moves with page when scrolled	scroll or fixed
background-color	Sets the background color of an element	RGB, hex, name or transparent
background-image	Sets an image in the background	URL or none
Background-position	Sets the starting position of an image in the background	top left top center top right center left center center center right bottom left bottom center bottom right x-% y-% x-pos y-pos
background-repeat	Sets the repetition of an image used in the background	repeat repeat-x repeat-y no-repeat

Table 4-1 The background property

Checkpoint!

We now know how to:

■ link a style sheet to a Web page, or embed CSS within a document

■ change background properties such as color or add an image

■ manipulate a background image so it can be repeated (or tiled) over an area, or remain static in relation to scrolling contents.

4.6 MANIPULATING TEXT

As we have seen it is also possible to set the color of text, in this case using the header selector:

```
<html>
<head>

<style type="text/css">
h1 {color: #00ff00}
h2 {color: yellow}
h3 {color: rgb(255,20,40)}
p {color: rgb(0,0,255)}
</style>

</head>

<body>
<h1>A colored header 1</h1>
<h2>A colored header 2</h2>
<h3>A colored header 3</h3>
<p>And a paragraph!</p>
</body>
</html>
```

This document uses a built-in style sheet to determine the color of various parts of the text. Here, a set of headers are each given a different color, along with a separate paragraph, which is also given its own individual color. A variety of ways of choosing and setting the values are used, including giving a hex value, a name and RGB values between 0 and 255.

The background color of text can also be changed:

```
<head>
```

```
<style type="text/css">
h1 {color: #00ff00; letter-spacing: -3px}
h2 {color: yellow; letter-spacing: 0.6px}
h3 {color: rgb(255,20,40); background-color: yellow}
p {color: rgb(0,0,255)}
</style>

</head>
```

Also, in this example the spacing of the letters is manipulated on specific text. The spacing is decreased on <h1> and increased on <h2>.

When controlling layout, it is often adequate to say whether you want text to be aligned to the left, center or right. This can also be done within CSS:

```
<html>
<head>

<style type="text/css">
h1 {text-align: center}
h2 {text-align: left}
h3 {text-align: right}
</style>

</head>

<body>

<h1>This is header 1</h1>
<h2>This is header 2</h2>
<h3>This is header 3</h3>

</body>
</html>
```

4.6.1 Text Decoration

Often text needs to be underlined. This can be done with text decoration, which also has several other styles:

```
<html>
<head>

<style type="text/css">
h1 {text-decoration: overline}
```

```
h2 {text-decoration: line-through}
h3 {text-decoration: underline}
a {text-decoration: none}
</style>

</head>

<body>

<h1>This is header 1</h1>
<h2>This is header 2</h2>
<h3>This is header 3</h3>
<p>
<a href="http://www.w3schools.com/default.asp">
This is a link</a>
</p>

</body>
</html>
```

4.6.2 Text Indentation

Text can also be indented:

```
<html>
<head>

<style type="text/css">
p {text-indent: 1cm}
</style>

</head>

<body>

<p>
This is some text in a paragraph
This is some text in a paragraph
This is some text in a paragraph
This is some text in a paragraph
This is some text in a paragraph
This is some text in a paragraph
</p>

</body>
</html>
```

4.6.3 **Text Case**

Sometimes you may want to control the case of text in a section or paragraph:

```
<html>
<head>

<style type="text/css">
p.uppercase {text-transform: uppercase}
p.lowercase {text-transform: lowercase}
p.capitalize {text-transform: capitalize}
</style>

</head>

<body>

<p class="uppercase">
This is some text in a paragraph
</p>

<p class="lowercase">
This is some text in a paragraph
</p>

<p class="capitalize">
This is some text in a paragraph
</p>

</body>
</html>
```

4.7 **USING FONTS**

The following example shows many of the font features available in CSS:

```
<html>
<head>

<style type="text/css">
h3 {font-family: times;
    font'size: 150%;
    font-style: normal }
p {font-family: courier;
    font-size: 100%;
    font-style: oblique}
```

```
p.sansserif {font-family: sans-serif;
    font-style: italic}
</style>

</head>

<body>

<h3>This is header 3</h3>

<p>
This is a paragraph</p>

<p class="sansserif">
This is a paragraph</p>

</body>
</html>
```

The first thing to look at is how fonts are set. This is, not surprisingly, with the font-family property. The property font-size will set the size of the text, either as a percentage or a relatively worded value such as small, medium, large. The other property used in the example is font-style which allows fonts to be set to normal, italic or oblique (slanted).

Test Yourself!

- Develop a simple Web page, maybe by altering an old one with lots of HTML presentation tags in. Convert any manipulation of text via HTML, such as fonts and colors, into CSS.
- Initially embed the style detail within the same page as the HTML.
- Take out the CSS and place in a separate file.

4.8 BORDERS AND BOXES

The border properties allow many styles of border to be placed around areas. There is a large degree of control over the type of border, such as solid, dashed, doubled or ridged. Along with this, colors, width and thickness can be applied.

The summary of properties is given in Table 4-2.

Property	Description	Values
Border	Sets all properties for four borders in one declaration	border-width border-style border-color
border-bottom	Sets all properties for bottom border in one declaration	border-bottom-width border-style border-color
border-bottom-color	Sets bottom border color	border-color
border-bottom-style	Sets bottom border style	border-style
border-bottom-width	Sets bottom border width	thin, medium, thick length
border-color	Sets the color of the borders	color
border-left	Sets all properties for left side	border-left-width border-style border-color
border-left-color	Sets left border color	border-color
border-left-style	Sets left border style	border-style
border-left-width	Sets left border width	thin, medium, thick length
border-right	Sets all properties for right side	border-right-width border-style border-color
border-right-color	Sets right border color	border-color
border-right-style	Sets right border style	border-style
border-right-width	Sets right border width	thin, medium, thick length

Table 4-2 The border *property*

Property	Description	Values
border-style	Sets style of the four borders	none hidden dotted dashed solid double groove ridge inset outset
border-top	Sets all properties for top border	border-top-width border-style border-color
border-top-color	Sets color for top border	border-color
border-top-style	Sets style for top border	border-style
border-top-width	Sets width for top border	thin, medium, thick length
border-width	Sets width for all borders	thin, medium, thick length

Table 4-2 *(continued)*

4.9 MARGINS

The margin is the space between one element and another, in addition to and outside of any padding (section 4.10) or border around an element:

```
<html>
<head>

<style type="text/css">
p.margin {margin-top: 5cm}
</style>

</head>

<body>
```

```
<p>
This is a paragraph This is a paragraph
This is a paragraph This is a paragraph
</p>

<p class="margin">
This is a paragraph with a top margin
This is a paragraph with a top margin
</p>

</body>
</html>
```

It is possible to set margins for top, bottom, left and right. You can use the margin property alone to set all the properties in one single declaration:

```
<style type="text/css">
p.margin {margin: 2cm 4cm 3cm 4cm}
</style>
```

4.10 PADDING

Padding allows you to insert extra space around the contents of an element but inside the border. You can change only the padding zone's thickness but not its color.

```
<html>
<head>

<style type="text/css">
    td {padding-bottom: 2cm; padding-top: 2cm}
</style>

</head>

<body>

<table border="1">
<tr>
<td>
A table cell with top and bottom padding
</td>
</tr>
</table>
</body>
</html>
```

The summary of properties is given in Table 4-3.

Property	Description	Values
padding-bottom	Adds padding at bottom	length, %
padding-top	Adds padding at top	length, %
padding-left	Adds padding at left	length, %
padding-right	Adds padding at right	length, %
padding	All of above in one declaration	padding-top padding-right padding-bottom padding-left

Table 4-3 The *padding* property

4.11 LISTS

There is some degree of control over the lists you create. It is possible to alter the list item marker and where the marker is placed:

```
<html>
<head>
<style type="text/css">
ul.disc
{ list-style-type: disc}
ul.circle
{list-style-type: circle}
ul.square
{list-style-type: square}
ul.none
{list-style-type: none}
</style>
</head>

<body>
    <b>Pizzas!</b><br><br>
    <ul class="disc">
    <li>Vegetarian</li>
    <li>Mozzarella</li>
    <li>Al Fungi</li>
    </ul>
```

```
<ul class="circle">
<li>Vegetarian</li>
<li>Mozzarella</li>
<li>Al Fungi</li>
</ul>

<ul class="square">
<li>Vegetarian</li>
<li>Mozzarella</li>
<li>Al Fungi</li>
</ul>

<ul class="none">
<li>Vegetarian</li>
<li>Mozzarella</li>
<li>Al Fungi</li>
</ul>

</body>
</html>
```

The summary of properties is given in Table 4-4.

Property	Description	Values
list-style-image	Use an image as marker	none, url
list-style-position	Positioning of marker	inside, outside
list-style-type	Type of marker	none, disc, circle, square, decimal ...
list-style	Set all properties	All above properties

Table 4-4 The *list* property

4.12 POSITIONING USING CSS

Unlike HTML, CSS allows good control over the positioning of elements. Ordinarily elements in a Web page flow in the order they appear. So, as you work down from the top of an HTML page the elements will appear: an image placed before a paragraph will appear on the page in just that way. Using CSS it is possible, instead, to break this normal flow and position elements out of this order. In fact it is possible to control exactly where elements will appear.

4.12.1 **Absolutely!**

The example in Listing 4–2 shows what is called absolute positioning. In this case the positioning sets the top left of the element, although it is also possible to set an element's position by the bottom right. It is labeled absolute position as it is not relative to where it would have been in the natural flow and uses the window positioning for exact coordinates.

```
<html>
<head>
<style type="text/css">
h1 {
position: absolute;
top: 100px;
left: 100px
}

p {
position: absolute;
top: 200px;
left: 100px
}
</style>

</head>

<body>
<h1>A heading</h1>
<p>
The <b>heading</b> is placed 100px
down from the top of the document,
and 100px to the right from the
left side of the document.
The <b>paragraph</b> is placed 200px
down from the top of the document,
and 100px to the right from the
left side of the document.
</p>

</body>
</html>
```

Listing 4-2 *Absolute positioning*

4.12.2 **It's All Relative**

Elements can also be placed relatively; that is, not in relation to other objects but in relation to where they would have been in the natural flow of the page. To do this the selector position: relative is used, along with top, right, bottom or left and :n where n is the offset from its natural location.

4.12.3 **The Z-Index**

Not only is it possible to position elements in the x and y coordinates but it is also possible to position them in terms of depth of the screen so things can appear to be behind or in front of others! To do this, a z-index is introduced. A z-index property has a number that describes where the object is in the stack of visible elements. The higher the number, the closer to the top and more visible the object is:

```
<html>

<head>
<style type="text/css">
p.ap {
position: absolute;
left: 55px;
top: 70px;
z-index: 0;
}
img.x
{
position:absolute;
left:0px;
top:0px;
z-index:1;
}
h1 {
position:absolute;
left:5px;
top:5px;
z-index: 2;
}
</style>
</head>
<body>

<h1>This is a Heading</h1>
<img class="x" src="cat.gif" width="100" height="180">
```

```
<p class="ap">Default z-index is 0. Z-index -1 has lower
                priority.</p>

</body>
</html>
```

This example shows three layers at depths 0, 1, 2. The heading is at depth 2 so is most visible (highest in the stack), followed by the image at 1 and finally the furthest back is the paragraph. Be aware that Netscape 4 does not support the z-index.

The height and width of an element can be set quite easily too, so it can be manipulated into a given space. To do this we use the dimension properties width and height, which can be set with percentage or pixel values:

```
<style type="text/css">

p.small {
height: 30px;
width: 50px
}

p.other {
height: 50%;
}
</style>
```

In p.small the width and height are given of the box to contain the paragraph. In p.other 50% of the container area will be used for the element's box size.

If the contents of the element do not fit in the box then it is possible to use the overflow property to explain what you want to happen. For example, using the value visible, (or simply not using the overflow property at all) makes the box expand so that its contents will fit. The value hidden will hide any contents that don't fit in the box; whereas the scroll value will add scroll bars to the element box so that there is a choice by the user as to whether the content can be looked at. Using auto as the value for the overflow property will make scroll bars only appear when they need to.

4.12.4 Shaping an Element

An element, such as an image, can also be usefully shaped with the clip property. For example:

```
img
{
```

```
position:absolute;
clip:rect(0px 50px 200px 0px)
}
```

4.12.5 Floating Elements

Sometimes you want an element, such as an image, to float so that other elements will flow around it. This happens, for example, when you want a picture to be surrounded by text on one side or another. To do this the `float` selector is used together with `left` or `right` as the value. Unfortunately a lot of browsers tend to be inconsistent with whether this is implemented properly!

4.12.6 Layout and Structure

The idea behind CSS was to separate the formatting and styling rules from the content. It is important to maintain structure within the document that will be styled by CSS. A way to do this is to break the page into logical sections with `div` (*division*) elements. You may break a page down, for example, into banner, navigation, news and content divisions as shown in Listing 4-3.

```
<html><head>
    <title>A Simple Web Page</title>
    <style type="text/css">
        #banner {
            font-family: Tahoma;
            background-color: #84a563;
            padding: 2px 2px 2px 10px;
        }
        #navigation {
            padding: 10px;
            border: 1px dotted;
            font-family: courier;
            font-size: 100%;
            background-color: #5c892e;
        }
        #news {
            padding: 4px;
            font-family: Tahoma;
            background-color: #5c922e;
        }
        #content {
            padding: 2px;
```

```
            font-family: Tahoma;
            background-color: #84a563;
        }
        a:hover {
            font-weight: bold;

        }
        a:link, a:visited {
            text-decoration: none;
            color: #550039;
        }
    </style>
</head>
<body>
<div id="banner">
    <h1>My Special Page</h1>
</div>
<div id="navigation">
    <a href="home.html">home</a>
    <a href="resources">resources</a>
    <a href="links.html">links</a>
    <a href="feedback.html">feedback</a>
</div>
<div id="news">
    NEWS:
</div>
<div id="content">
<pre>
 Stone walls do not a prison make,
 Nor iron bars a cage;
 Minds innocent and quiet take
 That for an hermitage;
 If I have freedom in my love
 And in my soul am free,
 Angels alone, that soar above,
 Enjoy such liberty.

<i>To Althea from Prison</i>
  - Colonel Lovelace
 </pre>
</div>
</body>
</html>
```

Listing 4-3 Using *div* sections

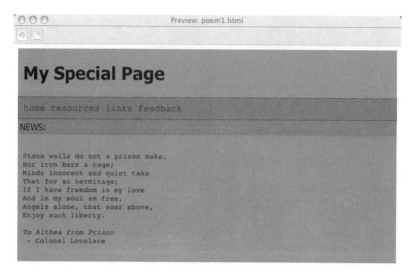

Figure 4-2 *The finished page*

Notice in this example the various div sections with identifiers; these are then used to plug in or connect the desired styles.

We can see the output in Figure 4-2.

Test Yourself!

- Write a Web page that has several blocks of text.
- Add borders, margins and padding.
- Position the text components as you want them.
- Place one on top of the other; what happens?
- Now add z-index properties and alter which one is on top.
- Try adding color or maybe a tiled image as a background.

4.13 CSS2

CSS level 2 was published as a recommendation in May 1998 and has already had a revision to CSS 2.1. CSS2 mainly covered improvements to absolute, relative and fixed positioning of elements. It also concerned manipulation of media types including aural style sheets, bidirectional text and new font properties.

CSS 2.1 improves features further that are currently badly supported. It also adds already implemented browser extensions to the specification.

CSS2 aural style sheets are an interesting addition, allowing accessibility for those who are visually impaired. They allow the features of speech processing of a document to be controlled. It is possible, for example, to add features that manipulate the frequency of speech, stress, how words are to be put together and also manipulate format to be speech friendly. For example, it is possible to say where the speech process proceeds when it encounters a table; does it read data downwards or across?

CSS2 also allows print-specific instructions to be added. This allows page control during hard copy output, such as breaks, margins and doubled-sided printing instructions.

Checkpoint!

We now know:

- display positioning of objects within a document usually occurs as a natural flow from top to bottom in an HTML document
- it is possible to use CSS positioning to move an element relatively to its normal position or absolutely by providing pixel coordinates
- as well as x and y positioning there is the z-index, which allows depth to be added to the display so objects can be layered and their position in this stack determined
- CSS level 2 has further improved CSS and added features too.

4.14 CHAPTER SUMMARY

- Initially HTML had a large number of presentation and formatting features.
- The need for CSS was based on the separation of presentation from HTML.
- HTML was redefined to be concerned with structural markup.
- CSS works by providing a selector and a set of rules to be applied.
- The selector identifies a particular element or logically defined section.
- A pseudo-class allows links to have styles applied.
- A style sheet can be embedded within the page or in a separate file with the `.css` extension, then linked in.
- A style sheet can control background images, colors and properties.
- Text can also be manipulated in terms of font, size, decoration, alignment and spacing.

- Style sheets can also control borders and various spacing possibilities around an element or section.
- Lists are capable of being styled.
- CSS can control positioning more precisely, both absolutely and relatively.
- Using the z-index feature it is possible to control positioning in terms of the order of items when overlapped. This adds a depth control to the display.
- Images can be clipped and manipulated.
- Elements can be floated so text flows around them.
- The div element provides the ability to break HTML into logical elements that can be manipulated using CSS.
- CSS2 has improved CSS further and enhanced many features while providing some that are new, such as aural style sheets.

Chapter Quiz

- One of the best ways to learn CSS is to actually experiment with using it. Take a previous design or Web page that was developed in HTML and redevelop it using CSS.
- The Zen Garden project is extremely interesting (see `http://www.csszengarden.com/`). The idea is that you download their HTML page and develop your own CSS to give it a new presentation. First of all look at other people's attempts at showing off CSS, then try and see what you can come up with.

Key Words and Phrases

Absolute When applied to CSS positioning, refers to the specifying of exact coordinates for an element

Border Defines all aspects of a border

Class For giving a name to each class of divisions

Div Divides a page into logical sections

ID For giving a unique name to a particular division

Margin For setting the amount of space between the sides of an element's border and the parent element

Padding For specifying the distance between the sides of an element's content area and the border

Relative When applied to CSS positioning, refers to specifying coordinates that are relative to the natural positioning of an element within a Web page

RGB Red Green Blue, a model used for color definition

Z-index Allows the setting of the depth of an element in relation to the overlapping of other elements

Useful Web Addresses

http://www.csszengarden.com/

http://en.wikipedia.org/wiki/Cascading_Style_Sheets/

http://www.w3schools.com/css/

http://www.w3.org/TR/REC-CSS1-961217.html

http://www.w3.org/TR/REC-CSS2/

5

This chapter will prepare you for developing with this popular scripting language, showing you the syntax and possibilities of use. The aims here are to show you how it is placed within a page, variables, strings, arrays and loops. Program flow is also discussed and how conditional operators and commands are used.

This chapter gives you an initial grounding in JavaScript, exploring why it is needed, where it came from and its basic language structure. It also looks at several important differences between JavaScript and other programing languages and how to start developing dynamic Web pages for interactivity with users.

Scripting may sound like a diminished aspect of programing but JavaScript is a complex, fully featured programing language. Like any programing language it may appear to be fairly simple but in fact it can be more complex than most. If there is not a good basic understanding it can be very frustrating to write even simple programs.

There is a myth too that JavaScript is in some way related to Java. This is in fact incorrect and, although there are some similarities, there is a great deal of difference between the two, as will be shown in this chapter. JavaScript does use objects but there is some argument as to whether it can in fact be called object oriented rather than object based.

JavaScript has been around for many years and has quite a history, but this chapter will explore how it has matured to become a sophisticated companion to any Web designer who wants to make their pages rich and dynamic.

5.1 WHAT IS JAVASCRIPT?

HTML and CSS concentrate on a static rendering of a page; things do not change on the page over time, or because of events. To do these things, we use scripting languages, which allow content to change dynamically. Not only this, but it is possible to interact with the user beyond what is possible with HTML. Scripts are programs just like any other programing language; they can execute on the client side (the one with the browser) or the server. In these initial chapters we will concentrate on the client side before moving on to the server.

It is important to realize there are advantages to running scripts on either side. For example, running a script on the client saves processing time on the server (and vice versa!). Doing some processing on the client before sending information may be advantageous: you could, for example, check information before it is sent.

These are the advantages of client side scripting:

- The Web browser uses its own resources, and eases the burden on the server.
- It has fewer features than server side language.

These are the disadvantages of client side scripting:

- Code is usually visible.
- Code is probably modifiable.
- Local files and databases can't be accessed (as they are stored on the server).

The main two client side scripting languages are JavaScript and VBScript. The more popular of the two is probably JavaScript. There is also JScript, a Microsoft version of the same language. The need for a common specification led to ECMA 262 and the development of a standardized version of the language called ECMAScript.

JavaScript was originally called LiveScript (and before that Mocha!), and was developed by Netscape Communications. Despite the name it has little in common with the programing language Java, which sometimes leads to confusion. JavaScript is an object-based language, rather than an object-oriented one, based on the idea of prototypes. The main similarity is that they share common syntax, which bears some relation to C.

JavaScript is embedded in Web pages and interpreted by the browser.

5.2 **HOW TO DEVELOP JAVASCRIPT**

It's possible to develop JavaScript programs using a simple editor and your browser in the same way as you would HTML and CSS. It's also possible to use IDEs such as Dreamweaver, which can help with development and speed up your writing of client side scripts.

There are a large number of JavaScript programs on the Web, so it's not always necessary to write your own and reinvent the wheel. You may like to modify someone else's code for your requirements or study how they did it.

JavaScript can be used to make your site more interactive and liven up your pages, creating an active user interface. You can validate incoming information from forms and improve the way your navigation interface works. JavaScript has the ability to create HTML pages on the fly, which could be dependent on choices that the user makes.

5.3 **SIMPLE JAVASCRIPT**

There are a few options as to where you place your JavaScript within the HTML; it can also be external to the HTML but linked in.

5.3.1 **Embedded**

JavaScript can be embedded in an HTML document. The media type for JavaScript is `application/x-javascript` but, more commonly, to embed it in HTML you must begin it with:

```
<script type="text/javascript">
```

and end with:

```
</script>
```

You may also see code for older browsers begin with:

```
<script language="Javascript" type="text/javascript">
<!-
```

and end with:

```
//-->
</script>
```

The script tag has the effect of stopping the JavaScript being printed out as well as identifying the code enclosed. The JavaScript can be placed in the head section of your HTML or the body.

```
<html>
<head>
     <title>A small piece of JavaScript</title>
</head>
<body>
     <script type="text/javascript">
          document.write("hello, JavaScript user!");
     </script>
</body>
</html>
```

Listing 5-1 A simple JavaScript program

Listing 5-1 shows a complete, but small, example program. As you can see it is embedded in an HTML page within the body section. The script is first of all identified with the `<script>` tag. The only piece of JavaScript here is the output to the browser, using the `document.write` statement.

Scripts placed in the body section are executed as the page loads and can be used to generate the content of the page.

As well as the body section, JavaScript can also be placed in the head part. The advantage of putting a script in there is that it loads before the main body. This makes sure it is loaded before anyone wishes to use it, so it would be good for functions, for example, or event driven programing.

5.3.2 **External Scripts**

If you want to use the same script on several pages it could be a good idea to place the code in a separate file, rather than writing it on each. That way, if you want to update the code, or change it, you only need to do it once.

Simply take the code you want in a separate file out of your program and save it with the extension `.js`. The script tag is not needed in the external file, just the code. The JavaScript must then be linked to at the point you want it to be inserted in your HTML. If the script was saved as `myscript.js`:

```
<html>
<head>
</head>
<body>
<script src="myscript.js"></script>
</body>
</html>
```

Checkpoint!

■ **JavaScript has a history that stretches back to the early days of the Web.**

■ **There are advantages to running scripts on the client side.**

■ **JavaScript is the main client side scripting language.**

■ **JavaScript has been standardized as ECMAScript.**

■ **JavaScript can be developed with simple software tools such as an editor and browser, or using an IDE.**

■ **It can be embedded in a Web page inside the body or head section.**

■ **It can also be linked in as an external script.**

5.4 VARIABLES

As in many programing languages, JavaScript lets you store information in named variables, which are just storage memories so you can access the data later by using a name you have assigned. A variable's value can change as the script runs too.

A variable can contain several types of value:

- number – a numeric value, e.g. 156, 1000, 1.2
- string – characters wrapped in quotes, e.g. "Cat", "The house is red"
- boolean – a value of true or false
- null – an empty variable
- function – a function
- object – an object

These are known as primitive data types, with only a single value. JavaScript also supports a composite data type known as an object. An object represents a collection of values, ordered or unordered. In JavaScript an object can also be a function; that is, an object with some associated code that is attached to it.

A JavaScript variable name has a few other attributes to take note of:

- It is case sensitive – mynum and MyNum are different variables.
- It cannot contain punctuation, spaces or start with a digit.
- It cannot be a JavaScript reserved word.

An important difference between languages such as C and Java is that variables can contain any type and also change between types through the course of the program. Although you can declare a variable with the var statement you do not have to give a type anywhere to make it only hold a specific kind of value. This property makes the language *untyped*.

5.4.1 Scope

A JavaScript variable can have either local or global scope; however, this is not quite the same as other languages that have block-level scope. Block-level variables are, as the name suggests, contained and not accessible outside of the block they were created in.

If a variable is created with the var statement such as:

```
var a;
```

or:

```
var a,b,c;
```

then the scope will either be global (available throughout the program) or local depending on where declared. JavaScript contains, like C, functions that can be called from anywhere in the main program. If a variable is inside a function then it will be local to that function and only available there. If declared in the main program then it will be available throughout the program.

If var is not used at all then the variable will have a global scope whether in a local function or not. It's possible to have a global variable and a function (local) variable with the same name and they will not interfere with each other, although inside the function only the local version will be available.

```
<html>
<body>

<script type="text/javascript">
var myname = "Fred";

tester();
document.write(myname);
tester();
```

```
        document.write(othername);
        document.write(hername);


        function tester( ) {
        var myname="Bert";
        var hername="Jane";
        othername="Sid";
        document.write(myname);

        }
        </script>
        </body>
        </html>
```

Listing 5-2 *Script showing use of scope for variables*

Try and follow the program in Listing 5-2 by dry running it yourself without the computer.
The output from it running is:

        BertFredBertSid

This should demonstrate the various scopes quite well! Notice in particular that Jane never
gets printed as it does not exist outside the function.

Test Yourself!

- Write a simple JavaScript program as your first attempt at scripting; add code to
  the head and body sections of a Web page.
- Now take out the JavaScript code and put it into an external script and link it into
  an HTML file.
- Write a script to make sure you understand how the scope works in JavaScript,
  using the program in Listing 5-2 as a starting point.

5.4.2 Assignments

As we can see from Listing 5-2, variables are assigned their values with the equals operator
'='. This is true for all types of value, whether it be string or numerical data. So, the X could
be set to 123 or "Bert" by:

            X = 123;
            X = "Bert";

If X was made equal to 123 how would you add one?

```
X = X + 1;
```

would work but so would:

```
X++;
```

which means increment the value. You can also:

```
X--;
```

to subtract.

There are other short cuts too, for example x = x + y can also be stated as x += y.

Table 5-1 shows the various assignments possible.

Assignment	Equivalent to
X+=Y	X=X+Y
X-=Y	X=X-Y
X*=Y	X=X*Y
X/=Y	X=X/Y
X%=Y	X=X%Y

Table 5-1 *Special assignment operators*

5.4.3 Strings

A string can be defined as a sequence of letters, digits, punctuation and so on. A string in JavaScript is wrapped in single or double quotes. There is no special type for a single character like in C (with char); it is simply a string with a length of one. When you assign a string it must only take up one line and not be broken up over several and if you want to include a newline character you would use \n which is similar to C, C++ and Java.

You can incorporate HTML into your strings, possibly for output to the browser. It must be remembered that some characters that you would like to include in a string need special attention and just like newline need a backslash to 'escape' them. For example, if you want to include a single or double quote within the string you would have to use a backslash before it – in this case to say to JavaScript that this is actually not the end of the string!

A few more useful escape sequences are shown in Table 5-2.

Sequence	Character
\t	Tab
\n	Newline
\r	Carriage return
\"	Double quote
\'	Apostrophe or single quote
\\	Backslash

Table 5-2 Escape sequences

Strings can be joined together with the + operator, which is called *concatenation*. For example, it is possible to:

```
mystring = "my name is " + "fred";
myother = "my name is " + name;
```

where name is a string variable with possibly a name as its contents.

As a string is an object type it also has some useful features. For example, if you wanted to find the length of a string you can use the length property:

```
lenStr = mystring.length;
```

There are also a number of methods available. If you wanted to get a specific character from a string you could use this:

```
nChar = mystring.charAt(3);
```

This would return the third character. There are other methods that will extract a substring or find the position of a letter in a string, as shown in Table 5-3.

5.4.4 **Arrays**

An array is a collection of data. Each item in the array has an index to access it with and they begin at zero. So, the first item will be at i[0] if i is the name of the array, whereas the fourth item will be at i[3].

Arrays are created using the Array( ) constructor:

```
var myArray = new Array( );
a[0] = 1;
```

Method	Description
charAt	Return the character at a specific index
indexOf	Find the first index of a character
lastIndexOf	Find the last index of a character
substring	Return a section of a string
valueOf	Return the numeric value of a string
toLowerCase	Convert a string to lower case
toUpperCase	Convert a string to upper case

Table 5-3 *Some methods attached to the string object*

```
a[1] = 2;
a[2] = "three";
a[3] = false;
```

Notice here that any type can be assigned.

It's also possible to define initial values with the constructor:

```
var myArray = new Array(1, 2, "three", false);
```

Or, you can declare the number of elements that the array will have:

```
var myArray = new Array(15);
```

Test Yourself!

- Use some of the inbuilt functions of strings to search for a word within a sentence. It should then say whether the word is present.
- How would we convert an input string to all lowercase before validation?

Checkpoint!

- JavaScript uses variables similar to other languages but they are untyped.
- Although the type is undeclared there are specific rules for their names.

- There are scope rules for such variables, which are determined by position within the script and the use of the **var** command.
- Variables can be assigned to with the equals operator and some other special statements such as +=, *=. Variables can be incremented and decremented using ++ and --.
- Strings are classed as an object and can be manipulated with the built-in methods and properties.
- An array is an object that also has built-in properties and methods for manipulating its data.

5.5 FUNCTIONS

A function is a section of code that is separate from the main program. It is defined once but can be invoked many times. A function can be passed as parameters so that they can be used and a value can be returned back. There are some functions already built in to JavaScript, such as the Math.cos( ) function, which calculates the cosine of an angle.

An example function could be:

```
function multByTen(x)
{
     return x*10;
}
```

This can then be invoked by using the function's name complete with any parameters you want to pass:

```
mysum = multByTen(3);
```

```
<html>
<body>

 <script type="text/javascript">


var z = multXbyY(10, 15);

document.write("The result is "+z);
```

```
function multXbyY(x,y) {
  document.write("x is "+x);
  document.write("y is "+y);
  return x*y;

}
</script>
</body>
</html>
```

Listing 5-3 *Script showing use of function with parameters*

Listing 5-3 shows how the function can be placed at the end of the main code. It will only execute when called though. In this script two parameters are passed.

One feature of JavaScript that is different to some other languages is that the function is a data type in itself. So, it is possible to pass a function to other functions or store them in variables. They can also be assigned to object properties like other values can and become a method of that object.

5.6 CONDITIONS

When you want to do something depending on the value of a variable then the if statement is one way of approaching the solution. The syntax is much the same as a lot of programing languages:

```
if (a==10) {

 // execute this block if true

 }
```

The condition usually requires an operator which in this case is the check for equality; in JavaScript there are quite a few with many uses, as shown in Table 5-4.

The useful addition to an if statement is an else:

```
if (a==10) {

 // execute this block if true

 } else {
```

Operator	Description
<, <=	Less than, less than or equal to
>, >=	Greater than, greater than or equal to
!	Logical complement
!=	Test for inequality
==	Test for equality
===	Test for identity
!==	Test for non-identity
&&	Logical and
||	Logical or

Table 5-4 *Conditional operators*

```
// do this if not true

}
```

5.6.1 Switch

The switch statement is another useful construct that works on a conditional basis. It works well when there are a small number of set choices:

```
switch (expression) {

    case label1:
        // code to be executed if expression == label1
    break;
    case label2:
        // code to be executed if expression == label2
    break;
    case label3:
        // code to be executed if expression == label3
    break;
    default:
        // code to executed if all the above do not match
}
```

An example of use is shown in Listing 5-4.

```
<html>
<head></head>
<body>
<script type="text/javascript">
//This finds the current Month 0-11
//depending on this decides on a
//message
var m=new Date();
theMonth=m.getMonth();
document.write(theMonth);
switch (theMonth)
{
case 4:
  document.write("The Merry Month of May");
  break;
case 0:
  document.write("Cold January!");
  break;
case 6:
  document.write("Summer Time!");
  break;
default:
  document.write("When is it holiday time?");
}
</script>
</body>
```

Listing 5-4 *Script showing use of* **case** *statement*

5.6.2 Conditional Operator

As in other languages JavaScript also contains a conditional operator:

```
avariable = (condition) ?value1:value2;
```

An example of use would be:

```
hello=(lang=="french")?"bonjour":"hi";
```

In this case the variable hello is either set to bonjour or hi depending on how the variable lang is set. If it is set to french it will choose the french greeting, bonjour; if not it will choose hi.

5.7 **LOOPS AND REPETITION**

It's often the case when programing that you need to iterate (repeat) over a section of code several times. You may want to repeat a set number of times, or break out of the loop when something happens, or go on forever (unlikely, but possible, if you really want to!).

The **for** loop works by initializing a variable to a start value, checking for a condition which, while true, the loop will run and finally incrementing (or decrementing) a value. If you had an array you wanted to print out between 10 and 20 then you could:

```
for (i=10; i<=20; i++) {

        document.write(x[i]);
}
```

Using a **while** loop to do the same thing you could:

```
i=10;
while (i<=20) {

        document.write(x[i]);
        i++;
}
```

Finally, the **do while**:

```
i=10;
do {
        document.write(x[i]);
        i++;

} while (i<=20);
```

Table 5-5 shows the different kinds of loop construct available in JavaScript.

Test Yourself!

- Write a script that uses functions to calculate how many days it is to your birthday.
- Extend the above programs to output various messages depending on how long there is to go and a special message if it is your birthday.
- Alter the program so it will repeat through several birth dates for different people and tell you how long to go for each.
- Using a loop, search for a word in sentence held in an array, returning the index. This is similar to some inbuilt JavaScript functions.

Loop construct	Description
`for (initialize; condition; increment) {}` `for (x=0; x<10; x++) {}`	Use when you know how many repetitions you want to do
`while (condition) {}` `while (x<10) {}`	Loop through block of code while condition is true
`do {} while (condition)` `do {} while (x<10)`	Execute block at least once then repeat while condition is true

Table 5-5 *JavaScript loop structures*

Checkpoint!

■ JavaScript allows the use of functions.

■ Functions, although defined once, can be invoked many times.

■ It can be passed parameters and also return values.

■ The function is a data type in JavaScript, unlike other languages, and can be passed as an argument to other functions.

■ It can also be assigned to object properties.

■ There are several conditional language structures such as `if {} else`, `case` and the conditional operator.

■ There are also several loop structures such as the for, `while and do {} while`.

5.8 CHAPTER SUMMARY

■ Client side scripting has some benefits over static Web pages and server side scripting too.

■ JavaScript has been around since the early days of the Web.

■ JavaScript allows pages to become dynamic and interactive.

■ It has a similar language structure to C, C++ and Java, although there are some interesting differences.

■ JavaScript can be developed using just a simple editor and browser or a Web development IDE.

■ JavaScript can be embedded in a Web page or linked in as an external file.

■ Variables are untyped and do not have a block-scope as in some languages.

■ Strings and arrays are both objects in JavaScript, which have built-in properties and methods.

■ Functions are sections of code that can be invoked with parameters and return a value. They are also classed as an actual value type.

■ There are several language features that allow program flow to be changed on condition, or repeated.

Chapter Quiz

• What do you think JavaScript is particularly useful for, that HTML isn't?

• Try and find some good reference sources on the Web for JavaScript; you can start with the ones below.

• Do you think JavaScript is object oriented? Try and find out why some authors call it object based – why do they make the distinction?

Key Words and Phrases

Array In JavaScript, an object that contains data and has properties and useful methods such as `pop`, `push` and `join`. The data can be of mixed type

Assignment When variables take on a value

Decrement To reduce a variable by a specific amount

Dynamic Web page A page that reacts to events or user input and alters its output because of it

Escape sequence When a special character is included within a string, a backslash is required before it to enable it to be output. An example is the single quote

Function A section of named code that can be invoked many times during a program, can also be sent parameters and have a return value. A function is also a variable type in JavaScript

Increment To increase a variable by a specific amount

Invoke To start, or call, a function to enable it to execute

Iterate To repeat a section of code

Loop A section of code that is repeated

Object A collection of data and methods

Scope The containment of a variable within a specific area of code

Script Usually a program that is interpreted by a browser, e.g. JavaScript

Static Web page A page that simply formats its output without change or reaction to the user or other information

String An object that is a collection of characters wrapped by quotes and also has properties and methods

Untyped Variables are untyped when they do not declare their type before use

Useful Web Addresses

http://www.ecma-international.org/publications/standards/
Stnindex.htm

6

JAVASCRIPT: DEVELOPING MORE ADVANCED SCRIPTS

In this chapter you will learn about using objects in JavaScript, both the built-in types and creating your own. You will also learn about the Document Object Model (DOM), which allows HTML documents to be manipulated and accessed. Forms and ways of validating information submitted are explored here too.

Object-oriented programing is well established as a model and it shouldn't be a surprise to learn that many scripting languages have the ability to be used in this way. JavaScript has object features and here we look into how both its built-in objects and ones you develop yourself can be used in your Web programs. There are many objects inside JavaScript already that are used when normally developing Web sites, for example the **document** object in **document.write**. Another that it is encountered frequently is the **Math** object. As in Java it is also possible to construct your own, complete with constructors, properties and methods. JavaScript's objects do vary from most object-oriented paradigms though and the differences will be discussed and highlighted here.

The DOM is used to both access information contained in HTML documents, such as forms, and build such documents dynamically. This allows content to be built interactively, harnessing JavaScript's ability to control format and presentation.

Finally, it is discussed how JavaScript can validate incoming information from the user, such as email addresses, using various techniques to search and manipulate string data.

6.1 JAVASCRIPT AND OBJECTS

6.1.1 What Is an Object?

In JavaScript, as in most programing languages, an object is a collection of named values and associated methods. The named values are usually known as properties or fields. This is similar to thinking about physical objects, such as a tree, which has height, type, and leaf shape. An object's properties contain information about that object. A property is usually named according to what it represents, so height would contain information about the vertical size of the object. The object's properties can be extended by adding new properties although there are static properties that cannot be altered.

To refer to an object's properties we use this syntax:

```
objectRef.propertyName
```

Where objectRef is the name of the object and propertyName is the property. The objectRef can also be the name of a variable that an object has been assigned to and you would still access its property by placing the dot followed by its name.

Methods are used in a similar way:

```
objectRef.methodName(parameters)
```

The idea is that methods are functions that can process the object's data. JavaScript has built-in objects as well as the ability to have user-defined objects.

6.2 JAVASCRIPT'S OWN OBJECTS

JavaScript has its own objects too. A good example of this is the Math object. It has several properties and methods, as shown in Table 6-1.

The properties such as PI are accessed like this:

```
Math.PI
```

So, you could for example print out the value of PI by writing:

```
document.write(Math.PI);
```

The value PI is also what is known as a *constant* so it can't be changed by assignment. As you can see there are also lots of useful methods attached to the Math object too. These are accessed in a similar way:

```
myValue = Math.round(10.2);
```

Properties available	Methods available
E	abs
LN_2	acos
LN_{10}	asin
LOG_2E	atan
$LOG_{10}E$	$atan_2$
PI	ceil
$SQRT_{1\_2}$	cos
$SQRT_2$	exp
	floor
	log
	max
	min
	pow
	random
	round
	sin
	sqrt
	tan

Table 6-1 *The JavaScript* Math *object*

These have brackets to contain values, which are passed to the method.

Test Yourself!

- Experiment with the Math object by writing a simple calculation program that will do a range of operations such as addition, subtraction, division and multiplication. You could also add some trigonometry functions, the PI constant and memories, if you wish!

6.2.1 User-Defined Objects

JavaScript allows you to create your own objects. The first step is to use the new operator:

```
var myObj = new Object( );
```

This creates an empty object! This can then be used to start a new object that you can then give new properties and methods. In object-oriented programing such a new object is usually given a constructor to initialize values when it is first created. However, it is also possible to assign values when it is made with literal values. This is shown in Listing 6-1. Notice how the values are assigned in one block, wrapped in braces and each property:value pair is separated by a comma. These can be spread over more than one line to help readability.

```html
<!DOCTYPE HTML PUBLIC "-//W3C//DTD HTML 4.01
            Transitional//EN">
<html>
<head>
<title>JavaScript Objects</title>
<meta http-equiv="Content-Type" content="text/html;
            charset=iso-8859-1">
</head>
<body>
<script language="JavaScript" type="text/JavaScript">
var line = { xorigin:10, yorigin:15, xend:100, yend:100 }
var person = {
                firstName: "fred",
                lastName: "Smith",
                age: 28,
                married: true,
                telephone: 234656
            }

document.write(person.firstName+" "+person.lastName+
            " "+person.age+" "+person.married);
document.write(line.xorigin, line.yorigin);

 </script>
</body>
</html>_
```

Listing 6-1 Using object literals

Another way of adding property values is to simply tag them to the object after you have created it. This is shown in Listing 6-2. A new object is created with the name person, this person object has certain attributes or properties ascribed to it such as first name, last name and age. It also has a property of hair which in turn has two additional attributes – length and color. To do this, person.hair is assigned a blank object, which in turn has the two properties required. In this way it's possible to see how a hierarchy of objects can be built up.

```
<!DOCTYPE HTML PUBLIC "-//W3C//DTD HTML 4.01
              Transitional//EN">
<html>
<head>
<title>JavaScript Objects</title>
<meta http-equiv="Content-Type" content="text/html;
              charset=iso-8859-1">
</head>
<body>
<script language="JavaScript" type="text/JavaScript">
var  person = new Object();

person.firstName = "Jane";
person.lastName = "Smith";
person.age = 32;

person.hair = new Object();
person.hair.length = "long"
person.hair.color = "red";

document.write(person.firstName+" "+person.lastName+
              " "+person.age);
document.write(person.hair.length+" "+person.hair.color);
</script>_</body>
</html>_
```

Listing 6-2 *Making a first object*

6.2.2 **Adding a Constructor**

A constructor is a pre-defined method that will initialize your object. To do this in JavaScript a function is used that is invoked through the **new** operator. Any properties inside the newly created object are assigned using the **this** keyword, referring to the current object being created.

```html
<html>
<head>
<title>JavaScript Objects</title>
<meta http-equiv="Content-Type" content="text/html;
                charset=iso-8859-1">
</head>
<body>
<script language="JavaScript" type="text/JavaScript">
function person(firstname, lastname, age, length, color)
{

this.firstName = firstname;
this.lastName = lastname;
this.age = age;

this.hair = new Object();
this.hair.length = length;
this.hair.color = color;
}


var person1 = new person("jane","smith", 32, "long",
                "red");

document.write(person1.firstName+" "+person1.lastName+
                " "+person1.age);
document.write(person1.hair.length+" "+person1.hair.color);
</script>
</body>
</html>
```

Listing 6-3 Using a constructor

In Listing 6-3 the function person becomes the constructor invoked through the new keyword on assignment to the person1 variable. Here the values are passed as parameters to the constructor. Inside the constructor the this keyword takes on the value of the newly created object and therefore applies properties to it.

6.2.3 **Methods**

In JavaScript a method is a function that is invoked through an object. Earlier it was mentioned that a function can be assigned to a variable, or in the same way, as a property of an object. A method can be assigned to an object, quite simply:

```
myObject.method = f;
```

Where f is the name of the function you want as a method of the object. To actually invoke the method:

```
myObject.method();
```

If the method expected parameters they would be put into the brackets:

```
myObject.method(x,y,z);
```

In Listing 6-4 methods are associated with an object and are used to change properties. First of all the functions are defined, beginning with the constructor, person. The next function is showPerson, which accesses the properties of the object it is attached to and prints out the details. The final function is changeAge, which will alter the age property of the person object.

In the main part of the program an object is instantiated (created and assigned a reference variable) as person1. The details set by the constructor are then printed out with person1.details, followed by the age being changed. To show an alteration has taken place the details are again printed out.

```html
<html>
<head>
<title>JavaScript Objects</title>
<meta http-equiv="Content-Type" content="text/html;
             charset=iso-8859-1">
</head>
<body>
<script language="JavaScript" type="text/JavaScript">
function person(firstname, lastname, age, length, color)
{
this.firstName = firstname;
this.lastName = lastname;
this.age = age;
this.hair = new Object();
this.hair.length = length;
this.hair.color = color;
this.details = showPerson;
this.alterAge = changeAge;
}
function showPerson()
{
    document.writeln("Name:"+this.firstName+
                     " "+this.lastName+"<br>");
```

```
            document.writeln("Age:"+this.age+"<br>");
            document.writeln("Hair:"+this.hair.length+
                            " "+this.hair.color+"<br>");
    }
    function changeAge(age)
    {
            this.age = age;
    }

     var person1 = new person("jane","smith", 32, "long",
                    "red");
    person1.details();
    person1.alterAge(30);
    person1.details();
    </script>
    </body>
    </html>_
```

Listing 6-4 *Attaching methods to an object*

Test Yourself!

- Develop your own object-based program using user-created objects to form a database of books in a library.
- Add a customer loaning system, complete with menu.

Checkpoint!

- JavaScript has its own built-in objects such as `Math`.
- JavaScript also can have user-defined objects.
- Objects are created with the `new` keyword.
- They can have properties.
- Objects also possess methods that can be passed as parameters.
- User-defined objects can use an initializing constructor function.
- When instantiated, object properties can be accessed or changed and methods can be invoked.

6.3 **THE DOM AND THE WEB BROWSER ENVIRONMENT**

As we have seen, JavaScript has inbuilt objects as well as those you can make yourself. The inbuilt objects also include complete object models suitable for the context of Web programing.

The `window` object is the primary point from which most other objects come. From the current `window` object access and control can be given to most aspects of the browser features and the HTML document. When you write:

```
document.write(''hello, world'');
```

You are actually writing:

```
window.document.write(''hello, world'');
```

The `window` is just there by default. This `window` object represents the window or frame that displays the document and is the global object in client side programing for JavaScript. If you want to refer to the `window` object you can use the two self-referential properties, `window` and `self`. In fact all client side objects are connected to the `window` object.

Figure 6-1 shows the hierarchy linked to the level under the `window` object.

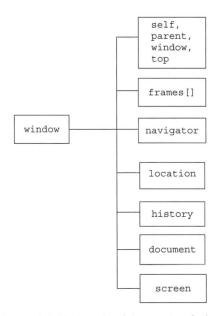

Figure 6-1 *The hierarchy of objects under* `window`

```
<html>
<head>
<title>JavaScript Objects</title>
<meta http-equiv="Content-Type" content="text/html;
            charset=iso-8859-1">
</head>
<body>
<script language="JavaScript" type="text/JavaScript">
defaultStatus = "Welcome to the JavaScript test program";
alert("Welcome to the Amazing JavaScript test program!");
confirm("Ready to proceed?");
ans = prompt("Do you like JavaScript?");
if (ans=="yes") {

    document.write("<h1>okay!</h1>");

} else {
    document.write("<h2>Oh dear :-(</h2>");

}

</script>
</body>
</html>
```

Listing 6-5 Using the **window** object

In Listing 6-5, a few of the window properties and methods have been used including `alert`, `confirm`, `prompt`, `document.write` and `defaultStatus`. The window properties are listed in Table 6-2. One of the more useful properties of the `window` object is a reference to a `screen` object, which allows information to be gained about the size of a user's display and color depth. Given this, it's possible to tailor the presentation of content to match how the user is viewing it. The `screen` object contains `width`, `height`, `availWidth`, `availHeight` and `colorDepth` properties. The `width` and `height` properties specify the width and height of the display size in pixels but the `availWidth` and `availHeight` properties specify the space actually available excluding task bars and other screen borders.

Other `window` object features are useful too. For example, you can open a new Web browser window with the `open( )` method:

```
var win = window.open("testJSlit.html", "testJS",
        "width=400,height=350,status=yes,resizable=yes");
```

Property	Description
closed	True if the window has been closed
defaultStatus, status	Status line text
document	A reference to the **document** object
frames[ ]	Array of **window** objects, one for each frame
history	A reference to the **history** object, which holds the history of the user's visits
location	A reference to the **location** object, which holds the current URL
name	The current windows name; used for targeting output with `<a>` tag
opener	A reference to the **window** object, which opened this one or null if opened by the user
parent	A reference to the frame of window that contains it (if the window is a frame)
self	The current **window** object
top	For a frame, the top-level window that contains it
window	The current **window** object
alert( ), confirm( ), prompt( )	Warnings to user; **confirm** and **prompt** are interactive
close( )	Close the window
focus( ), blur( )	Make the window active or inactive
moveBy( ), moveTo( )	Move the window to a particular position
open( )	Open a top-level window with a specified URL
print( )	Print the window or frame
resizeBy( ), resizeTo( )	Change the size of the window
scrollBy( ), scrollTo( )	Scroll the current document
setInterval( ), clearInterval( )	Set an interval that a function will be repeatedly called; or cancel it
setTimeout( ), clearTimeout( )	Set a time period for calling a function once; or cancel it

Table 6-2 *Some important* **window** *object properties*

Here a new `window` object is returned and created with the initial features passed as parameters. The first of these is the URL of the document to display in the new window, the second is the name of the window which is useful for targeting output with `<a>` or `<form>` tags. The third parameter contains features such as `width`, `height`, `status bar` available and whether the window can be resized.

Notice in this example that `window.open` is explicitly used rather than just `open( )`. This is to stop confusion with the `document` object's `open( )` method.

Having opened the new window it is also possible to close it with, in this case:

```
win.close();
```

Test Yourself!

- Write some JavaScript that will open browser windows set to various URLs with specific display sizes.
- Experiment with some of the other `window` object properties listed above.

6.3.1 The document Object

There are lots of objects that descend from the `document` object forming a large sub-tree known as the Document Object Model (DOM), which has become standardized. The `document` object represents the HTML displayed in the window. The `write` method that you have probably already used allows HTML to be dynamically written to this object as it is parsed. Using this object it is possible to access information about the document itself and also about the information content.

Using this object it is possible to control certain parameters of the current document like background, foreground and link colors:

```
document.bgColor="#9F2020";
document.fgColor="#FAF519";
document.linkColor="#9781B7";
document.write("<h2>Hello There!</h2>");
document.write("<a href=\"http://www.w3.org\">W3C
          Organization</a>");
```

This code would produce a dark red background with yellow writing and purple link text.

It is also possible to access any form information in a document by using the forms[ ] array. This contains all the form objects that are in the document. Likewise, the images[ ] array contains objects that represent all the images in the document.

For example, a form can be constructed with:

```
<form name="userDetails">
<input type="text" name="fname"/>
<input type="text" name="lname"/>
<input type="submit" name="submit"/>
</form>
```

The form data can then be accessed with various DOM syntax constructions. The form itself can be accessed through:

```
document.forms[0]
```

It can also be referred to by:

```
document.userDetails
```

An individual element can then be accessed:

```
document.userDetails.fname
```

Listing 6-6 shows how to access form elements using the names given in the input field.

```
<html>
<head>
<title>JavaScript Objects</title>
<meta http-equiv="Content-Type" content="text/html;
                charset=iso-8859-1">
</head>
<body>
<form name="userDetails" onSubmit="processForm()">
<input type="text" name="fname"/>
<input type="text" name="lname"/>
<input type="submit" name="submit"/>
</form>

<script language="JavaScript" type="text/JavaScript">

function processForm() {
    myform = document.userDetails;
```

```
            document.write("hello, "+myform.fname.value+
                        " "+myform.lname.value);

    }

</script>
</body>
</html>
```

Listing 6-6 *One way to access form fields*

Another way to access the form details is through the enumerated form elements themselves, as shown in Listing 6–7.

```
<!DOCTYPE HTML PUBLIC "-//W3C//DTD HTML 4.01
                Transitional//EN">
<html>
<head>
<title>JavaScript Objects</title>
<meta http-equiv="Content-Type" content="text/html;
                charset=iso-8859-1">
<script language="JavaScript" type="text/JavaScript">

function processForm( ) {
    myform = document.userDetails;
    first = document.forms[0].elements[0].value;
    last  = document.forms[0].elements[1].value;
    document.write("hello, "+first+" "+last);

}

</script>
</head>
<body>
<form name="userDetails" onSubmit="processForm( )">
<input type="text" name="fname"/>
<input type="text" name="lname"/>
<input type="submit" name="submit"/>
</form>
</body>
</html>
```

Listing 6-7 *Extracting form information*

Notice in this example you don't actually have to know the names of the data fields, just where they occur in the form, which is at element positions 0 and 1.

Test Yourself!

- Write a script to set up a Web page, complete with a form to take user details, add foreground and background color using the **document** object. Access the user details and produce a new Web page with the data formatted in a suitable manner.

Checkpoint!

- Many of the built-in objects in JavaScript contain the ability to change or access the browser environment to allow control.
- These often have many properties and are part of large hierarchies of objects.
- Part of one sub-tree is the **document** object, also known as being part of the DOM.
- The DOM is a standardized model for accessing HTML documents' various parts.
- Using the DOM it is possible to change formatting.
- It is also possible to extract information that the user enters.

6.4 FORMS AND VALIDATION

There are advantages to doing some processing of submitted information on the client side, mainly in terms of resources – by not sending the data over to the server you are saving resources. For example, you could write JavaScript that will check an age with a limit imposed or check an email address looks like it might be correct, with a simple syntax check.

```html
<html>
<head>
<title>JavaScript Forms</title>
<meta http-equiv="Content-Type" content="text/html;
          charset=iso-8859-1">
</head>
<body>
<form method="post" action="mailto: Webmaster@localhost"
          name="logon" onSubmit="return
          processForm( )">
```

```
<input type="text" name="password"/>
<input type="submit" value="log in" name="Login"/>
</form>

<script language="JavaScript" type="text/JavaScript">

function processForm( ) {
    var check=false;
    myform = document.logon;

    if (myform.password.value=="letmein") {
        document.write("hello, you are now in the secret
                        area!");
        check=true;
    } else {
        alert("Wrong Password!");
        myform.password.focus( );
    }
    return check;

}
</script>
</body>
</html>


</script>

</body>
</html>
```

Listing 6-8 *Validating a user*

The simple program in Listing 6–8 allows a user to enter a password via a form that is then accessed in the JavaScript program. If it is the same as the string within the code then all is okay; otherwise an alert box comes up and warns the user. An interesting thing here to note is that the form will only be submitted when the processForm( ) function returns true to the event handler, otherwise it will keep on the form page.

While this program serves to make a point about how to pick up details from the form it wouldn't be feasible to check a password in this way as it would be insecure. JavaScript could be used to validate other details that are not as important.

If you wanted to check the input from a user of an email address how would you do it? The first thing to decide is what the format of such an address could be in all possible and legal cases. There are a few different formats of email address. Here are some examples:

```
bert@yahoo.co.uk
sid@mycompany.com
andrew.murphy@leeds.ac.uk
```

At first glance, you can tell that these are probably correct and do have a structure that looks like a local address followed by a domain name. One of the first things you could do would be simply to check that a supplied email address has an '@' (at) symbol somewhere! After this you could do more detailed checking as to where it is placed (for example, not at the start!), and you could also look at the local part and the domain to see if they conform to what is expected.

A routine to validate an email should check for invalid characters, check the existence of the single '@' and its positioning. It should also check the '.' (dot) is present in the domain name and again its positioning (there must be at least two characters after the period in the address).

Given all these rules to check for, it's important that there are some good string manipulation and access functions built in to JavaScript. The presence of a character and its position can be checked with:

```
strpos = stringName.indexOf("@",startPos);
```

The `indexOf` function returns the position of a character in a string beginning at (in the above example) `startPos`. If it doesn't exist in the string then it returns a –1.

Another useful function will return the character at a given point in the string:

```
whichChar = stringName.charAt(index);
```

`index` is the position of the character you want in the string `stringName`. These two functions should allow a routine to be written that can check an email.

Test Yourself!

- Using the above ideas and hints write a JavaScript function that will check for a valid email address.

6.4.1 Using Regular Expressions for Validation

Another way of checking for valid information is to use regular expressions. This allows a kind of template to be created, which patterns can be checked against. It is probably best described using an example such as Listing 6–9.

```html
<html>
<head>
<title>JavaScript Forms</title>
<meta http-equiv="Content-Type" content="text/html;
            charset=iso-8859-1">
</head>
<body>
<form method="post" name="getinfo"
   onSubmit="return processForm( )">
<input type="text" name="email"/>
<input type="submit" value="log in" name="Login"/>
</form>
<script language="JavaScript" type="text/JavaScript">
function processForm( ) {
var myform = document.getinfo;
var check=myform.email.value;
document.write(testEmail(check));
}
function testEmail(chkMail) {
    var emailPattern =
    "^[\\w-_\.]*[\\w-_\.]\@[\\w]\.+[\\w]+[\\w]$";
    var regex = new RegExp(emailPattern);
    return regex.test(chkMail);
}
</script>
</body>
</html>
```

Listing 6-9 Using a regular expression to validate an email

This will check for a valid email as described; note how compact it is compared to other ways of doing the same thing! You should be able to follow the basic idea of the information being extracted and the call to the function, which checks it is valid. As you can probably tell, the `testEmail( )` function returns true or false. The way it determines this end result is built on the template/pattern in the string `emailPattern`. This is used to work out the order of expected characters, how many times they repeat and any specially occurring punctuation. The string in this case that is used as a template is:

```
"^[\\w-_\.]*[\\w-_\.]\@[\\w]\.+[\\w]+[\\w]$"
```

The first section is:

```
^[\\w-_\.]
```

This sequence, beginning with ^, means check the first character is a word character (that is, in the range a–z and 0–9) represented by \\w. It can also be an underscore, hyphen or period, which are not normally used but are legal. The next part is:

```
*[\\w-_\.]
```

The * means that the next series of characters described can be repeated many times or not at all. The characters themselves are the same as before; that is, word characters, underscore, hyphen or period.

```
\@[\\w]\.+
```

This section begins by checking for the @ (at) character. Following this should be the word characters and then at least one 'dot'. In other words it would not accept a dot straight after the @ character.

The last part is:

```
[\\w]+[\\w]$
```

The first set in square brackets makes sure that there are some characters after the dot and the last part checks that the last character is a word character (as described earlier).

In the program after the string is declared, a regular expression object is created with the pattern:

```
var regex = new RegExp(emailPattern);
```

The pattern can then be tested against the incoming parameter with the object's test method:

```
return regex.test(chkMail);
```

This will return true or false depending on whether there is a match or not.

Test Yourself!

- Write a script to validate:
  - telephone numbers in the form 012-345-678 (three numbers, hyphen, three numbers, hyphen, three numbers)

- an identity number in the form AB 01 02 03 CD (two uppercase letters, A–Z, followed by three sets of two-digit numbers, followed by two more uppercase letters, A–Z).

Checkpoint!

- Information that is entered by the user can be accessed, processed and checked by JavaScript.
- Validation can take place using special string handling methods.
- Validation can also be done using regular expressions and the associated object.
- Regular expressions can be used to write compact, rule-based templates.

6.5 CHAPTER SUMMARY

- JavaScript contains many built-in objects that contain useful methods that you can use.
- JavaScript has object-based features, allowing the creation of user-defined objects.
- The Web browser environment can be controlled and accessed.
- The DOM further extends this capability into the HTML document itself.
- Using the DOM, form information can be accessed and processed.
- Form information can be validated using inbuilt string methods.
- Form information can also be validated using regular expressions and the associated object.

Chapter Quiz

- Find some more objects that are built in to JavaScript and attempt to use them.
- Regular expressions are used in many languages. Try and find out some more details on how they can be used.
- From a security point of view JavaScript is not much use for validating passwords, so what can be used?

Key Words and Phrases

Constructor A method that is used to initialize an object

DOM The Document Object Model, a standardized hierarchy for accessing parts of an HTML document

Method An associated piece of code that, in JavaScript, is actually a function, attached to an object

Object A collection of properties and methods

Object based/Object oriented A programing language that uses objects

Property A piece of data attached to an object

Regular expression A string that describes or matches a set of strings according to specific syntax rules

Validate A process by which information is checked to determine its correctness

Useful Web Addresses

`http://www.w3.org/DOM/`

`http://www.mozilla.org/docs/dom/domref/`

`http://www.w3schools.com/htmldom/dom_reference.asp`

`http://www.ietf.org/rfc/rfc2822.txt`

7

DHTML

The aim of this chapter is to bring dynamic aspects of site design together. You will learn about animation, caching, event driven scripting and browser compatibility. It's in this chapter you will also find out more about compatibility and the need to provide alternatives for different browsers.

To ensure you make your site 'sticky', that is, to make people return, you might want to make it richer in dynamic or media content. Web sites can be very attractive without adding movement but using animation and interactivity can add a whole new dimension to your content. It can also add very useful features that aid functionality such as the input of data. Whatever you add make sure you don't over do it; you want to capture your visitors' imagination and not make them annoyed by irritating gimmicks, like clashing colors, flashing or popups. Make sure whatever you place on your site is suitable for the majority of browsers and doesn't take an age to load up on a lower bandwidth connection, or at least has an option to skip it if users want to. Go for a design that will be fairly simple and effective and is compatible with as many browsers as possible.

An aspect of JavaScript programing that is very useful is event driven programing: the ability for some input from the user to be linked to a section of code that is then executed. In this chapter event driven scripts are developed to explain how these can simplify coding and add interactivity with the user.

You will notice that some of these scripts utilize techniques to detect the type of browser (this is called *browser sniffing!*) and then execute the appropriate section depending on which it is. This is an important aspect of programing as you need to make it work on as many browsers as possible.

7.1 COMBINING HTML, CSS AND JAVASCRIPT

DHTML, or *Dynamic HTML*, is really just a combination of HTML, JavaScript and CSS. The main problem with DHTML, which was introduced in the 4.0 series of browsers, is compatibility. It is not a standard, as such, but a range of technologies that the browsers were supposed to be able to support. The main focus generally when speaking of DHTML is animation and other such dynamic effects.

7.1.1 Animation

One of the more interesting things that can be done to liven up a Web site is to add animation of various kinds to enhance its content. DHTML is naturally the right way to do this, combining HTML, JavaScript and CSS.

First of all, let's have a look at some dynamic effects before going on to image use.

```
<html>
<head>
<title>!ALERT!</title>
</head>
<body>
<div id="urgent"><h1>Red Alert!</h1>The Web server is under
              attack!</div>
<script>
var e = document.getElementById("urgent");
var colors = ["white", "yellow", "orange", "red"]
var nextColor = 0;
setInterval(

"e.style.backgroundColor=colors
              [nextColor++%colors.length];",
                   500);
</script>
</body>
</html>
```

Listing 7-1 Dynamic effects

Listing 7-1 shows a fairly simple script that outputs a message to the browser and then changes the color of the background dynamically. The message is actually a named section in a div element and by this it is possible to alter aspects of it. The first thing the script does is find the element and make a variable as a reference. Once that is done a set of colors is defined and variables set up. The setInterval command runs the enclosed script at specific time slots, in this case every 500 milliseconds. The actual code that is executed alters the urgent element's background color by incrementing (adding one) the nextColor variable. You might wonder why it doesn't just keep going past the end of the array of colors. The trick here is the % (modulus) operator, which takes the colors.length (size of the array) and returns the remainder, which makes it never go above the total size.

To place an image on the screen with HTML the following markup can be used:

```
<img src="suki.jpg" alt="Suki the cat">
```

This places the image at the src URL specified in the document. The alt attribute will be output if the picture cannot be displayed; for example, the browser does not use graphics or it cannot be loaded. It is possible to manipulate the size of the image by specifying the width and height in pixels:

```
<img src="suki.jpg" alt="Suki the cat" width="50" height="50">
```

It is also possible to specify size by a percentage of the browser window size:

```
<img src="suki.jpg" alt="Suki the cat" width="50%" height="50%">
```

When you have created images in the page using the image tag they become stored in the DOM hierarchy as an array in document.images[ ]. If you specify a name within the <img> tag then that can be used to index the image in the array.

```
<html>
<head>
<title>Two Cats!</title>
</head>
<body>
<img src="suki.jpg" name="cats" width="25%" height="25%">
<form>
<input type="button" name="suki.jpg" value="Miss Suki"
        onClick="document.cats.src='suki.jpg';">
<input type="button" name="pooka.jpg" value="Miss Pooka"
        onClick="document.cats.src='pooka.jpg';">
</form>
</body>
</html>
```

Listing 7-2 Basic image flipping

The small Web document in Listing 7-2 shows how it is possible to manipulate the stored images in the document. Initially an image is set to source suki.jpg, a form then declares two buttons. Attached to each button is a JavaScript event onClick, which when activated

Figure 7-1 Select the picture

executes the attached piece of script. When a button is clicked the associated image is selected and the document is changed appropriately. The output is shown in Figure 7-1.

In a similar way, in animation, images are generally flicked between to give the impression of motion or change of some sort.

Checkpoint!

- DHTML, Dynamic HTML, usually refers to the combining of HTML, CSS and JavaScript.
- By referring to elements and utilizing the DOM of your browser it is possible to produce dynamic effects.
- Animation is fairly easy to do by swapping images.
- Images in a document can be accessed and swapped using the DOM, referring to the image array or a named element.

7.1.2 The Image Object

By associating an image source and an `Image` object it is possible to control images better using caching. This is a technique where the images are placed in memory. It's a good idea to cache images you want to use in an animation. This ensures they are ready and loaded up *before* the animation begins, otherwise it may not look very smooth!

An `Image` object is created in the same way as any other object with the new keyword:

```
anImage = new Image( );
anImage.src = "suki.jpg";
```

The second line there sets the source for the object. The properties for this object are given in Table 7-1.

Property	Description
border	Read-only property containing border width set by `<img>` tag
complete	A boolean value, true if completely loaded
height	Read-only property containing height of image set by `<img>` tag
hspace	Read-only property containing horizontal space set by `hspace` in `<img>` tag
lowsrc	URL of alternate low resolution image
name	Name assigned to tag
src	Source URL of the displayed image
vspace	Read-only property containing the amount of vertical space set by `vspace` attribute in `<img>` tag
width	Read-only property containing the width of the image specified in the `<img>` tag

Table 7-1 The Image *object*

However, it's not often we want just one image for animation! So, instead an array of `Image` objects is used, complete with a different image source in each:

```
var myimage = new Array(6);

for (var i=0; i<6; i++) {

    myimage[i] = new Image( );
    myimage[i].src = "anim"+i+".jpg";
}
```

When placed before the main code this will store the images before they are needed (they are cached). Note in the above code your image files should be named anim0.jpg, anim1.jpg, anim2.jpg … anim5.jpg.

To actually animate a set of image frames you need to flick through the images you have loaded up. Listing 7-3 shows how to do this. This code makes sure the images are available

```
<html><head><title>Animation</title>
    <script language="JavaScript">
    anims = new Array(4);
    var frame = 0;
    var timeout_state = null;
    function imageLoad( ) {
        for(i = 0; i<=3; i++) {
            anims[i] = new Image( );
            anims[i].src = "anim" + i + ".jpg";
        }
    }
    function animate( ) {
        document.animImage.src = anims[frame].src;
        frame = (frame + 1);
        if(frame > 3) {
            frame = 0;
        }
        timerId = setTimeout("animate( )",
                    document.animateform.speed.value);
    }
    function checkButton( ) {
        if(document.animateform.runAnim.value == "Start")
            {
            document.animateform.runAnim.value = "Stop";
            animate( );
        } else {
            document.animateform.runAnim.value =
                        "Start";
            clearTimeout(timerId);
            timerId = null;
        }
    }
    </script></head>
<body onLoad="imageLoad( )"><h1>Cat Animation</h1>
<P><img src="anim0.jpg" name="animImage" height=337
            width=256>
<form name="animateform">
```

```
<input type=button value=Start name="runAnim"
                onClick=checkButton( )>
<input type=text value=250
                name="speed">milliseconds</form>
<script>
document.animateform.runAnim.value = "Start";
document.animateform.speed.value = 250;
</script></body></html>
```

Listing 7-3 Simple animation

before the script tries to show them by using onLoad to call the image loader straight away. The form allows you to enter the delay gap between slide changes and start or stop the sequence. The button initially says 'start', and when clicked it sets up a timer that calls the animate function after a given period using:

```
timerId = setTimeout("animate( )",
document.animateform.speed.value);
```

This sets up continuous calls to the animate function that are only canceled when the button is again toggled to its stopped state and the timer is cleared with:

```
clearTimeout(timerId);
```

Note here that the timerId needs the reference to it that was returned when it was called above with setTimeout.

The next example, Listing 7-4, shows how it is possible to incorporate CSS to allow for the positioning of moving objects. Ten ball objects in an array are initialized with random positions. Each ball has properties such as x and y position, its direction and an associated ball graphic in markup as a div element. The graphic it uses is actually called ball.gif.

When the page is loaded up the movement loop begins, which goes through each ball updating its position according to the direction vectors it contains (xdirn, ydirn).

If this script doesn't work on your browser you may like to find out and adapt it to the version of DOM it works with but make sure you try to use browser sniffing to detect which browser needs specific code!

The program shows how it is possible to use JavaScript and CSS together to liven up a static Web site.

```
<html>
<head>
<script>
function ball(bx, by, bxdir, bydir, bid) {
    this.xpos = bx; this.ypos = by;
    this.xdirn = bxdir; this.ydirn = bydir;
    nam = "ball"+bid;
    s='<div id=ball'+bid+'
      style="left: 100px; position: absolute; top:
                    100px"><img
    src="ball.gif"
    border=0></div>';
    document.writeln(s);
    this.gr = document.all[nam].style; this.setball =
                    setball;
    this.moveball = moveball;
}
function setball(bx, by) {
    this.xpos = bx; this.ypos = by;
    this.gr.left=bx; this.gr.top=by;
}
function moveball( ) {
        this.ypos+=this.ydirn;
        if (this.ypos>ymax) this.ydirn=-this.ydirn;
        else if (this.ypos<10)
                    this.ydirn=Math.abs(this.ydirn);
        this.xpos+=this.xdirn;
        if (this.xpos>xmax) this.xdirn=-this.xdirn;
        else if (this.xpos<10)
                    this.xdirn=Math.abs(this.xdirn);
        this.setball(this.xpos, this.ypos);
}
function onMove( ) {
        for (j=1; j<=numballs; j++) {
            aball[j].moveball( );
        }
        setTimeout("onMove( )",1);
}
</script>
</head>
<body>
<div id=test2 style="left: 140px; position: absolute; top:
            110px">A simple animation demo</div>
<script>
  numballs=10; aball = new Array( );
```

```
    for (j=1; j<=numballs; j++) {
      xdirRange = (Math.random( )*8)-4;
      ydirRange = (Math.random( )*8)-4;
      aball[j] = new ball(12+(Math.
                    random( )*400),13+(Math.random( )*400)
          ,xdirRange,ydirRange,j);
    }
  xmax=document.body.clientWidth-30;
  ymax=document.body.clientHeight-30;
  window.onload = onMove;
</script>
</body>
</html>
```

Listing 7-4 *Moving objects around the browser window*

Checkpoint!

- ▪ JavaScript contains the **Image** object, which possesses useful properties and methods and can be associated with an image source.
- ▪ It's possible to cache the images in an **Image** object, 'ahead of time', to make sure they are available when needed to allow smooth movement for animation.
- ▪ JavaScript has the ability to execute code at specific timing intervals using **setTimeout( )**.
- ▪ Positioning for animated objects can be achieved using CSS.
- ▪ Awareness of compatibility between browsers is essential so test and code for each where possible especially where the DOM is concerned.

Test Yourself!

- • Write your own basic animation with a graphic that swaps images on the spot, but does not move from its position.
- • Use the **Image** object.
- • Add caching to try to make the transition between images smoother.
- • Finally, add movement around the browser window.

7.2 EVENTS AND BUTTONS

One of the interesting things about JavaScript is its ability to be event driven. Events are actions that the user performs when they visit your page. They may, for example, move the mouse around or click on buttons. When an event happens it triggers objects that are associated with that kind of event. Event handlers catch these events and execute code in response. See Table 7-2 for a list of the available event handlers.

Event	When does it happen?
onabort	Visitor aborts page loading
onblur	Visitor leaves an object
onchange	Visitor changes the value of an object
onclick	Visitor clicks on an object
ondblclick	Visitor double-clicks on an object
onfocus	Visitor makes an object active
onkeydown	Key is being pressed down
onkeypress	Key is pressed
onkeyup	Key is being released
onload	Page has finished loading
onmousedown	User presses a mouse-button
onmousemove	Cursor moves on an object
onmouseout	Cursor moves off an object
onmouseover	Cursor moves over an object
onmouseup	Visitor releases a mouse-button
onreset	Visitor resets a form
onselect	Visitor selects content on a page
onsubmit	Visitor submits a form
onunload	Visitor closes a page

Table 7-2 JavaScript events

7.2.1 The Window

The window itself has its own events, which trigger when a new page is starting up (onLoad), shutting down (onUnload), being resized (onResize), moved (onMove), canceled (onAbort) or when an error occurs (onError). There is also an event triggered when the window moves to the foreground (onFocus) or changes to the background (onBlur).

7.2.2 The Mouse

The mouse has a few events associated with it when a button is pressed (onMousedown) on top of an element and when it is released (onMouseup); when the mouse moves and the pointer is already over an element (onMousemove) and when it moves away from the element (onMouseout). Events are triggered also when the pointer is over an element (onMouseover) and when it is clicked once (onClick) or twice (onDblclick).

7.2.3 The Keyboard

Events can be triggered when the key is pressed down (onKeydown) and when it is released (onKeyup). The complete key sequence, down press and up release, triggers another event (onKeypress).

7.2.4 Using Events

Each of the events can be used to trigger scripts to run. Listing 7-5 shows how it is possible to trap the exiting of the user from a page.

```
<html>
<head>
<title>JavaScript Forms</title>
<meta http-equiv="Content-Type" content="text/html;
            charset=iso-8859-1">
</script>
</head>
<body bgcolor="green"
onUnload="alert('Bye, see you again!')">
<h1>Hello, this is my new web page</h1>
</body>
</html>
```

Listing 7-5 *A basic window event being captured*

The event itself is captured by the onUnload embedded in the body tag, which triggers an alert box. The onLoad event can be captured in a similar way but is triggered, as the name suggests, when the page first loads. No doubt you have probably seen such things before on commercial sites that either trigger popups as you enter or leave, which are done in just this way. This can prove to be very annoying with over use, so employ with care!

In the script in Listing 7-6, the event handler is embedded in the (X)HTML tag that the event depends on, which in this case is a link to another page. When the link is clicked the onclick event is triggered and an alert box comes up with the Date( ) function's information included with the message. This can also be done with a button rather than a link.

```
<html>
<head>
<title>JavaScript Forms</title>
<meta http-equiv="Content-Type" content="text/html;
             charset=iso-8859-1">
</script>
</head>
<body bgcolor="green">
<h1>Hello, this is my new web page</h1>
<p>Click for the <a href="mytime.html" onclick="alert('the
             time and date is '+Date( ))">time!</a></p>
</body>
</html>
```

Listing 7-6 *Using a mouse click*

Listing 7-7 shows how you can use buttons to activate scripts rather than a link. Notice here that single quotes are used inside the double quotes to help stop it getting confusing!

```
<html>
<head>
<title>JavaScript Forms</title>
<meta http-equiv="Content-Type" content="text/html;
             charset=iso-8859-1">
</script>
</head>
<body bgcolor="green">
<h1>Hello, this is my new web page</h1>
<button type="button" name="findtime" onclick="alert('Today
             is '+Date( ))">
     Time and Date info</button><br>
```

```
<button type="button" name="red" onclick=
            "document.bgColor='red';">red</button><br>
<button type="button" name="blue" onclick=
            "document.bgColor='blue';">blue</button><br>
<button type="button" name="green"
onclick= "document.bgColor='green';">green</button><br>
</body>
</html>
```

Listing 7-7 *Buttons for events*

Mouse events can be picked up in the same way and associated with some code. In Listing 7-8, the event of the mouse passing into and out of an element is captured.

```
<html>
<head>
<title>JavaScript Forms</title>
<meta http-equiv="Content-Type" content="text/html;
            charset=iso-8859-1">
</script>
</head>
<body bgcolor="green">
<h1 onmouseover="style.color='yellow'"
onmouseout="style.color='black'">Hello, this is my new web
            page</h1>
</body>
</html>
```

Listing 7-8 *Using* `mouseover`

In this example, when the event is triggered, the color of the element is changed. Not only can the clicking event be used but the individual components of the click itself; that is, the downward and upward movement of the mouse click itself. To do this, you utilize **onMousedown** and **onMouseup**. This is shown in Listing 7-9, which swaps two images depending on whether the mouse is pressed down or released up.

```
<html>
<head>
<script type="text/javascript">
function imageOne( )
{
```

```
document.getElementById('theimage').src="image1.gif"
}
function imageTwo( )
{
document.getElementById('theimage').src="image2.gif"
}
</script>
</head>

<body>
<img id="theimage" onmousedown="image1( )"
onmouseup="image2( )" src="image1.gif">
<p>Click to change image</p>
</body>
</html>
```

Listing 7-9 *More mouse events*

An image can be made to follow the mouse pointer around the screen by linking the mouse movement events and location to the actual image's positioning. This is shown in Listing 7-10.

```
<html>
<head>
<title>Follow me</title>

<script language="javascript">
  function onMove(e) {

    if (IE) {
        ex = event.clientX;
        ey = event.clientY;
    } else {
        ex=e.pageX;
        ey=e.pageY;
    }

    gr.left =ex+"px";
    gr.top  =ey+"px";


  }
  function setup( ) {
    if (!IE) document.captureEvents(Event.MOUSEMOVE);
```

```
        window.document.onmousemove = onMove;

    }
</script>

</head><body>
  <DIV ID="catpic2" STYLE="position:absolute; top: 100;
                left: 100;">
    <IMG SRC="catscratch.jpg">
  </DIV>

  <script language="javascript"   >
    var IE = document.all ? true : false;

    gr=document.getElementById("catpic2").style;

    window.onload = setup;
  </script>

</body></html>
```

Listing 7-10 *Using* **onmousemove** *and compatibility checks*

This script should work for several browsers, such as Safari, Firefox and Internet Explorer, because of the way it is written to take account of the differences between them. In the main JavaScript an image is placed within a div element with a name to identify it so it can be referenced later on. The main JavaScript program begins with a variable being set up, IE, which is set to true if the test that document.all is available (only if it is an IE browser). A reference variable is then declared to point at the picture's style attribute. The next line makes the function setup run when the page has properly finished loading.

The setup function connects the mouse movement event to calling a function to actually move the image. There is a slight variation here between browsers in that non-IE types (well, Firefox in particular!) need the line:

```
document.captureEvents(Event.MOUSEMOVE);
```

which will switch the event on for capture. The function onMove is then called when an event happens with:

```
window.document.onmousemove = onMove;
```

The onMove function needs to again check for the browser type in use as there is a variation in how the actual event is accessed. You may have noticed that there is an incoming parameter, 'e'. This is the event that is automatically passed into the mouse handler function; it is not used for IE but for others it is required. If it is an IE browser the position of the mouse is accessed by:

```
ex = event.clientX;
ey = event.clientY;
```

If it's another browser it uses the event object, 'e', that has been passed in:

```
ex = e.pageX;
ey = e.pageY;
```

This completes getting the actual position of the mouse. All we need to do now is transfer that information to the image and, by doing that, reposition. To do this the reference we initially set is used:

```
gr.left = ex + "px";
gr.top = ey + "px";
```

This sets the style attributes of the image object, adding 'px' to make sure it is understood that it is absolute pixels that are being set.

As well as window and mouse events there are also ways to find out key presses using **onkeypress**, as well as **onkeydown** and **onkeyup**. This is very similar to the mouse event in that **onkeypress** will be triggered when the event happens but **onkeydown** and **onkeyup** are triggered individually. Listing 7-11 is an example that shows the code values of key presses and particularly reacts to the lowercase 'q' letter in a different way to any other. Notice in this example that instead of the actual code being placed in the event line it is removed to a function. A calling function header is used with a parameter being passed, which is the key press from the event.

```
<html>
<head>
<title>Untitled Document</title>

<script type="text/JavaScript">

function processKey(key) {
  if (key == 113) {
        alert("You pressed key the q key!");
  } else {
        alert("You pressed a key: "+key);
  }
```

```
    }

</script>
</head>
<body onKeyPress="processKey(window.event.keyCode)">
<h1>Press a key!</h1>
<br><br>
</body></html>
```

Listing 7-11 *Keyboard input*

There are a few other events such as **onsubmit**, which has been used before in this book. It simply triggers a script when the visitor to your page presses submit. For example the form:

```
<form onSubmit="processform(this.name.value)">
<input name=myname type="text" ROWS=1 SIZE="20">Enter your
                name:
<input name=submit type="submit">
<input name=reset type="reset">
</form>
```

This sends the contents of the input field **myname** when the submission button is pressed. Again, as in the earlier example, the code executed is a call to a function with a parameter rather than the script itself.

Test Yourself!

- Use the animation script you developed earlier as the basis for a new program in which you control your animation via the mouse and/or keyboard.
- With the animation still running make it change its position to follow the mouse.
- Add keyboard control to change its position.

7.3 CONTROLLING YOUR BROWSER

The **window** object has some useful features that you can use to control your browser. For example, sometimes you want an entirely new browser window to open rather than disturbing the content you have in the current one, perhaps because you want to show a new site. To do this:

```
    myWindow =
```

```
window.open("apage.html","pageName","width=330,height=200,
            scrollbars=yes");
```

myWindow contains the new window object. The new window is loaded with the page pointed to in the first parameter. pageName is the reference to the new window so you can target it later if you want to change the content. Finally, the size of the window is given and the option of adding a scrollbar is selected.

It is possible to also scroll the new window to a certain part of the page if you wanted to select a specific bit of information for the visitor. To do this, first of all make sure the window is selected:

```
myWindow.focus();
```

Then, to do the actual scroll itself:

```
myWindow.scroll(0,200);
```

This would make the window scroll 0 pixels horizontally and 200 pixels vertically. Instead of loading a page into the new window it is possible to leave that parameter as an empty string and write an entirely new page into the window using JavaScript. First, set up the page:

```
myWindow = window.open("","pageName",
         "width=330, height=200, scrollbars=yes, resizable=yes");

myWindow.document.write("<html><head><title>JS Generated
            Window!<\/title><\/head><body><h2>This is a
            JavaScript produced
            page...<\/h2><\/body><\/html>");
```

If you open a child window from your original window how would you refer back from that child to the parent to get some information like a form field? The answer is to use the opener property, which gives a reference to the parent opening window. So, within that child to refer to a form value in the parent:

```
opener.document.dataForm.inField.value
```

In this example, dataForm is the name of the form in the parent and inField is the name of the field. Using this method it is possible to either access a value or set it.

Finally, to close a window, use the appropriate method:

```
myWindow.close();
```

Checkpoint!

- ■ JavaScript can utilize event driven programing.
- ■ Events that can trigger execution of code include the mouse, keyboard and window.
- ■ Window events can be used to trigger code on loading.
- ■ User input can add to dynamic interaction.
- ■ It's possible to start up new browser windows and interact with them.

Test Yourself!

- • Experiment with starting up new windows.
- • Pass information between them, in response to a user form on one of them.
- • Another idea is to make one a control or navigation panel and the other the output for content; try and implement this.
- • Finally, make it possible to shut down the child windows when finished.

7.4 CHAPTER SUMMARY

- ■ DHTML can be used to enrich a static Web site, on the client side.
- ■ It is a combination of HTML, CSS and JavaScript.
- ■ It can be used to provide animation and greater interaction with the user.
- ■ There are specific techniques for improving animation.
- ■ Event driven scripting can be usefully employed for picking up user input.
- ■ JavaScript contains mechanisms for controlling the browser and its interface.

Chapter Quiz

- • Write a simple game using DHTML such as the classic Pong, ball and bat game.
- • Consider how difficult it would be to develop a more complex game such as a Space Invaders or Pac Man types; what would be the useful features of JavaScript?

Key Words and Phrases

Animation The process of producing the illusion of motion, usually by flicking between image frames

DHTML Dynamic HTML, the combination of HTML, CSS and JavaScript to enrich a Web site

Event driven Using events to trigger the execution of specific code

Image caching A technique for improving animation by loading and storing the images to be used ahead of the time of use

Useful Web Addresses

`http://www.w3schools.com/dhtml/`

`http://www.dhtmlcentral.com/`

`http://www.webreference.com/dhtml/`

8

In this chapter you will learn about the basics of XML and how it can be used to store information away from the mechanism of processing or formatting of such data. You will learn how to build simple XML files, and be able to manipulate and refer to them.

The primary use of XML is the description of data rather than presentation. Initially this would be to extract data away from HTML and focus on the *semantics* (the meaning!) rather than the formatting. XML has far more to it than just this though. XML is, as the name suggests, a language, or rather a meta-language, which can be used to store data and act as a mechanism to transfer information between dissimilar systems.

XML does not actually do anything by itself, it simply describes data. To have anything happen with that data it needs to be processed or transmitted or whatever it is that needs to be done.

Here we explore its basic use and capabilities before moving on to more advanced topics.

8.1 **INTRODUCTION TO XML**

XML is a language to describe other languages. It's possible to use it to actually make up other markup languages and in this book we have met it before in the chapters describing XHTML. You can use it to describe any kind of data that you can think of, whether it be mathematical, genealogical, scientific or business data. Several languages are based on XML including SVG, XHTML, RSS, MathML, RDF, WAP and WML.

XML came about in the mid-nineties as a solution to perceived problems with the WWW. Practitioners of SGML saw that it held some answers to these problems and in 1996 activity commenced into researching the possibilities by an 11-member working group. In 1998 XML 1.0 became a W3C recommendation.

Its main purpose is to allow the sharing of data across different systems and it is particularly useful in this sense for applications that do this over the Internet.

These are the main features of XML:

- It is in a format that both humans and machines can read. There is nothing special about XML, it's just plain text, made up of normal characters and angled brackets.
- It supports unicode, which is capable of encoding all human languages.
- It supports data structures well.
- It is self-documenting.
- It has a strict format that makes it easy for parsing to take place.
- It can be understood and exchanged between dissimilar systems.
- It can be useful in swapping data between different applications.

8.2 **THE MANY USES OF XML**

In a Web context XML can be used to separate the data away from HTML, which should be concerned with presentation. The HTML is then concerned with the layout of such data and it doesn't matter if that data changes. In this way you would not change your HTML if you wanted to add or amend the data.

8.3 **SIMPLE XML**

An XML document has a simple and self-describing syntax. Listing 8-1 shows a simple example containing an item described in XML for a database containing people information.

```
<?xml version="1.0" encoding="ISO-8859-1"?>
<person>
<first>Fred</first>
<last>Bloggs</last>
<birthdate>20th March 1977</birthdate>
<birthplace>Leeds</birthplace>
<employed started="12/12/04">Leeds City Library</employed>
</person>
```

Listing 8-1 *A simple XML document*

The first line is the XML declaration and gives the XML version and character encoding used. The next line contains the root element, `<person>`. All XML documents contain a root element, defining an element that is descriptive of that document as a whole, which in this case says 'this is a person'. The next few lines contain the data and also describe that data. For example, the next line after the root element is:

```
<first>Fred</first>
```

In this case the line contains a first name, Fred, which is wrapped in a descriptive element, `<first>`. Similarly, the next few lines describe the data containing the last name, the birth date, birth place and current employer until the root element is finally closed on the last line:

```
</person>
```

As you can see this is fairly self-descriptive and readable by you!

8.4 XML KEY COMPONENTS

One of the key aspects of XML is how strict the syntax is. Here we go into more detail regarding how the language is constructed.

8.4.1 Elements

The strict syntax of XML contains a few rules about elements that must be adhered to:

- Elements must have a closing tag.
- Tags are case sensitive.
- Elements must be nested correctly.
- XML documents must have a root element.

The closing tag in XML is important; for example, older forms of HTML allowed elements to miss out the closing tag but this would be illegal with XML and therefore XHTML! It's also important to remember that XML is case sensitive so:

```
<birthdate>20th March 1977</birthdate>
```

would not be the same as:

```
<Birthdate>20th March 1977</Birthdate>
```

In HTML it is sometimes possible to improperly nest elements inside each other:

```
<b><i>Some text</b></i>
```

whereas it should be more properly done like this:

```
<b><i>Some text</i></b>
```

In XML it is essential to nest elements in the correct order.

8.4.2 Attributes

There is an attribute in Listing 8-1 containing the person's start date at his job. Attributes can be added to elements in XML but must always be quoted. For example, this would be incorrect:

```
<employed started=12/12/04>Leeds City Library</employed>
```

To make it legal XML syntax, the attribute must be enclosed in quotes:

```
<employed started="12/12/04">Leeds City Library</employed>
```

8.4.3 Other Essentials

There are a few other important aspects to keep in mind when working with XML.

For example, white space is preserved in XML where as in HTML it is truncated down to just a single space. So, you may have text in HTML like this:

```
Hello World, this is a simple document
```

which will be displayed as:

```
Hello World, this is a simple document
```

In XML the spaces would be kept as they are.

Another interesting XML fact is that a carriage return (CR) and linefeed (LF) combination, sometimes produced at the end of text lines by word processors, becomes translated to just a linefeed with XML.

One thing does remain in common with HTML though: comments can be added using the triangle brackets like this:

```
<!--  here are some remarks -->
```

8.4.4 Namespaces

Sometimes in XML there is a danger of conflicting names between documents; for example, it would be quite easy for two different documents to contain the same named element. It's even more likely if you are sharing documents with someone else. It may be that you have used the word 'name' for an animal database and the other person has used it for a region identity. A problem like this can be resolved by adding a prefix to the elements, such as `animal:name`, or even your own name for that particular document. However, these may also not be unique enough.

It is possible instead to associate a namespace with the elements in use, providing a unique name. When a namespace is used it is not for looking up information by the parser but simply to provide the unique name. It is sometimes used though to give a Web site address about the namespace.

Namespaces usually take the form of a URL, beginning with a domain name, an optional namespaces label in the form of a directory name and finally a version number, which is also optional:

```
xmlns="http://www.mydomain.com/ns/animals/1.1"
```

Checkpoint!

- **XML means Extensible Markup Language; a meta-language that describes other languages.**
- **Where HTML deals with the presentation and formatting of Web documents, XML is concerned with the semantics or meaning of data.**
- **It stores data in such a way as to be understandable and readable by both humans and computers.**
- **It has a strict syntax; for example, tags must be closed and nested properly. It is also case sensitive.**
- **It's useful for both storing information and the transmission of information.**

> ■ To help prevent name conflicts between documents it is possible to use a prefix or a namespace.

Test Yourself!

- Develop an XML document that will hold a music collection with fields for artist name, record company, date released and format (CD, Minidisk, DVD).

8.5 DOCUMENT TYPE DEFINITIONS AND SCHEMAS

XML is particularly concerned with being *well formed* or correct in syntax. There are two ways of checking whether a document follows the expected order and structure: Document Type Definitions (DTDs) and schemas. These template schemas are checked as the parser scans the document.

8.5.1 DTDs

DTDs can be declared in the XML document itself, or as an external file.

In Listing 8-2 the first line declares the XML version and then proceeds into the DTD. DOCTYPE defines that this is a document of type memo. It is then defined as having four

```
<?xml version="1.0"?>
<!DOCTYPE memo [
  <!ELEMENT memo (to,from,title,message)>
  <!ELEMENT to       (#PCDATA)>
  <!ELEMENT from     (#PCDATA)>
  <!ELEMENT title (#PCDATA)>
  <!ELEMENT message     (#PCDATA)>
]>
<memo>
  <to>Alan</to>
  <from>Sid</from>
  <title>Meeting</title>
  <message>Don't forget the meeting today at 12</message>
</memo>
```

Listing 8-2 *A simple DTD*

elements, to, from, title and message. These elements are each in turn defined as having type PCDATA, which stands for parsed character data, which refers to everything except markup; this includes numbers, letters, symbols and entities. A DTD describes an XML document in terms of elements, tags, attributes, entities, PCDATA and CDATA. Most of these have been described before apart from CDATA, which is the equivalent of a comment that will not be processed.

The DTD can also be stored in an external file, as shown in Listing 8-3, allowing many documents to use the same structure check.

```
<!ELEMENT memo (to,from,title,message)>
<!ELEMENT to (#PCDATA)>
<!ELEMENT from (#PCDATA)>
<!ELEMENT title (#PCDATA)>
<!ELEMENT message (#PCDATA)>
```

Listing 8-3 *DTD as an external file*

The actual XML document can be then stored in a separate file that refers to it (Listing 8-4).

```
<?xml version="1.0"?>
<!DOCTYPE memo SYSTEM "memo.dtd">
<memo>
<to>Alan</to>
<from>Sid</from>
<title>Meeting</title>
<message>Don't forget the meeting today at 12</message>
</memo>
```

Listing 8-4 *The referring XML document*

In the above DTDs there are two different kinds of definition:

```
<!ELEMENT memo (to,from,title,message)>
```

or

```
<!ELEMENT message (#PCDATA)>
```

The first is an element followed by a list of children elements; the second is an element named message followed by parsable data. The other possibilities include the ability to say exactly how many elements should occur; for example, at least one, none or one occurrence, none or multiple occurrences, or one or more occurrences (Table 8-1).

Number of occurrences	Syntax	Example
Only one	`<!ELEMENT element-name (child-name)>`	`<!ELEMENT memo (message)>`
One or more	`<!ELEMENT element-name (child-name+)>`	`<!ELEMENT memo (message+)>`
Zero or more	`<!ELEMENT element-name (child-name*)>`	`<!ELEMENT memo (message*)>`
Zero or one	`<!ELEMENT element-name (child-name?)>`	`<!ELEMENT memo (message?)>`
Either/or	`<!ELEMENT element-name (child-name|child-name)>`	`<!ELEMENT memo (note|message)>`

Table 8-1 DTD

In a similar way it is possible to declare attributes:

```
<!ATTLIST element-name attribute-name
attribute-type default-value>
```

For example, in using DTD:

```
<!ATTLIST payment type CDATA "card">
```

a typical XML example could be:

```
<payment type="card" />
```

The attribute type can have other values, as shown in Table 8-2.

The specified default value can have several values, as specified in Table 8-3.

For example, to use #REQUIRED, the DTD would include:

```
<!ATTLIST product idcode CDATA #REQUIRED>
```

For the correct XML:

```
<product idcode="28177"/>
```

it would be an error to not include an ending tag:

```
<product />
```

Value	Description
CDATA	Character data
(enum1|enum2|...)	Must be from enumerated list
ID	Unique ID
IDREF	ID of another element
IDREFS	List of other IDs
NMTOKEN	XML name
NMTOKENS	List of XML names
ENTITY	Entity
ENTITIES	List of entities
NOTATION	Notation name
xml:	Predefined XML value

Table 8-2 DTD attribute types

Value	Description
value	Default value of an attribute
#REQUIRED	Attribute must be included
#IMPLIED	Doesn't have to be included
#FIXED value	This value is fixed

Table 8-3 Attribute required or default

8.5.2 **Schemas**

A schema performs the same function as a DTD; that is, it defines what is legal in an XML document. Schemas are largely replacing DTDs as they are extensible, richer and generally more useful. They became an official W3C recommendation in May 2001.

Going back to the memo example, the XML schema in Listing 8-5 is the equivalent of the DTD in Listing 8-2 for the XML memo document.

```
<?xml version="1.0"?>
<xs:schema xmlns:xs="http://www.w3.org/2001/XMLSchema"
targetNamespace="http://www.myXMLnspace.com"
xmlns="http://www.myXMLnspace.com"
elementFormDefault="qualified">
<xs:element name="memo">
    <xs:complexType>
      <xs:sequence>
        <xs:element name="to" type="xs:string"/>
        <xs:element name="from" type="xs:string"/>
        <xs:element name="title" type="xs:string"/>
        <xs:element name="message" type="xs:string"/>
      </xs:sequence>
    </xs:complexType>
</xs:element>
</xs:schema>
```

Listing 8-5 *Equivalent XML schema*

The schema in Listing 8-5 would be stored as `memo.xsd`. Most elements contained in this schema are simple types, as they do not contain other elements. However, the element `memo` is complex as it contains a lot of the simple types. To use this schema, a link is placed inside the original document as shown in Listing 8-6.

```
<?xml version="1.0"?>
<memo
xmlns="http://www.w3schools.com"
xmlns:xsi="http://www.w3.org/2001/XMLSchema-instance"
xsi:schemaLocation="http://www.myXMLnspace.com memo.xsd">

<to>Alan</to>
<from>Sid</from>
<title>Reminder</title>
<message>Don't forget the meeting today at 12</message>
</memo>
```

Listing 8-6 *Referring to a schema in an XML document*

The schema begins properly at its root element:

```
<xs:schema> ... </xs:schema>
```

As you can see the `<schema>` element can contain several attributes, the first part of which (`xmlns`) declares the namespace that the elements and data types (such as `schema`, `element`, `complexType`, `sequence`, `boolean` …) used in this schema come from. All these are to be prefixed with `xs:`. The `targetNamespace` indicates where elements defined in this schema (such as `to`, `from`, `title` and `message`) come from.

8.5.3 Elements

Elements in XML schemas are defined in a similar way to the DTDs but with a different syntax. For example, you may have:

```
<firstname>Greg</firstname>
<lastname>Hurst</lastname>
<age>35</age>
```

which could have some schema element definitions:

```
<xs:element name="firstname" type="xs:string"/>
<xs:element name="age" type="xs:integer"/>
<xs:element name="lastname" type="xs:string"/>
```

These are some simple element types:

- `xs:string`
- `xs:decimal`
- `xs:integer`
- `xs:boolean`
- `xs:date`
- `xs:time`.

Complex elements can be built that contain other elements and attributes. The following parts of a schema use a complex type named `productinfo`. This in itself contains a sequence of elements, hence the complex type. The `productinfo` complex type can then be used for elements:

```
<xs:element name="food" type="productinfo"/>
<xs:element name="magazines" type="productinfo"/>
<xs:element name="clothes" type="productinfo"/>
<xs:complexType name="productinfo">
  <xs:sequence>
    <xs:element name="item" type="xs:string"/>
    <xs:element name="itemcode" type="xs:string"/>
  </xs:sequence>
</xs:complexType>
```

8.5.4 **Attributes**

To define an attribute a similar style is adopted; for example for the XML element:

```
<firstname lang="English">Greg</firstname>
```

the schema definition could be:

```
<xs:attribute firstname="lang" type="xs:string"/>
```

The data types used are the same as those defined as above. It is possible to have an attribute assigned automatically should no other be given; in other words it is possible to give a default value:

```
<xs:attribute name="lang" type="xs:string" default="English"/>
```

If an attribute is to be attached that cannot be changed then a fixed value can be ascribed:

```
<xs:attribute name="lang" type="xs:string" fixed="English"/>
```

Attributes can also be made optional or required:

```
<xs:attribute name="lang" type="xs:string" use="optional"/>
<xs:attribute name="lang" type="xs:string" use="required"/>
```

This should give some idea of XML schemas. There is much more to learn in this area so you could try the W3C Web site for more information or w3schools.

8.6 **WELL FORMED?**

XML documents should be well formed and utilize rules set out in DTDs or schemas to define them. A parser can use these rule sets to work out whether a document is correct or not. Parsers can be stand alone software, part of a browser or an object in a programing language. JavaScript, for example, includes the ability to access parsers, such as Microsoft's XMLDOM, utilize them and report any errors generated. Some Web sites will let you paste XML into a text area and will check it for you, while others will verify a specified site is valid.

For example, if you visit:

```
http://www.w3schools.com/dom/dom_validate.asp
```

you can check whether XML is correct using both methods mentioned earlier.

Checkpoint!

■ There has to be some way of verifying that an XML document is correct or well formed.

■ There are two ways to do this, DTDs and schemas.

■ Schemas are probably better and more commonly used.

■ Both give a set of rules for the parser to verify the XML code.

■ They are composed of descriptions of the order, sequence and description of the various elements, attributes and other parts of the document.

Test Yourself!

• Try and develop a DTD for your XML music collection document.
• Develop a schema for your XML music collection document.
• Find a browser that will parse and validate your document.
• Find out more about the JavaScript mechanism for accessing and using an XML parser.

8.7 USING XML WITH APPLICATIONS

So, if you have managed to get your data into order with XML what can you do with it? Well, it's possible to look at XML with a browser and it will show it in a hierarchical form, which it has derived by scanning through it with its own parser.

It's also possible to utilize XML inside HTML. For example, XML can be stored as a separate file as we have seen. It can also be embedded within an HTML document using the unofficial <xml> tag. It is also possible to bind XML to HTML elements using *data islands*, although this does not work with all browsers.

Listing 8-7 shows an example of using a data island. First the XML file with the data island is loaded using the <xml> element then the <table> element is bound to the data island using the datasrc attribute. This code will output all the entries in that file that are in the fields ARTIST and TITLE.

Many applications now use XML as a storage or transfer mechanism. For example, you could easily make a database of books and store the data as XML. It is possible to use parsers to scan

```
<html>
<body>
<xml id="cdcat" src="cd_catalog.xml"></xml>
<table border="1" datasrc="#cdcat">
<tr>
<td><span datafld="ARTIST"></span></td>
<td><span datafld="TITLE"></span></td>
</tr>
</table>
</body>
</html>
```

Listing 8-7 *Using data islands*

through the tags and hierarchy to extract the information your application requires. Java, JavaScript and the .NET programing languages among others all contain ready-built parsers for this, although is also possible to write your own!

8.8 CHAPTER SUMMARY

- **XML is a language that can be used to describe other markup languages.**
- **Its main purpose is to give meaning to data.**
- **It can be used as both a store and a transfer mechanism for information.**
- **It is readable by humans as it is simply held in plain text format.**
- **The syntax is strict and case sensitive.**
- **Conflicts between names in XML documents can be resolved with prefixes or namespaces.**
- **XML can be verified with a parser that uses an associated DTD or schema.**
- **DTDs and schemas consist of a set of rules that determine the correct order and type of included parts of the document.**
- **XML can be used with many applications, which can use it to store or transfer data; for example, to store information on a music collection or library of books.**
- **XML can be utilized in many programing and scripting languages that already contain components to manipulate such documents.**

Chapter Quiz

- Would it be possible to develop an entire database from XML? What would be the problems and advantages in doing so?
- If you are used to writing computer programs (or scripts!) and you had to parse XML, how could you do it?

- Use a few different browsers and point them at your XML. Which ones process the XML and which ones don't? (Some should display a kind of hierarchical tree.)

Key Words and Phrases

Data islands A way of including information stored in an XML file inside an HTML page

DTD Document Type Definition, a document containing a set of rules that determine how an XML file should be structured. Can be inadequate for some XML documents, the alternative being the schema

Enumerated An ordered sequence, or list, of information

Schema Another way of providing a description for an XML document so it can be checked

XML The Extensible Markup Language, a markup language that can be used to define other markup languages. Used to give meaning and a description of data rather than providing formatting as HTML would

Useful Web Addresses

http://www.w3schools.com/dom/dom_validate.asp

http://www.w3schools.com/xml/

http://www.w3.org/XML/

http://en.wikipedia.org/wiki/XML

9

XML, XSL AND XSLT: TRANSFORMING XML

The aim of this chapter is to learn about and explore the possibilities of using XML as the starting point for data to be transformed into other target formats using XSLT. Style sheets are used and linked to documents. It is shown here that it is possible to process XML with a browser or a programing language on the client side.

XML allows the capture of meaning, or semantics, but it also has the ability to store data in a format that can be transformed into other types of document. This could be simply another XML document but with a different structure, or a totally different kind, such as XHTML, text or even PDF. By doing this you are keeping the meaning of the data away from forms it can be represented in and therefore increasing the flexibility. The XML document becomes the central store for information, which can then be output in whatever form is required for a particular context.

For example, if you choose to output your data in XHTML form you can harness the power of the markup to display that information in tables, frames or forms and highlight any information of particular interest with colors and emphasis.

In this chapter we explore the basics of how this is done so it is possible to transfer XML documents onto the Web and increase the usefulness of data stored in this way.

9.1 INTRODUCING XSL

Where CSS is used as a style sheet language for HTML, XSL could be considered as the equivalent for XML. This is correct but it's not just a style sheet language. XSL is in fact really a name that covers a family of different languages:

- XSLT This is XSL Transformations and will be the main area covered in this chapter. It concerns the transforming of XML documents from one syntax to another.
- XSL:FO This is XSL Formatting Objects and is a way to visually transform XML to several formats such as PDF, PostScript and text files.
- XPath This is used by XSLT to access, or to refer to, parts of XML documents.

Each of these is described in the W3C recommendations.

9.2 XML TRANSFORMED

XSLT could be considered one of the most important parts of XSL and became a W3C recommendation on 16 November 1999. It can be used to render XML into another kind of document. This could be another XML document or some other type, such as HTML or XHTML. Several browsers support an actual implementation of XSLT; these include Internet Explorer (using MSXML), Mozilla, Firefox and Netscape (using TransforMiiX). As usual, though, there is some variation in how well they do implement XSLT so it is wise to check with the specific browser and version. XSLT is used to change, and rearrange elements, add and sort to build a new document. In effect it transforms a source XML tree into a resulting XML tree.

To do this, XSLT also uses another language that has already been mentioned in this chapter, XPath. This allows elements and attributes in the tree to be navigated. Using XPath, XSLT defines parts of an XML document that match a template. Once found and matched to the template the elements can then be transformed.

Checkpoint!

- **XSL is the style sheet language for XML.**
- **The name covers several other language components such as XSLT, XSL:FO and XPath.**
- **XSL is concerned with transforming a source document to another type or format as a resulting document.**

- **XSLT will transform a document using XPath to specify and address parts of the source document's XML tree.**
- **Most browsers support an implementation of XSLT.**

9.3 **A SIMPLE EXAMPLE**

The best way to begin is with a simple example. The following code is part of a simple XML document:

```
<?xml version="1.0" encoding="ISO-8859-1"?>
<library>
  <book>
    <title>A Scanner Darkly</title>
    <author>Philip K. Dick</author>
    <publisher>Gollancz</publisher>
    <price>6.99</price>
    <year>1985</year>
    <isbn>1-85798-847-7</isbn>
  </book>
  .
  .
  .
</library>
```

The next step is to create an XSL style sheet that will transform the XML document to the format we want, which in this case will be XHTML:

```
<?xml version="1.0" encoding="ISO-8859-1"?>
<xsl:stylesheet version="1.0"
xmlns:xsl="http://www.w3.org/1999/XSL/Transform">
<xsl:template match="/">
  <html>
  <body>
    <h2>My Library</h2>
    <table border="1">
    <tr bgcolor="#9acd32">
      <th align="left">Title</th>
      <th align="left">Author</th>
    </tr>
    <xsl:for-each select="library/book">
    <tr>
      <td><xsl:value-of select="title"/></td>
```

```
            <td><xsl:value-of select="author"/></td>
          </tr>
          </xsl:for-each>
          </table>
        </body>
        </html>
      </xsl:template>
      </xsl:stylesheet>
```

Just like connecting the CSS style sheet to XHTML or HTML there needs to be a link between the two. This is done in the XML document:

```
<?xml version="1.0" encoding="ISO-8859-1"?>
<?xml-stylesheet type="text/xsl" href="libstyle.xsl"?>
<library>
  <book>
    <title>A Scanner Darkly</title>
    <author>Philip K. Dick</author>
    <publisher>Gollancz</publisher>
    <price>6.99</price>
    <year>2002</year>
    <isbn>1-85798-847-7</isbn>
  </book>
  .
  .
  .
</library>
```

As you can see the second line has been added, which links to your XSL style sheet libstyle.xsl.

To actually see the result you will have to load the XML back into your XSLT-compliant browser! Figure 9-1 shows the output after adding a few more records (Listing 9-1).

My Library

Title	Author
A Scanner Darkly	Philip K. Dick
Dr BloodMoney	Philip K. Dick
Ubik	Philip K. Dick

Figure 9-1 Output from Listing 9-1

```
<?xml version="1.0" encoding="ISO-8859-1"?>
<?xml-stylesheet type="text/xsl" href="libstyle.xsl"?>
<library>
  <book>
    <title>A Scanner Darkly</title>
    <author>Philip K. Dick</author>
    <publisher>Gollancz</publisher>
    <price>6.99</price>
    <year>2002</year>
    <isbn>1-85798-847-7</isbn>
  </book>
  <book>
    <title>Dr BloodMoney</title>
    <author>Philip K. Dick</author>
    <publisher>Gollancz</publisher>
    <price>6.99</price>
    <year>2001</year>
    <isbn>1-85798-952-X</isbn>
  </book>
  <book>
    <title>Ubik</title>
    <author>Philip K. Dick</author>
    <publisher>Gollancz</publisher>
    <price>6.99</price>
    <year>2002</year>
    <isbn>1-85798-853-1</isbn>
  </book>
</library>
```

Listing 9-1 *A simple XML document*

Checkpoint!

■ XML can have an associated style sheet to transform its output.

■ This is linked in to the XML document using a special style sheet reference.

■ Apart from adding the reference there is no difference to the XML document.

■ The style sheet must be available to perform the transformation.

9.3.1 The XML

As you can see from the XML used in this example, Listing 9-1 is not that different to what has been used before; there is a root element, library, followed by several book elements. Other items could belong to the library too, such as DVDs or music CDs.

9.3.2 The Style Sheet

The style sheet provides the template that transforms the document from one structure to another. In this case the <xsl:template> starts the definition of the actual template, as the name suggests. The match="/" attribute makes sure this begins applying the template to the root of the source XML document. Inside the template is the formatting for the output document, which is HTML and in this case a table. Probably the most interesting part of this is how it manages to visit each record of data stored in the XML. Here we can see a structure after the initial HTML that begins <xsl:for-each select="library/book">; this makes sure each book element is visited in turn and the code inside the for-each structure repeated in turn. Note where this structure ends and the code in-between. The data in each record is accessed by using:

```
<xsl:value-of select="title" />
```

and:

```
<xsl:value-of select="author" />
```

This is wrapped in the formatting commands for the HTML table that separate each item.

9.3.3 Linking

The style sheet is linked into the XML by adding the connecting statement to the XML document:

```
<?xml-stylesheet type="text/xsl" href="libstyle.xsl"?>
```

Test Yourself!

- Experiment with the above XML and XSL documents.
- Alter the output format so it simply lists all the data in the XML document.
- Alter the output again to create a table that contains all the stored data, complete with field headings at the top of the table.

9.4 **XSL ELEMENTS**

XSL contains many elements that can be used to manipulate, iterate and select XML for output. Some of the more important ones are discussed here.

9.4.1 `value-of`

Value-of allows information to be extracted and added to the resulting document. The actual **select** attribute consists of an XPath expression that is similar in addressing parts to an operating system's file hierarchy with the forward slash selecting sub-directories.

9.4.2 `for-each`

The for-each element can be used to iterate and select through every XML element; again the **select** attribute contains an XPath.

9.4.3 `sort`

Information can also be sorted for output, simply by adding an <xsl:sort> element inside a for-each.

```
<?xml version="1.0" encoding="ISO-8859-1"?>
<xsl:stylesheet version="1.0"
xmlns:xsl="http://www.w3.org/1999/XSL/Transform">
<xsl:template match="/">
  <html>
  <body>
    <h2>My Library</h2>
    <table border="1">
    <tr bgcolor="yellow">
      <th align="left">Title</th>
      <th align="left">Author</th>
    </tr>
    <xsl:for-each select="library/book">
    <xsl:sort select="year"/>
    <tr>
      <td><xsl:value-of select="title"/></td>
      <td><xsl:value-of select="author"/></td>
    </tr>
    </xsl:for-each>
    </table>
```

```
    </body>
    </html>
  </xsl:template>
</xsl:stylesheet>
```

Listing 9-2 *Using* `<xsl:sort>`

In Listing 9-2 **sort** is used to sort the information by year, although this could be used on any of the fields.

9.4.4 `if`

The `<xsl:if>` element allows the specifying of a query to extract information you may want. For example, Listing 9-3 has the `<xsl:if>` element:

```
<xsl:if test="year &gt; 2001">
```

This simply checks whether the year is greater than 2001 and in this case will only output those items that qualify, which is two of them.

```
<?xml version="1.0" encoding="ISO-8859-1"?>
<xsl:stylesheet version="1.0"
xmlns:xsl="http://www.w3.org/1999/XSL/Transform">
<xsl:template match="/">
  <html>
  <body>
    <h2>My Library</h2>
    <table border="1">
    <tr bgcolor="yellow">
      <th align="left">Title</th>
      <th align="left">Author</th>
    </tr>
    <xsl:for-each select="library/book">
    <xsl:if test="year &gt; 2001">
    <tr>
      <td><xsl:value-of select="title"/></td>
      <td><xsl:value-of select="author"/></td>
    </tr>
    </xsl:if>
    </xsl:for-each>
    </table>
```

```
    </body>
    </html>
  </xsl:template>
</xsl:stylesheet>
```

Listing 9-3 *Using a condition*

9.4.5 Choices

Sometimes a multiple condition is required, or a default, in case the main condition is not met. For this it is possible to use the `<xsl:choose>` element, which is used with the `<xsl:when>` and `<xsl:otherwise>` elements. Using this structure it is possible to change output according to whether an item is found or highlight specific information. Listing 9-4 shows the structure and gives an example of use.

```
<?xml version="1.0" encoding="ISO-8859-1"?>
<xsl:stylesheet version="1.0"
xmlns:xsl="http://www.w3.org/1999/XSL/Transform">
<xsl:template match="/">
  <html>
  <body>
   <h2>My Library</h2>
   <table border="1">
   <tr bgcolor="yellow">
     <th align="left">Title</th>
     <th align="left">Author</th>
   </tr>
   <xsl:for-each select="library/book">
   <xsl:choose>
   <xsl:when test="year = 2001">
   <tr>
     <td bgcolor="red"><xsl:value-of
                 select="title"/></td>
     <td><xsl:value-of select="author"/></td>
   </tr>
   </xsl:when>
   <xsl:otherwise>
   <tr>
     <td bgcolor="green"><xsl:value-of
                 select="title"/></td>
     <td><xsl:value-of select="author"/></td>
   </tr>
```

```
                </xsl:otherwise>
              </xsl:choose>
            </xsl:for-each>
          </table>
        </body>
      </html>
    </xsl:template>
  </xsl:stylesheet>
```

Listing 9-4 *Multiple choices*

The structure follows this basic pattern:

```
<xsl:choose>
  <xsl:when test "test expression">
     output if true
  </xsl:when>
  <xsl:otherwise>
     output in other cases
  </xsl:otherwise>
<xsl:choose>
```

9.4.6 **Applying Templates**

The next example shows how to use `<xsl:apply-templates>`, which allows control over how templates can be applied, either to the current element or, if using **select,** to a specific element's nodes. Listing 9-5 initially applies a template to the root and then three other templates to control output to the screen for title, author and pricing information.

```
<?xml version="1.0" encoding="ISO-8859-1"?>
<xsl:stylesheet version="1.0"
xmlns:xsl="http://www.w3.org/1999/XSL/Transform">

<xsl:template match="/">
    <html>
    <body>
        <h2>Book Library</h2>
        <xsl:apply-templates/>
    </body>
    </html>
```

```
        </xsl:template>

        <xsl:template match="book">
                <p>
                <xsl:apply-templates select="title"/>
                <xsl:apply-templates select="author"/>
                <xsl:apply-templates select="price"/>
                </p>
        </xsl:template>

        <xsl:template match="title">
        Title: <span style="color:red">
        <xsl:value-of select="."/></span>
        <br />
        </xsl:template>
        <xsl:template match="author">
        Artist: <span style="color:blue">
        <xsl:value-of select="."/></span>
        <br />
        </xsl:template>
        <xsl:template match="price">
        Price: <span style="color:green">
        <xsl:value-of select="."/></span>
        <br />
        </xsl:template>
        </xsl:stylesheet>
```

Listing 9-5 *Applying multiple templates*

The initial template match is with the root '/'. Within this there is a further <xsl:apply-templates> that activates the other templates, starting with the book-matching template. This then calls the others in sequence to give the desired output. Again, it is possible to use the usual HTML formatting to color and highlight the information.

Checkpoint!

- XSL uses templates, targeted by XPath, to change the resulting output document.
- XSL contains many elements to process XML; these include sorting, iteration and conditional selection.
- Templates can be applied in specific orders and output formatted as required.

Test Yourself!

- Expand the library XML document to include DVDs and CDs.
- Experiment with how you can look for specific information in an XML document, for example just the books or just the DVDS.
- Output each as a separate table.

9.5 TRANSFORMING WITH XSLT

As has been shown, it is possible to convert an XML document to XHTML using the browser's own parser. However, this is not always possible:

- The browser at the client end may not be suitable or equipped to do the transformation.
- It may not be a good idea to include the reference to the style sheet or even have the style sheet available!

In the case of the browser, it may be that it lacks the features required; for example, the actual transformation may be aimed at Braille or aural presentation. In the second case, including a reference within an XML document actually limits the XML to only that particular transformation and therefore gains flexibility.

The answer to this is to process the document and style sheet outside of the browser's own mechanisms for doing this task. This can be done either on the client side or the server side (which we will look at later).

9.5.1 Using JavaScript

One way to process and transform XML on the client side is using JavaScript, which has several features for doing the task very well.

```
<html>
<body>
<script type="text/javascript">
// Load the XML document
var xml = new ActiveXObject("Microsoft.XMLDOM")
xml.async = false
xml.load("lib.xml")
// Load the XSL document
```

```
var xsl = new ActiveXObject("Microsoft.XMLDOM")
xsl.async = false
xsl.load("libstyle.xsl")
// Do the actual transform
document.write(xml.transformNode(xsl))
</script>
</body>
</html>
```

Listing 9-6 Processing XML with JavaScript

Listing 9-6 shows one way to transform with JavaScript using Microsoft's proprietary Application Programing Interface (API) for the Internet Explorer browser. As you can see this is very simple indeed. It is also possible to process XML using the DOM, although as usual you have to be careful with compatibility between browsers. Using both of these mechanisms it is possible to also traverse an XML document and process either according to a style sheet or simply using the JavaScript to make the stylistic decisions.

Apart from JavaScript, it is also possible to use other programing languages (such as Java and .NET) to process and then output a transformed document.

Checkpoint!

■ Client side transforming of XML does not have to be limited to the browser's implementation of XSLT.

■ It is also possible to process XML using XSLT through languages such as JavaScript utilizing DOM or proprietary language features.

■ It's also possible to process XML with languages without a style sheet at all.

■ Separate processing allows a certain degree of flexibility as there is no need to reference a set XSL document within the XML.

9.6 CHAPTER SUMMARY

■ XSL is a special style sheet language for XML.
■ XSL is composed of several languages, XSL, XSL:FO and XPath.
■ XSL allows the transformation of XML from an initial source document to another kind of document, which can be XML, XHTML, text or some other type.
■ XPath is used to refer to specific parts of the source XML document.

- Most browsers implement a version of XSLT and so can be used to transform documents from one format to another, given the XML document with its referenced style sheet.
- Templates are used to match and then change part of the resulting document.
- XSL contains many useful elements to sort, iterate and conditionally select parts of the XML document.
- It is also possible to process XML outside of the browser, using client side languages. This can utilize the style sheet, which does not have to be referenced in the original XML, leading to more flexibility.
- It is also possible to process XML without a style sheet with languages such as Java and JavaScript that contain special language features to parse the XML source tree.

Chapter Quiz

- Consider how easy it would be to develop a complete database in XML with XSLT for output.
- Develop a simple query system for checking whether an XML document contains the information you want; how could you do this with a Web form as the main input page?
- See if you can find out more on the Web about XSL:FO and XPath; w3schools and Wikipedia are good places to start.

Key Words and Phrases

Template In XSLT a template is a set of rules that activate when a specific node is matched

XPath Used to address parts of an XML document by XSLT

XSL:FO XSL Formatting Objects, another way of transforming objects, converting description into presentation

XSLT XSL Transformations, an XML-based language used for transforming XML documents

Useful Web Addresses

http://www.w3.org/Style/XSL/

http://www.w3.org/TR/xslt

http://en.wikipedia.org/wiki/XSLT

http://www.w3schools.com/xpath/

10

WEB SERVICES, FEEDS AND BLOGS

Here you will learn about three important areas of Web activity: how it is possible to create language- and platform-independent services that utilize common Web protocols and XML; how information can be disseminated automatically to interested people; and finally, the phenomenon of the blog!

This chapter elaborates on how it is possible to build Web services, a means of communicating between distributed applications via the Internet. This allows a move toward a service-based (even subscription-based) computing model where it would be possible to access small parcels of functionality from distributed systems to add to your own application. For example, when writing on a word processor you may access a spell checker (which could be for a specific language) through a Web service rather than having a local version.

Web feeds are detailed here as a means of providing information to interested parties without having them even visit a Web site. Instead, an agent links them to the data source and collects preferred data, which is kept updated.

Lastly in this chapter, the idea of the blog is explored and the areas it has impacted upon are looked at. Some direction is given into how you would develop your own and either integrate it with your own Web site or use a service.

10.1 **THE NEED FOR WEB SERVICES**

Often there is a need to swap information with a distant computer that is running an application of some sort, to maybe process some information or retrieve data. This kind of distributed programing led to several problems becoming apparent:

- It was often difficult for information to be sent between platforms such as Unix or Windows.
- Special ports were required for applications that firewalls block for security reasons. For example, an application may use port 135 but will be blocked by a firewall that only has port 80 in use for the Web. Systems administration would not like to just open ports without good reason!

There is a need then for a service that is platform independent, will work between systems that are distributed and can communicate through firewalls without raising security issues.

10.2 **SOAP**

SOAP is an acronym meaning Simple Object Access Protocol. The idea behind SOAP is to provide a mechanism that allows access to objects across the Net. For example, a system may have a procedure belonging to an object that fulfills a purpose that an application requires. This sounds a little more complicated than it is but the idea is fairly simple. For example, you could require some processing to be done on data or have a request for information. SOAP can do the following:

- cross platform boundaries
- go through firewalls set up for normal Web browsing (i.e. default port 80)
- pose little security risk.

SOAP does this by using XML. It therefore becomes very lightweight and easy to understand; after all it is just a text file! There are several types of messaging pattern in SOAP. One of the most common is the RPC (Remote Procedure Call) where the client node sends a request to another node (usually the server), which then responds.

Figure 10-1 shows simple communication using SOAP.

10.3 **SOAP, XML AND HTTP**

As you can probably tell:

$$SOAP = XML + HTTP$$

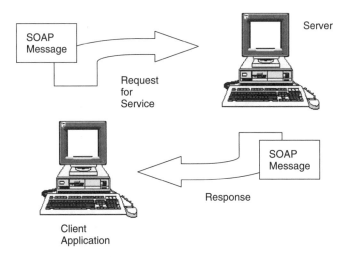

Figure 10-1 *SOAP communication*

The main idea behind SOAP is to wrap the message you want to send to the remote application in XML and then transport it over HTTP in the usual manner. Doing this allows SOAP to share the same ports as any other Web communication over port 80.

The actual protocol used in the SOAP dialog is the usual HTTP request/response described before. However, the `Content-Type` header for a SOAP request and response states:

```
POST / item HTTP/ 1.1
Content-Type: application/soap+xml; charset=utf-8
```

Notice the mime type is `application/soap+xml`. The `Content-Length` header for a SOAP request and response specifies the number of bytes in the body. For the MIME type again `application/soap+xml` must be specified.

The SOAP message itself is XML, giving some benefits over other binary distributed protocols such as DCOM (Distributed Component Object Model). Possibly the only disadvantage to using XML is its lengthy syntax, which could also be considered an advantage. XML can slow down processing time in comparison to binary formats, which tend to be shorter. There are, however, ways of speeding up this processing with hardware appliances and binary XML.

Using SOAP with XML contains several elements:

- `Envelope` – identifies the XML document as a SOAP message (required)
- `Header` – contains header information (optional)
- `Body` – contains call and response information (required)

- Fault – provides information about errors that occurred while processing the message (optional).

A SOAP message must use the SOAP Envelope and Encoding namespaces:

```
<?xml version="1.0"?>
<soap:Envelope
xmlns:soap="http://www.w3.org/2001/12/soap-envelope"
soap:encodingStyle="http://www.w3.org/2001/12/soap-encoding">
```

It's important to remember though that DTD references and XML processing instructions should be left out.

In Listing 10-1 the request is being made for information from a remote application about a product whose stock code is 289387. As you can see the request is made up from XML. Notice here how the namespaces are being used and the way the SOAP utilizes the Envelope element to encapsulate the message.

```
<?xml version="1.0"?>
<soap:Envelope
xmlns:soap="http://www.w3.org/2001/12/soap-envelope"
soap:encodingStyle="http://www.w3.org/2001/12/soap-
                encoding">
  <soap:Body xmlns:m="http://www.stock.org/stock">
  <m:GetProductDescription>
    <m:ProductCode>289387</m:ProductCode>
  </m:GetProductDescription>
  </soap:Body>
</soap:Envelope>
```

Listing 10-1 *A SOAP request*

Listing 10-2 is the response back from the remote application. Note the format, which is very similar to the request message. Here we see that the server-based application has responded with the answer of 'DVD recorder' to the question of which item is 289387.

Checkpoint!

■ **Web services allow functionality to be provided over the Internet for various tasks.**

- SOAP (Simple Object Access Protocol) allows the transfer of information to such services using normal Web-based protocols (HTTP) and script languages (XML).
- This provides a safe and effective mechanism for data exchange.
- Many scripting and programing languages have the capability to develop applications with SOAP.

```
<?xml version="1.0"?>
<soap:Envelope
xmlns:soap="http://www.w3.org/2001/12/soap-envelope"
soap:encodingStyle="http://www.w3.org/2001/12/soap-
              encoding">
  <soap:Body xmlns:m="http://www.stock.org/stock">
    <m:GetProductDescriptionResponse>
      <m:ProductDescription>DVD
                  Recorder</m:ProductDescription>
    </m:GetProductDescriptionResponse>
  </soap:Body>
</soap:Envelope>
```

Listing 10-2 *A SOAP response*

10.4 **WEB FEEDS**

A Web feed is a document, often based on XML, which provides content such as news items, weather and blogs. Usually, this can be summarized with a link to the main source itself. You may encounter the terms *publishing a feed* or *syndication* when making such a source available. This simply refers to the idea of sharing the data with other sites. The main feed formats used are RSS and Atom. RSS has a few different meanings! One of the more popular is Really Simple Syndication, although others include Rich Site Summary and Real-Time Simple Syndication.

The information from a Web feed is usually retrieved using an aggregator, which will read the stream. The idea here is to stop a person having to frequently check a site for renewed content. In a way, by gathering subscribed information from various feeds, they can create a kind of personal newspaper. It is usually an easy matter to subscribe and unsubscribe from streams. For example, as well as news feeds, the BBC Web site has the following:

- Album Reviews
- Backstage

- Comedy
- *Doctor Who* News
- Radio 1 News
- *Top of the Pops* Daily News
- Weather.

Aggregators with the ability to consolidate information in this way have started to be incorporated into Web sites and portals as well as desktop applications. Email clients, Web browsers, blog creation systems and media players can all incorporate aggregators. Some devices such as TV/video systems and mobile phones may also incorporate them.

10.4.1 Reading a Web Feed

Web feeds usually have a static URL to access them by; for example, the Ask Yahoo feed can be seen with:

```
http://ask.yahoo.com/index.xml
```

When this is read with a normal browser the text doesn't make much sense (Listing 10-3)! You have to use a special reader to look at it properly. However, if the feed you are looking at is RSS, or some other XML format, it is possible to see its structure by using your browser's view source function.

```
<?xml version="1.0" encoding="iso-8859-1" ?>

<rss version="2.0">
<channel>
  <title>Ask Yahoo!</title>

  <link>http://us.rd.yahoo.com/ask/rss/?http://
             ask.yahoo.com/</link>
  <description>Answers to some of life's little
             mysteries.</description>
  <language>en-us</language>
  <copyright>Copyright (c) 2006 Yahoo! Inc. All rights
             reserved.</copyright>
  <lastBuildDate>Mon, 08 May 2006 03:00:32
             PDT</lastBuildDate>
  <image>

   <url>http://us.i1.yimg.com/us.yimg.com/i/us/ask/gr/
             ask75x25.gif</url>
        <title>Ask Yahoo!</title>
        <link>http://ask.yahoo.com/</link>
```

```
            <width>75</width>
            <height>25</height>
      </image>
      <item>
         <title>What exactly is "white noise"?</title>
<link>http://us.rd.yahoo.com/ask/rss/*http://
              ask.yahoo.com/20060505.html</link>
         <description>In addition to being a rather forgettable
                      thriller starring Michael Keaton, white
                      noise refers to an "acoustical or
                      electrical noise of which the intensity
                      is the same at all frequencies within a
                      given band." Now, unless you have a Ph.D.
                      in acoustics, that definition probably
                      makes no sense. So, let's add a little
                      color to today's column with some help
                      from our old friend  ...</description>
         <pubDate>Thu, 04 May 2006 21:00:00 PDT</pubDate>
         <guid isPermaLink="false">ask/20060505</guid>
      </item>
   </channel>
   </rss>
```

Listing 10-3 *An RSS Feed*

Some feeds require information to deal with your request. For example, for a weather feed (such as is shown in Listing 10-4) it may require a location identifier for the place you want the report for. Using the Yahoo weather RSS for London would need the URL:

```
http://xml.weather.yahoo.com/forecastrss?p=UKXX0085"u=f
```

Everything after the question mark is a location ID.

```
<?xml version="1.0" encoding="UTF-8" standalone="yes" ?>
<rss version="2.0" xmlns:yweather=
              "http://xml.weather.yahoo.com/ns/rss/1.0"
              xmlns:geo="http://www.w3.org/2003/01/geo/
              wgs84_pos#">
<channel><title>Yahoo! Weather - London, UK</title>
<link>http://us.rd.yahoo.com/dailynews/rss/
              weather/London__UK/*http://xml.weather.
              yahoo.com/forecast/UKXX0085_f.html</link>
<description>Yahoo! Weather for London, UK</description>
```

```
<language>en-us</language>
<lastBuildDate>Mon, 08 May 2006 12:20 pm
                BST</lastBuildDate>
<ttl>60</ttl>
<yweather:location city="London" region="" country="UK" />
<yweather:units temperature="F" distance="mi"
                pressure="in" speed="mph" />
<yweather:wind chill="57" direction="150" speed="5" />
<yweather:atmosphere humidity="88" visibility="999"
                pressure="29.83" rising="0" />
 <yweather:astronomy sunrise="5:20 am" sunset="8:35 pm" />
 <image>
<title>Yahoo! Weather</title>
<width>142</width>
<height>18</height>
<link>http://weather.yahoo.com/</link>
<url>http://us.i1.yimg.com/us.yimg.com/i/us/nws/
                th/main_142b.gif</url>
</image>
<item>
<title>Conditions for London, UK at 12:20 pm BST</title>
 <geo:lat>51.51</geo:lat>
<geo:long>-.08</geo:long>
<link>http://us.rd.yahoo.com/dailynews/rss/
                weather/London__UK/*http://xml.weather.yahoo.
                com/forecast/UKXX0085_f.html</link>
<pubDate>Mon, 08 May 2006 12:20 pm BST</pubDate>
<yweather:condition text="Light Drizzle" code="9"
                temp="57" date="Mon, 08 May 2006 12:20 pm
                BST" />
<description><![CDATA[
<img src="http://us.i1.yimg.com/us.yimg.com/i/us/we
                /52/9.gif" /><br />
<b>Current Conditions:</b><br />
Light Drizzle, 57 F<BR /><BR /><b>Forecast:</b><BR />
 Mon - Showers. High: 58 Low: 48<br />
 Tue - Showers. High: 63 Low: 51<br /><br />
<ahref="http://us.rd.yahoo.com/dailynews/rss/
                weather/London__UK/*http://xml.weather.yahoo.
                com/forecast/UKXX0085_f.html">Full Forecast
                at Yahoo! Weather</a><BR/>
(provided by The Weather Channel)<br/>
]]></description>
<yweather:forecast day="Mon" date="08 May 2006" low="48"
                high="58" text="Showers" code="11" />
```

```
<yweather:forecast day="Tue" date="09 May 2006" low="51"
              high="63" text="Showers" code="11" />
  <guid isPermaLink="false">UKXX0085_2006_05
              _08_12_20_BST</guid>
  </item>
</channel>
</rss>
<!-- p5.weather.dcn.yahoo.com uncompressed/chunked Mon May
              8 04:51:36 PDT 2006 -->
```

Listing 10-4 *A weather RSS feed*

10.4.2 **Making Your Own RSS Feeds**

It is a fairly easy matter to make your own RSS feed so that people can stay up to date with your Web site or interests! The first thing to do is to decide which version of RSS to use; older versions such as 1.0 and lower tend to be harder to understand. Here we will look at version 2.0.

The examples from Yahoo in this section so far have used RSS version 2.0 and as you can see it is fairly easy to follow with your knowledge of XML from this book so far.

```
<?xml version="1.0" encoding="ISO-8859-1" ?>
<rss version="2.0">
<channel>
  <title>Ralph's Web </title>
  <link>http://ralph-moseley.co.uk</link>
  <description>Personal interests</description>
  <item>
    <title>Teaching</title>
    <link>http://ralph-moseley.co.uk/teaching</link>
    <description>Information on teaching modules
</description>
  </item>
  <item>
    <title>Sound</title>
    <link>http://ralph-moseley.co.uk/sound</link>
    <description>Web pages on sound synthesis</description>
  </item>
</channel>
</rss>
```

Listing 10-5 *RSS feed: individual parts*

You should be able to recognize some characteristics of an XML document in Listing 10-5, which is a simple RSS feed. The first line is the XML declaration, which states the XML version and character encoding used. The following line identifies the RSS version to be used, which in this case is 2.0. The channel element is next, which must contain `<title>`, the title of the channel; `<link>`, the hyperlink to the channel, which in this case is my home page URL; and `<description>`, which is a textual description of the channel. An `<item>` element then follows on from this, which is a single article of news and also contains these elements too but in the context of the news or story item. There can then be more `<item>` elements or none.

Finally, the document is closed for both the `<channel>` and `<rss>` elements. Remember to follow all the rules for XML when writing and experimenting with your RSS, closing elements, being consistent with case sensitivity and properly nesting elements too.

As well as the main elements listed here there are also several optional elements within the channel element itself, as listed in Table 10-1.

For the `<item>` element you also have a list of optional and required further elements, as listed in Table 10-2.

Once you have developed a simple RSS feed, save it to a suitable location on your site to test. Something like:

```
http://ralph-moseley.co.uk/feed.xml
```

could work for mine.

The next thing you can do once you have uploaded it is validate it and check that it is correct. Suitable validation services are available such as:

```
http://feedvalidator.org/
```

Aggregator services allow you to register your feed so that clients can find them; several are available:

- Syndic8 – `http://www.syndic8.com/`
- NewsIsFree – `http://www.newsisfree.com/`.

Finally, to complete your feed you need to put some kind of notice on your site saying how the feed can be viewed. This is usually accompanied by the RSS icon:

RSS element	Description
category	Defines categories for the feed
cloud	Update notifications for the feed
copyright	Copyright notifications
description	Description of the channel. Required
docs	Documentation format used in the feed
generator	Specifies the program that generates the feed
image	Image to be displayed when aggregator presents a feed
language	The language the feed is written in
lastBuildDate	Last modified date
link	Hyperlink to channel. Required
managingEditor	Email address of editor of feed content
pubDate	Last publication date of feed content
rating	PICS rating of the feed
skipDays	Number of days that aggregators can skip updating the feed
skipHours	Number of hours that aggregators can skip updating the feed
textInput	A text input field that should be displayed with the feed
title	Title of the channel. Required
ttl	Minutes before a feed can be refreshed
webMaster	Email address to the Web master of the feed

Table 10-1 RSS `<channel>` *elements*

You can update the RSS feed you make yourself or use a special content manager to do the job for you such as the following:

- MyRSSCreator – http://www.myrsscreator.com/
- FeedFire – http://www.feedfire.com.

It is possible to write your own scripts or use other people's to update the RSS feed too. Many scripting languages are capable of parsing XML and therefore are suitably equipped for handling RSS both for reading and writing content.

RSS element	Description
author	Email address of author
category	Defines categories for the item
comments	Link to comments about item
description	Description of the item. Required
enclosure	Media file to be included with item
guid	Unique identifier for the item
link	Hyperlink to item. Required
pubDate	Last publication date of item content
source	Third party source for item

Table 10-2 RSS *<item>* elements

Checkpoint!

■ Web feeds allow information to be captured by interested parties without the need for them to continually visit a site. The sharing of this information is called syndication.

■ The two most popular formats for Web feed files are RSS and Atom.

■ RSS can stand for Really Simple Syndication, among other things!

■ Aggregators are used to subscribe to RSS feeds. These can be an application or a Web-based service.

■ By gathering just the information required, personalized content can be delivered.

■ RSS uses XML.

■ Content has a fairly simple structure.

■ It's possible to update RSS files automatically.

Test Yourself!

• Find a site with an RSS stream, and try and read it using a normal browser.
• Once you have loaded the feed, look at it with the view source option on your browser.

- Find out how you can subscribe to feeds with aggregators; you can use a site-based service or an application (sometimes embedded within a browser!).
- Try and write your own feed and if possible upload it to your site, validate it and finally view it with a reader.

10.5 BLOGS

The word 'blog' comes from Web log or Weblog, which is the publication of regular articles over time in some area of personal or professional interest. A blog can be in the style of a simple diary, made up of time-stamped entries, or be more complex with multimedia either supplementing or taking the place of text. Often it can allow readers to comment on entries, making it more of a dialog with the outside world.

Blogs started appearing around the mid-nineties with a only a few people initially writing online diaries but this soon became a mainstream and popular practice by 2004, with a wide range of subject areas beyond personal use alone:

- business – used to disseminate information relating to business activities, such as stocks
- Clog – a community blog, with some basis in the physical world; for example to act as a forum about where a group of people live
- collaborative – a blog where more than one member writes entries
- cultural – generally about music, arts, theater, sports and other aspects of popular culture
- educational – there are many educational uses for blogs such as logging activities of students or as learning journals
- Moblog – a blog that is updated while on the move with some suitable device such as laptop, mobile phone or PDA
- paid – a blog is created on behalf of a company
- Photoblogs – galleries of photographs make up the blog, instead of text
- political – a blog with a particular political slant, which can be made up of many links to news articles
- professional – this type of blog engages the career or even interest of the person. Not generally about the particular employer of the individual
- science – a means of spreading data or discussing activities or results
- social – used to maintain social networks between people.

Obviously, this list does not cover all types of blog, but it does give some idea of the diverse scope of areas that blogs are active in.

Blogs can be authored manually, simply by writing entries to a Web site with an editor; they can use scripts you have developed yourself or from other people. Increasingly, bloggers use automated software on sites where all that is required is that you either join or register. You can then set preferences for your blog site and start making entries, complete with attachments, links and multimedia.

The software for writing blogs can be divided into user hosted (software applications installed by web log authors to run on their own systems) and developer hosted (software services operated by the developer, requiring no software installation for the blog author). An example of user hosted is b2evolution (`http://b2evolution.net/`) and an example of the developer-hosted services is Blogger (`http://www.blogger.com/`).

Checkpoint!

- Blog is a contraction of the phrase Web log.
- It's a method of recording periodic entries, which can be written in text or via multimedia formats.
- The method of recording such entries can be from a static PC or on the move, from some other device such as PDA or mobile phone.
- There are many themes for such logs: they can be similar to a personal diary, or can highlight some interest or business ideas.
- Blog software can be user hosted or developer hosted (via a Web site for example).

Test Yourself!

- Look up some blogs using a search engine.
- Try and get an idea of the scope of interests used as subjects for blogs.
- How would you integrate a blog into your own Web site?
- What daily subjects could you write about?
- Go to Blogger (`http://www.blogger.com/`) and see how you would use their blogging system.

10.6 CHAPTER SUMMARY

- There is a need for a simple way of calling for functionality over networks.
- This must be able to work within the normal protocols to avoid security problems.

- It's possible in the future that applications will be available as subscription services.
- SOAP allows functionality to be remotely called for from distributed applications.
- It uses XML + HTTP to provide platform independence, language independence, cross-platform boundaries and communication through firewalls.
- Web feeds provide information to interested parties via subscription rather than through visiting a Web site.
- The agent that accomplishes the gathering of preferred data is called an aggregator.
- The aggregator can be a piece of desktop software or a Web site service.
- It's relatively easy to create your own feed on a Web site using an XML-based format such as RSS or Atom.
- A created feed should be registered so aggregator services know about its presence.
- Blogs provide a way of communicating interests, links and personal events to the broader world.
- Blogs utilize software that is based on a user's Web site or via a Web service.

Chapter Quiz

- Consider the types of application you could develop using SOAP.
- How would you change an application you have written (or use) so that it works via a Web service?
- How would you develop a Web feed for your own site? Would it be possible to write a Web feed system that updates everyone as to where you currently are?
- What motivates someone to write a daily blog?
- What is the difference between a forum and a communal blog?

Key Words and Phrases

Aggregator A type of software that retrieves syndicated Web feeds according to the preferred desires of its user. It can also be applied to Web sites or portals that offer this service

Atom A file format based on XML and used for various tasks such as Web feeds and blogs

Blog A web-based publication of periodic articles that are updated on a regular basis

RPC Remote Procedure Call, a protocol that allows software on one machine to cause code to run on another

RSS Really Simple Syndication, a name for a group of file formats, based in XML, which are used for Web feeds and blogs

SOAP Simple Object Access Protocol, a standard for exchanging XML messages over a network

Web feed A periodically updated document that can contain summaries, blogs and links to longer articles

Web service A collection of protocols and standards used for exchanging data between applications

Useful Web Addresses

http://en.wikipedia.org/wiki/SOAP

http://www.w3.org/TR/soap12-part0/

http://www.w3schools.com/rss/

http://www.myrsscreator.com

http://www.feedfire.com/

http://www.syndic8.com/

http://www.newsisfree.com/

http://feedvalidator.org/

http://www.blogger.com/

http://b2evolution.net/

11

THE SERVER SIDE

This chapter aims to give you your first contact with the server side and introduces you to the server; the various possible packages and platforms; how to set up and the options involved; testing your server; logging users and dealing with dynamic IPs.

The leap to the server side is an interesting and exciting one, if all you have experienced is client side development or browsing. It allows much more capacity for dynamic interaction with your users and control over how your pages are delivered.

Here we introduce the basic ideas behind servers generally and then specifically for the Web, which was begun in Chapter 1. Various server software packages are looked at and the differences highlighted. The operating system platforms are also looked at and comparisons offered which, although they may not be needed for initial learning, will be important should you want to set up even a modest Web server.

Once a suitable server is chosen, hints and tips are given about the various options involved, configuration and testing. It is shown how Web pages can be delivered and development work can take place on your own computer with the help of an installed server.

The subject of tracking your visitors is begun here with a brief introduction to server logs and their importance in investigating loading and which pages are producing hits.

11.1 WHAT IS A SERVER?

The word 'server' can have several slightly different meanings and contexts. Generally, in computing, it refers to a software application that provides a service on behalf of another piece of software called a client. It can also refer to the machine that runs the software or even in some instances the company that provides the service.

In the case of the software application, there can also be different kinds of server providing various services. For example, you can have a Web server but you can also have file servers and application servers. There are also mail and database servers. Here is a list of some of the possible server types:

• Web
• file (possibly using FTP, for example)
• application
• Instant Messaging
• image (many formats of images, including video streaming)
• sound (audio and audio streaming).

A server, as a piece of software, can reside on a normal computer that you may be doing some other task on at the time, such as writing a report or working on a spreadsheet. In other words it can be a background task (also known as a process or in Unix language, a *daemon!*), serving files, Web pages, audio streams or other multimedia. Some viruses install such software to set up a file server on your machine for illicit use of your computer resources over non-standard ports.

All these servers have one thing in common: they respond to incoming requests and provide a service, as was described in Chapter 1. In the case of a Web server, a request is made using the HTTP protocol over port 80 to the server, which will then respond either with the requested item or an error message. A file server will respond, maybe through the FTP protocol, in a similar way. This model is known as client–server (as shown in Figure 11-1) where there is a client making requests and a server that deals with those requests. An example of another kind of model is *peer-to-peer*; here each node or computer is equal, in that they are both a server and client. This is popular for file sharing where a computer will respond to requests as to what files it has and, if asked to, will send a file to any members of that network. The real power lies in the effective distribution of computing power and bandwidth, rather than concentrating it in only a few servers.

A server can run on a fairly adequate computer that you would have at home or in the office but it can be a dedicated piece of hardware with high speed Internet links, tetrabytes of storage and massive memory. It can also have a multiple processor motherboard. This kind of server may have to deal with a great number of requests in quick succession and is typical

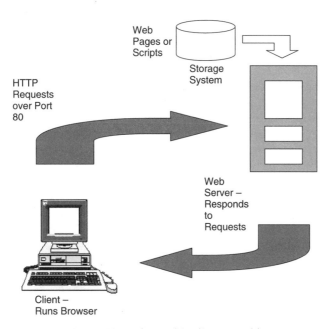

Figure 11-1 *Client and (Web) server model*

of the kind of machine that may work at a Web hosting company or ISP for example. It's also possible to build a server using a stripped-down, maybe slightly out-of-date, machine because as long as the load isn't too heavy it can be quite a simple computer system. For example, it doesn't need heavy duty graphics processing so really it does not need a graphics card. It also doesn't need sound or complex hardware interfaces. All it really needs is a network connection, a decent amount of memory and disk space.

An interesting question at this point is: which do you think is more complex, the client or the Web server?

Generally, the answer is that the server has a much more simple task, as all it has to do is respond to requests, whereas the client (in the case of a Web server) has to render the graphics, deal with input from the user etc. Scripting on the server side has increased the complexity of its requirements though!

11.2 **CHOICES**

There are a number of software Web servers that can be set up on personal computers. Quite a few exist in the public domain and so cost little, if anything, to install. Here are a few of the many available:

- Apache HTTPd Server from the Apache Project
- Internet Information Services (IIS) from Microsoft
- Personal Web Server from Microsoft (superseded by IIS)
- Sun Java System Web Server (formerly Sun ONE Web Server) from Sun Microsystems
- Zeus Web Server from Zeus Technology
- Abyss Web Server from Aprelium Technologies
- AOLserver from America Online, open source
- BEA WebLogic from BEA Systems
- Lighttpd.

Some exist as part of a package that also includes scripting language module extensions (such as PHP) and a database technology (such as MySQL). These packages have been known under the acronyms LAMP, WAMP or XAMPP depending on which platform they are based on. For example, the Linux package is LAMP, standing for Linux, Apache (the Web server), MySQL and PHP (and/or Perl + Python) although even more variations exist.

There follows an overview of some of the most popular software.

11.2.1 **Apache HTTPd Server**

This is the most popular server on the Internet and is developed and maintained by an open community of developers under the Apache Software Foundation. Apache is highly configurable with many compiled modules available, ranging from server side programing support to authentication schemes. Perl (Practical Extraction and Report Language), Python and PHP are supported, along with the authentication modules such as `mod_access`, `mod_auth`, and `mod_digest`. Other features include SSL and TLS support as `mod_ssl`, among many other options. Apache exists as two major versions: the older 1.x series and the more recent 2.x, which has several major enhancements including Unix threading and better support for non-Unix platforms such as Windows.

Available from: `http://httpd.apache.org/`

11.2.2 **Internet Information Services**

The main competitor to Apache is Microsoft's IIS or Internet Information Services (sometimes Server or System). This is a set of Internet based services for Windows machines that were originally part of Windows NT as an option pack and were then subsumed and integrated with Windows 2000 and Windows Server 2003. It includes servers for FTP, SMTP, NNTP and HTTP. Windows XP Professional includes a restricted version of IIS.

Available from: Microsoft (it could be built into your current Windows OS)

11.2.3 **PHP, Perl, Python . . .**

There are quite a few server side languages available that can be downloaded and installed as you need them. In this book PHP is focused on as a popular, modern server side language, although we will look at some of the others to familiarize ourselves with important features.

PHP main site: `http://www.php.net/`
Perl main site: `http://www.perl.org/`
Python main site: `http://www.python.org/`

11.2.4 **MySQL**

One of the most popular relational database servers, utilizing SQL, on the Web is MySQL. It is multi threaded and multi user. It is open source software that is available under the GNU General Public License (GPL) as well as other kinds of license.

MySQL main site: `http://www.mysql.com/`

Checkpoint!

- A server is the software system that deals with incoming requests.
- It sometimes refers to the whole hardware computer (or even the ISP!).
- There are different kinds of server: Web, file, application, Instant Messaging, multimedia (image, sound or video, sometimes streaming).
- A server can reside on the computing device you use for other tasks or be dedicated.
- There are lots of servers available for a variety of workloads, prices and platforms (the OS).
- Apache is one of the most popular and is available in special packages, complete with server side languages and database systems.
- There are other models besides client–server; these include peer-to-peer, where each node (a computer) acts as an equal client–server.

11.3 SETTING UP

To get started developing on the server side you will need access to a Web server or to set up a server on your own computer. The server software can be downloaded and installed on your particular computer, the one you will be developing on. Alternatively, you may want to set up a computer on your LAN to be used specifically for this task. If you do want to set up a full server you may want to consider the system from the 'ground up': What operating system is best? What hardware configuration would be most suitable?

The first point you should be aware of when finding a server is that some OS come complete with them built in; these include: Mac OS X, Windows (limited on some versions), Linux distributions (such as SUSE) and also Unix. However, even if they are installed they may need 'switching on' and configuring. In some cases it may actually be easier to download packages. This may also create a more powerful server.

Each of the individual packages, such as Apache HTTPd Server and PHP, is available to download and install. Usually the main Web site holds a binary (pre-compiled) copy for your platform (Windows, Mac, Unix, Linux) which you then download and follow the precise instructions, which vary with each operating system.

Another way to set up your machine is to use a package that includes everything you need. XAMPP is one of the easiest packages to install and it is described here.

11.3.1 **XAMPP**

One of the easiest server packages to set up is XAMPP (available at Apache Friends: `http://www.apachefriends.org/en/index.html`). This package is available for many platforms such as Linux, Windows, Solaris and Mac. It is very easy to install and free. While package contents do change it generally contains at least the following:

- Apache HTTPd (the Web server)
- MySQL
- FileZilla FTP Server
- phpMyAdmin
- OpenSSL (for security)
- PHP . . .

First of all, download the XAMPP package from Apache Friends; you will also notice an XAMPP Lite package for smaller disk space use – the choice is yours. Extract the package to the root of a drive such as `C:\`. After this unpacking you will find a directory named `C:\xampp` (or `C:\minixampp` for the Lite version).

If you want to run the servers as actual services under Windows NT/2000 then start the install batch file. Otherwise, you can manually start and stop the servers, which is fairly easy anyway. The way to start the Apache server is to simply look for and run the `apache_start.bat` file and to stop it simply close the console window.

To start the MySQL server, use `mysql_start.bat` and `mysql_stop.bat`.

11.3.2 **Where Is the Server?**

Developing and experimenting with your own setup probably means you don't have to worry too much about your IP address and name resolution initially. You simply point at your own computer with the loopback (so called because it points back at the machine itself!) address, `http://127.0.0.1` or `http://localhost`. If your Web server is a separate machine you need to know the local LAN address such as `http://192.168.1.8` and point at that. If you don't know the IP address, there are a few ways to find it out, depending on which platform you are on. Go to the server machine and, depending on the OS, use the appropriate command. Windows machines will respond with a list of current IP addresses assigned if the `ipconfig` command is given at the command prompt window. Most Unix-based and Unix-like machines (including Linux!) will give you a clue if you use `ifconfig`.

Figure 11-2 shows the output from `ifconfig` on a Mac OS X machine within a terminal window. This contains a list of all the devices connected to networks in the computer. In this particular output, `lo0` is the loopback `127.0.0.1` as you can see. `en0` is the normal Ethernet connection via cable (see the entry, `100baseTX <full-duplex>`). `en1` is the wireless connection. You could cross-check these entries with `dmesg` output on a Unix-type machine by looking at the MAC (Media Access Control, unique identifier) addresses (in this case, `00:10:93:72:f3:e2` for en0 and `00:12:24:2b:1f:af` for en1).

11.3.3 **Testing**

Whatever package you choose the following testing should apply. To check that your server is running and actually serving pages you could try pointing your browser at `http://127.0.0.1` or `http://localhost`. You should see a welcome screen rather than an error message of *page not found!*

The next question is: once you have your server running how do you publish your pages?

No matter what server you install, there will be a directory that acts as the place you put displayable Web pages. Table 11-1 shows the sub-directories under XAMPP. To get your own pages delivered by the server, locate the directory `htdocs` under your main directory for XAMPP, or under the Apache directory you have installed. For example it could be `C:\xampp\htdocs` or `C:\minixampp\htdocs`. Any pages you want to be served should be placed in this directory. So, if you had a Web page called `myfirstpage.html`, you would place it in the `htdocs` directory and then point your browser at:

> `http://localhost/myfirstpage.html`

Hopefully, all being well, it should appear! Notice here that you do not mention `xampp` or `htdocs` in the browser address!? The reason is that `htdocs` is taken as the starting point for any Web materials. If you wanted one part of your Web site to be about your large collection

```
Ralph-Moseleys-Computer:~ ralphmoseley$ ifconfig
lo0: flags=8049<UP,LOOPBACK,RUNNING,MULTICAST> mtu 16384
        inet6 ::1 prefixlen 128
        inet6 fe80::1 prefixlen 64 scopeid 0x1
        inet 127.0.0.1 netmask 0xff000000
gif0: flags=8010<POINTOPOINT,MULTICAST> mtu 1280
stf0: flags=0<> mtu 1280
en0: flags=8863<UP,BROADCAST,SMART,RUNNING,SIMPLEX,MULTICAST>
        mtu 1500
        inet6 fe80::20d:93ff:fe72:e3e2 prefixlen 64 scopeid 0x4
        inet 192.168.1.2 netmask 0xffffff00 broadcast
                192.168.1.255
        ether 00:10:93:72:f3:e2
        media: autoselect (100baseTX <full-duplex>) status:
                active
        supported media: none autoselect 10baseT/UTP
                <half-duplex> 10baseT/UTP <full-duplex>
                10baseT/UTP <full-duplex,hw-loopback>
                100baseTX <half-duplex> 100baseTX
                <full-duplex> 100baseTX
                <full-duplex,hw-loopback>
en1: flags=8863<UP,BROADCAST,SMART,RUNNING,SIMPLEX,MULTICAST>
        mtu 1500
        inet6 fe80::211:24ff:fe2b:faf prefixlen 64 scopeid 0x5
        inet 192.168.1.3 netmask 0xffffff00 broadcast
                192.168.1.255
        ether 00:12:24:2b:1f:af
        media: autoselect status: active
        supported media: autoselect
fw0: flags=8822<BROADCAST,SMART,SIMPLEX,MULTICAST> mtu 2030
        lladdr 00:0d:93:ff:fe:72:e3:e2
        media: autoselect <full-duplex> status: inactive
        supported media: autoselect <full-duplex>
```

Figure 11-2 *Network details using* `ifconfig`

of tropical fish and another to be about your interest in golf, you may like to keep the different materials separate so you would probably make a directory called `fish` and another called `golf`. Any Web pages could then be accessed by:

    http://localhost/golf/

for golf materials and

    http://localhost/fish/

File or directory	Meaning
\xampp\apache\logs	Where log files go for Apache and PHP
\xampp\apache\bin\php.ini	Central configuration file for PHP with MOD_PHP
\xampp\cgi-bin\	CGI-BIN directory
\xampp\apache\conf\httpd.conf	Central configuration file for Apache
\xampp\htdocs\	Web document root for HTML, PHP, CGI . . .
\xampp\install\	Initializing documents
\xampp\mysql\	Directory for MySQL
\xampp\perl\	Perl directory
\xampp\php\	php.exe + dlls + pear
\xampp\phpmyadmin\config.inc.php	Configuration file for phpMyAdmin
\xampp\tmp	Temporary directory for PHP uploads and sessions etc
\xampp\moddav	MOD-DAV example

Table 11-1 *Directory for XAMPP*

for tropical fish. Don't forget that if someone writes in the address `http://localhost/golf/`, there must be a page with the name `index.html` or `index.php` in that directory in order for the start page to work.

11.3.4 External Access to the Web Server

To access the server from the outside world (beyond your LAN!) you need to know its external IP address. You can find this out from the computer or by using a Web service such as `http://www.whatismyip.com`. Once the address is known you would then point a browser at this address plus the directory you want to see; for example: `http://86.135.74.177/golf`.

An important point to mention here is that to access your pages you must configure any firewalls you have, either on your router/modem or your server machine itself, to allow access to port 80. Usually, firewalls have ways of letting the user configure so only the ports they want can be opened. Likewise, if you wanted to set up an FTP or other kind of server then you must open the appropriate port(s) for access. Don't forget also that some OS, such as Windows XP, have firewalls built in.

What if you wanted to associate a domain name with your server? To do this you need to purchase a domain name such as http://www.mygolfempire.org. This domain name is then registered through a DNS service such as http://www.dyndns.org/, which connects your IP with that particular name.

Checkpoint!

- Server software can be downloaded and installed singularly or as special packages for various OS platforms such LAMP, WAMP or XAMPP.
- A complete package may contain the server itself, server side languages and the database system, together with tools.
- A server you learn, or develop, on can be your usual work machine such as a laptop or a dedicated computer on your LAN.
- You can access a server on your own machine, usually through http://127.0.0.1, http://localhost or the LAN IP address.
- If you are using a dedicated server, use its LAN IP address. You can usually find this out through the network configuration system of that particular machine or through the command line: ifconfig (for Unix-like computers) or ipconfig (for Windows machines).
- Most servers have a test page when you initially point the browser at its address such as http://127.0.0.1.
- There is a Web document root address for the server and individual users so pages can be published on the connected network.

11.4 UNIX AND LINUX WEB SERVERS

Unix-based platforms usually have their own versions of the Web servers too. In fact Unix- and Linux-based systems are the most popular to form the basis of a Web server system. For example, Yahoo uses FreeBSD and Apache for its Web servers; the MP3.com Web site uses FreeBSD and Apache to serve pages and MP3 music files and Microsoft uses FreeBSD to power its hotmail email servers!

On Unix- and Linux-based systems the file structure is slightly different so you will probably find files in different places than on a Windows system. For example, on Windows you would usually find your Web documents either under your Apache directory or under the main packages tree, such as `C:\xampp\htdocs`. Unix-based systems do this a little differently. The main server Web root for example in my OpenBSD system is:

> `/usr/local/www/data`

Each user account on the system also has its own directory with its own Web folder:

> `/home/ralph/public_html`

How would you access these directories from the outside world? Well, the main server site in my case is simply its IP address, which locally is 192.168.1.4. So:

> `http://192.168.1.4`

Pointing the browser at this local address after the initial install brings up the test screen, as shown in Figure 11-3. Notice here that the server has its secure modules already added and mentioned as `mod_ssl` in this test page.

Hey, it worked !
The SSL/TLS-aware Apache webserver was
successfully installed on this website.

If you can see this page, then the people who own this website have just installed the Apache Web server software and the Apache Interface to OpenSSL (mod_ssl) successfully. They now have to add content to this directory and replace this placeholder page, or else point the server at their real content.

ATTENTION!
If you are seeing this page instead of the site you expected, please **contact the administrator of the site involved.** (Try sending mail to `<webmaster@domain>`.) Although this site is running the Apache software it almost certainly has no other connection to the Apache Group, so please do not send mail about this site or its contents to the Apache authors. If you do, your message will be **ignored**.

The Apache online documentation has been included with this distribution.
Especially also read the mod_ssl User Manual carefully.

Your are allowed to use the images below on your SSL-aware Apache Web server.
Thanks for using Apache, mod_ssl and OpenSSL!

Figure 11-3 *An Apache server test page*

How would an individual's pages be reached? If the person had a username of `brianjones` and the page was called `helloYou.html` then:

> `http://192.168.1.4/~brianjones/helloYou.html`

Notice here, there is a tilde symbol (∼) before the username.

Test Yourself!

- Find out which server would be best for your PC or laptop and its OS. If you want server side languages and a database system you may want to consider a complete package.
- When it's installed find out how you start and stop the server and maybe the database server too if you have one.
- Where do you put documents you want to publish on the Web?
- Try out starting the server and pointing the browser at its address.
- Find out how many ways you can point at the same address; for example what is the LAN address of your server? What is its external IP address?
- Use the `ping` command to check your server is still online. Use the command followed by the IP address. Check that the firewall will let the request through though if you have a problem!

11.5 WHICH OS?

If you have to build a dedicated Web server which OS would you choose? There are pros and cons for each:

- **Windows 2000** is an improvement on Windows NT, which underwent continuous evolution. It suffers the brunt of virus, spyware and hacking attacks. Windows Server 2000 also had a bundled IIS.
- **Windows Server 2003** was an advancement on previous Windows servers in stability and was delivered in various versions, based on the expected loading: Web, Standard, Enterprise and Datacenter. It can be expensive and may struggle in comparison to FreeBSD or NetBSD.
- **FreeBSD,** the Unix-based system, as we have seen, is used by large companies to deal with heavy loading. It is known to have one of the fastest TCP/IP stacks. It has some similarities with Linux (a compatibility mode for software, for example) but FreeBSD was built from the beginning for heavy-duty networking and it can handle the high-traffic situations that Linux (and Windows NT) cannot.
- **OpenBSD** is an ultra-secure OS with carefully audited and checked code for vulnerabilities. Strong cryptography and heavy-duty algorithms throughout the system ensure the best possible security found in an OS. Free and open source, it is available as a download or for purchase on CD.
- **NetBSD, DragonflyBSD**... are other flavours of BSD, with a variety of specialized features and philosophies.

- **Mac OS X** can form the basis of a stable system, as it is formed around FreeBSD to begin with! It has Apache pre-installed and it's fairly easy to get any modules such as PHP up and running. You can also install XAMPP as a complete package if you prefer. There is a specific server version of the system – Mac OS X Server – which is easy to install and use.
- **Sun Solaris** is the most widely known commercial Unix OS. It has a wide variety of tools and add-ons and support for Windows networks. It has a live update system, which is useful in an environment that is used round the clock. It can be more difficult to install and administer than most server OS.
- **Linux** has several distributions (sometimes abbreviated to *distro*!) suitable for a Web server: Slackware, Debian, Red Hat, SUSE and many more. The Slackware version is used by many for Web servers and has proven to be fairly stable with a limited number of reboots. For production-based Web servers, many businesses use Red Hat Enterprise Linux (RHEL).

So, which do you choose? If you are simply learning or even developing to some extent you can select whichever you feel suits you or your equipment! Even better you could try more than one out.

If want to try running a Web server there are a few points that do stand out. Both FreeBSD and OpenBSD are extremely stable and do not cost a lot to get set up. FreeBSD is probably slightly better supported in terms of applications but OpenBSD has incredibly secure features. Often these systems can go years serving Web pages without needing a reboot!

Resources!

This chapter is full of URLs for all the software you could need, whether it is Web servers, scripting languages, database systems or tools.

If you are interested in a separate server box and want a slightly more challenging project why not experiment with a FreeBSD-based setup? A good starting point is: `http://www.freebsd.org`.

11.6 LOGGING USERS

One of the ways (there are others, which we will look at) to keep track of who is visiting your site, and when/where from, is to look at your server logs. Every time someone visits your Web pages and therefore makes the HTTP requests the server logs activity. These files are held in a special logs directory. Consult your server documentation to find out where. With Apache running on Windows they are held in a directory below its root, e.g. `C:\Apache\logs` or, for XAMPP, `c:\ xampp\apache\logs`. In an OpenBSD system (probably the same for most Unix systems) it is: `/var/log/httpd-access.log`.

Figure 11-4 shows an example log of incoming requests. This is composed of the IP address of the visitor, followed by the date and time the actual HTTP request was made.

```
192.168.1.3 - - [10/Jan/2006:19:22:09 +0000] "GET /cmt3092
              HTTP/1.1" 301 366
192.168.1.3 - - [10/Jan/2006:19:22:10 +0000] "GET /cmt3092/
              HTTP/1.1" 200 343
192.168.1.3 - - [10/Jan/2006:19:22:17 +0000] "GET
              /cmt3092/xampp-win321.2.exe HTTP/1.1" 404 1243
192.168.1.3 - - [10/Jan/2006:19:22:47 +0000] "GET
              /cmt3092/xampp-win321.2.exe HTTP/1.1" 404 1117
192.168.1.3 - - [10/Jan/2006:19:23:29 +0000] "GET /cmt3092/
              HTTP/1.1" 200 344
192.168.1.3 - - [10/Jan/2006:19:23:36 +0000] "GET
              /cmt3092/xampp-win32-1.2.exe HTTP/1.1" 200
              28329331
192.168.1.3 - - [10/Jan/2006:19:33:08 +0000] "GET /cmt3092
              HTTP/1.1" 301 366
```

Figure 11-4 *Server logs*

11.7 DYNAMIC IPS

If you want to set up a Web server, the DNS needs to know where it is in terms of an IP address, as shown in Chapter 1, but what if it changes every now and again? You may know you have a dynamic IP either through your service agreement with your ISP, or simply by noticing it from the connection information available on your machine. With the IP changing, it would be quite hard to set a Web server up without specific techniques and mechanisms for dealing with it! However, there exist dynamic DNS services that update your DNS profile when your IP changes. One way this can be done is by using a small program (or process) that runs in the background and checks that your IP is the same as the last time it checked. If they don't match, it sends a message to the dynamic DNS service, which then updates the DNS system.

For example, a BSD Web server I have running uses a program that is available called `ddclient` to update my dynamic DNS service at dyndns.org, if a change is detected.

Checkpoint!

- Unix- and Unix-like Web servers have a different directory structure with a Web document root and separate Web publishing directory for each user.
- Each platform has pros and cons, robustness, loading, stability and price being a few of the attributes you should consider.
- Large companies tend to use very stable systems based on Unix, such as FreeBSD and OpenBSD (for security).
- Server logs are one way of checking your system's usage and seeing where visitors (may) originate from.
- It's possible to set up a server even from a dynamic IP address, using a dynamic DNS service and supporting software.

11.8 CHAPTER SUMMARY

- There are several types of server: Web, file, application, Instant Messaging and multimedia.
- A server in our context usually relates to the piece of software that is active and responds to HTTP requests for Web pages.
- There are a few models of Web architecture including client–server and peer-to-peer.
- A server can be run on fairly low specification hardware or, for much higher loads, a multi-processor system with large hard drive capacity and memory.
- There are many popular server packages and types of software to choose from, depending on your requirements.
- A server usually has a specific directory set up for publishing Web pages including a Web root directory.
- When you start your server you should be able to see that it is active by pointing a browser at the computer's IP loopback address, `http://127.0.0.1`, or `http://localhost`, as well as its local LAN IP.
- Separate content in your Web directory according to subject under appropriate directory names.
- There are many command line tools that will help you diagnose and analyze your server set up, including `ifconfig` (Unix-like machines) and `ipconfig` (Windows) as well as `ping` and `netstat`.
- It is important to consider the OS platform when setting up a dedicated server machine.

- A Web server can be associated with a specific domain name by purchasing the domain name and registering it with an IP address.
- The IP address may be dynamic but it requires a special DNS service and software for a server.

Chapter Quiz

- Why is OpenBSD considered a stable platform for a server?
- What database servers are available for your system?
- What firewalls protect your computers? If you work within a university campus or a company, which ports and services are accessible from the outside world?
- How does a streaming server differ from a normal file-serving arrangement?
- Find out what the most popular servers are on the Web and what the market share of each is.

Key Words and Phrases

Apache HTTPd A popular open source Web server for many platforms

Client–server A model for network application architecture in which there are defined clients and separate servers

Distro An abbreviation of distribution applied usually to versions of Linux

Dynamic DNS service A service that keeps the DNS up to date with changes in a dynamic IP address that is associated with a server

Dynamic IP An IP that changes from time to time, due to the ISP

Peer-to-peer A model for network application architecture in which each node can equally function as client or server

Server An application that responds to requests, in the case of a Web server using the HTTP protocol

Useful Web Addresses

http://www.lighttpd.net/

http://httpd.apache.org/

http://www.apachefriends.org/en/index.html

http://www.microsoft.com/WindowsServer2003/iis/default.mspx

http://www.dyndns.org/

http://www.linux.org/

http://www.freebsd.org/

```
http://www.openbsd.org/
http://www.php.net/
http://www.perl.org/
http://www.python.org/
```

12

PHP 1: STARTING TO SCRIPT ON THE SERVER SIDE

This chapter gives a basic introduction to PHP and dynamic programing on the server side.

You will learn how to develop simple PHP, how to structure your programs and embed script within HTML.

In this chapter we discover how to write scripts using PHP, a good choice for Web applications that need to interact and generate pages as required, depending on the user or processed data.

PHP is an acronym meaning 'PHP: Hypertext Pre-Processor'; you could call this *recursive* in that it refers to itself! This is a naming style borrowed from Unix's GNU – GNU's Not Unix.

First of all let's work out why we need a dynamic programing language such as PHP. As there are many different programing languages around why learn and develop in yet another?

PHP is a modern, Web-targeted language. It's modern because the people who have developed it have learnt from other languages and particularly suited it toward Web development. You may have picked up ideas and concepts from other languages such as C, C++ and Java that are in keeping with PHP's philosophy and implementation. Many of the programing structures and concepts shown in the JavaScript chapter are used here.

PHP is well suited for Web development particularly because of its ability to allow dynamic interaction with a Web page, building it up as real-time data is processed. This might be input from the user, database material, date sensitivity or other information which changes.

Test Yourself!

- Find out how PHP started by doing some research on the Web. What was its original name?

12.1 STARTING TO SCRIPT WITH PHP

PHP is a scripting language that is combined with HTML, either by embedding it within a Web document or by using it as a file that is processed alongside it, but on the server side!

Listing 12-1 shows an HTML page that has embedded PHP code. The code is sitting within HTML inside a special tag beginning with <?php and ending with ?>. Any code inside this tag is interpreted as PHP and must follow the syntax that is legal within a PHP program.

```
<html>
<head>
<title>Listing 12-1</title>
</head>
<body> Today's date is <?php print(date("l F d, Y")); ?>
</body>
</html>
```

*Listing 12-1 Script using the **date** function*

When embedding code in this way it is particularly important to pay attention to formatting the script to make it easy to follow. It would be possible for example to improve the above program as in Listing 12-2. Notice here there are several differences:

- code is indented
- comments are added
- more white space is added.

PHP can be indented and have white space (spacing) as required for your style and it is good programing practice. This improves readability and therefore adds a style that is quicker to follow.

Notice how adding white space and indentation does not interfere with the program's running or output. The only way such additions would be visible is if there were changes to the text within the print statement. In previous scripts echo was used instead of print, so what's the difference? Not much, except that print actually is a function that always returns 1 as a value, but it can be ignored. Echo is marginally faster as it doesn't do this.

```
<html>
<head>
<title>Listing 12-2</title>
</head>
<body> Today's date is
<?php
   /*
   * We can print today's date using PHP
   *
   *
   */

   print(date("l F d, Y"));
?>
</body>
</html>
```

Listing 12-2 *Tidying the script using the* **date** *function*

12.1.1 **Good Programing Practices Apply Here!**

In the program the HTML body contains text that is output to the Web page and then PHP code follows. This is sent to the PHP engine or interpreter within the Web browser. Any output from the PHP code will follow the text from the HTML. In this case the output from PHP is sent by the print command and utilizes the **date** function, which allows the current date to be output in a format determined by a special set of characters. In this case we have selected the weekday name, the full month name, the day of the month and the four-digit year.

Another way to improve readability and quick understanding of your program is to add comments. In PHP this is similar to Java, C and C++. Comments can take up one line only and use a double forward slash, or they can take up several lines.

```
// This is a comment

/*
*   And so is this...!
*   but this one is spread
*   over several lines
*/
```

A multi-line comment stretches over several lines by being enclosed within a starting /* and ending with */.

It is possible you want the output of the program to be purely from the PHP, rather than the HTML. The way to do this would be to place the actual text within the print statement along with the **date** function.

Listing 12-3 shows how the output can be placed directly within the PHP code. Notice though, the Web page generated is exactly the same. The way text output is combined with a function is by using a full-stop or period character. This is slightly different to other languages where concatenation (the joining of two items such as strings) is performed by characters such as addition or ampersand. In this example you will notice that the output of the year is slightly different as it is in a two–digit format. This has happened because Listing 12-3 has a lowercase 'y', rather than an uppercase one as in the previous program, meaning that there should be a four-digit year.

```
<html>
<head>
<title>Listing 12-3</title>
</head>
<body>
<?php
  /*
   * We can print today's date using PHP
   *
   *
   */

  print("Today's date is ".date("l F d, y"));
?>
</body>
</html>
```

Listing 12-3 Using concatenation

Test Yourself!

- You've encountered the **date** function but what other useful built-in functions exist? Look on the Web!
- Make a list of features you would consider to be good programing practices that you can apply to your PHP scripts.

12.2 **VARIABLES**

As described earlier in the chapter on JavaScript, programing languages often need somewhere to keep values that are being worked on. PHP, just like other languages, uses variables to do this.

When a variable is encountered for the first time a memory space is set aside for the contents. Unlike a lot of programing languages such as C and Java, you don't have to state explicitly what type will fit in that variable, it will work it out from the assignment statement. This language feature is called being 'loosely typed'. Listing 12-4 contains several variables with different kinds of content. In PHP all variables are prefaced with a dollar sign. The first two

```
<html>
<head>
<title>Listing 12-4</title>
</head>
<body>
<?php
    /*
     * This program shows how to output variable
     * data and mix it with other textual output
     *
     */

    // first declare the variables
    $filmName = "Minority Report";
    $cinema = "Blue Screens Multiplex";
    $screenNumber = 5;
    $ticketCost = 7.50;
    $todaysDate = date("l F d, Y");

    // now output the complete message
    print("Today, ".$todaysDate.", at the ".$cinema);
    print(" in screen ".$screenNumber." is ");
    print($filmName." which costs ".$ticketCost);

?>
</body>
</html>
```

Listing 12-4 Utilizing variables and output

in the listing, $filmName and $cinema, contain strings that can be any textual information built up of characters. The next variable, $screenNumber, contains an integer-type number while $ticketCost, because it is a monetary value, has a floating point type. Finally in this listing we have the assignment of a variable with the value of a function, in this case the **date** function. When the interpreter of the PHP encounters this it will first work out the function result and place that within the variable memory. It needs to do this first so it can allocate the correct memory space for the result.

The next section of the program outputs the variable contents. Notice here that although the output to the Web page is on one continuous line the program statements to do this are actually on three. The program is joining the text together, complete with variable output through the concatenation operator.

12.2.1 **Errors in PHP**

What happens if you miss out a dollar sign in front of a variable name? If you do this when the variable is being set up and declared then you will receive something like Figure 12-1.

Parse error: parse error, unexpected '=' in **/homepages/**
42/d33119297/htdocs/book/list12_4.php on line **1**

Figure 12-1 *Error in variable name*

If the error is lower down in the program after its declaration, then the program may run but with strange results. The output from Listing 12-4 with a missing dollar sign on the $cinema variable in the print statement is shown in Figure 12-2. If you look carefully at the output you will notice that instead of the cinema's name there is the word 'cinema'. In other words, the variable name itself has been printed rather than its contents.

Today, Monday August 02, 2004, at the cinema in screen 5 is
Minority Report which costs 7.5

Figure 12-2 *Error in variable at print out*

You can also define constants; names that are associated with a value using the define statement. They don't need the dollar sign to precede them and can't be changed once set up but otherwise they are used as variables:

```
define("pi", 3.14159);
```

Checkpoint!

We now know how to:

■ set up a variable by declaring it and assigning a value

■ create a constant

■ output the value stored in a variable

■ join text and variables together for output

■ use a simple built-in function

■ format for readability and good programing practice.

Test Yourself!

• Write a small program to output an HTML document via the PHP print command. Don't forget you can use all the usual format commands available in a Web document.

12.3 GETTING SOME INPUT

The next stage is to learn how to receive input from a user; after all, one of the benefits of using PHP is being able to dynamically build Web pages based on user data!

Listing 12-5 is an HTML document that calls a separate PHP file with collected input from the user. First of all there are the usual starting tags and title. Within the body is a form that has several parts. We can see there are a few input points consisting of a label such as 'Name:', 'Age:' and 'Date of Birth:', together with some input variables and associated types. The first and last lines of the form concern chaining the separate PHP file when the submit button is pressed. The `action` statement points to the program that will be able to access the user input through the various defined variables.

Listing 12-6 is a more complex program. It is not purely PHP but contains a mix of HTML and PHP. The listing begins with an insert outside of the main HTML code. This shows that it does not have to be contained within the HTML. It also shows that you can have PHP in separate fragments throughout a listing. This code sets the variable with the date function as before. The next section of the code is the usual HTML starting point, which leads into the main program.

```html
<html>
<head>
<title>Listing 12-5</title>
</head>
<body>
<form action="list12-6.php" method="post">
  Name: <input type="text" name="aName"><br>
  Age: <input type="text" name="anAge"><br>
  Date of Birth: <input type="text" name="dob"><br>
<input type="submit" value="Send Data">
</form>
</body>
</html>
```

Listing 12-5 Setting up a form

```php
<?php
    $Today = date("l F d, Y");
?>
<html>
<head>
<title>Listing 12-6</title>
</head>
<body>
Today's date:
<?php
    /*
    ** print today's date
    */
    print("<h3>$Today</h3>");

    /*
    ** print greeting message
    */
    print($_REQUEST['aName'] . ", you are ");
    print($_REQUEST['anAge']);
print(" years old and your date of birth is ");
    print($_REQUEST['dob']."<br>");
?>
</body>
</html>
```

Listing 12-6 Accessing the form variables

The main section initially prints out the date set up at the start of the listing. This is output through the print statement as before but this time it is formatted using HTML within the actual string. In this case the <h3> style is used as usual for a Web page. The best way to think about this is to imagine, correctly, that you are writing a Web page with the print output rather than, as you would with other languages such as C, outputting to a screen.

The following section of code accesses the variables set up in Listing 12-5 at runtime with $_REQUEST['variable_name']. When the submit button is pressed on the HTML form page the form fields are sent to the script noted in the **action** attribute. PHP takes these values and places them in an array called _REQUEST. An array is simply a series of memory locations accessed under one name. In this case each stored form field is placed in a memory location and accessed by the programer by placing the name of the required field in the square brackets. You may notice that when the form fields are described in the HTML code there is a type attached to each; if you enter a string where a number is expected then PHP will enter a zero for that field.

Another point to note in this listing is the use of newline and line breaks. This allows any output to continue on a line until you wish to output a break of some type. Remember all HTML formatting commands are available for use in your print.

Checkpoint!

This section has covered several key points:

- **input via variables**
- **transfer control to another script at runtime**
- **accessing the variables**
- **processing the user-entered data**
- **formatting output via HTML commands.**

Test Yourself!

- Write two scripts, one to pick up the details of a library customer and the other to store the details (in variables) and display them.

12.4 **DECISIONS**

When writing scripts and programs very often we need certain sections of code to execute only if certain conditions have been met. The idea is the same as was met in the JavaScript chapter. In the case of PHP, the ability to generate Web pages in certain formats or with particular features may be the outcome of such decisions.

Listing 12-7 shows how to control the flow of execution for your script based on certain conditions being present. First of all the program prints today's date using the date function as before but notice this time that the variable is embedded within the actual output string. If you are used to other programing languages you would probably think that the actual variable name itself would be printed out but in the case of PHP any reference to a known variable within such a string results in the contents, not the name, being printed out.

```
<html>
<head>
<title>Listing 12-7</title>
</head>
<body>
<h1>
<?php
      $Today = date("l F d, Y");
      print("Today is $Today -");

      /*
      ** Get this years leap year status!
      */
      $Today = date("L");
      if($Today == 1)
      {
          print("This year is a leap year!");
      }
      else
      {
          print("This year is not a leap year");
      }

?>
</h1>
</body>
</html>
```

Listing 12-7 Controlling execution flow

The next section of code again accesses the **date** function and re-uses the same variable, this time accessing the **date** function's leap year status value.

To access this value an 'L' is placed in the string. When this is done the return value is either a 1 if the current year is a leap year, or 0 if not. If you want to react in a program to whichever case is true then you could use the condition structure shown.

This particular method is the same as that described in the chapter on JavaScript. It has a structure that begins with the **if** statement itself, followed by brackets that contain a logical condition. The case here is that a variable is tested to see if it contains 1. Note that the test is done with double equal signs rather than a single equals, which is used for assigning values.

Table 12-1 shows other logical operators that are available; some of which are fairly obvious, others are more subtle.

The condition or test is performed and the result, if true, allows the next block of code to be executed. The **if** statement can also contain a block of code to be completed if the condition is false, contained after an **else** statement.

Operator	Operation performed	Example
<	Less than	$num < 12
>	Greater than	$num > 32
<=	Less than or equal to	$num <= 23
>=	Greater than or equal to	$num >= 78
==	Equal to	$num == 3
===	Identical	$num === NULL
!=	Not equal to	$num !=20
!==	Not identical to	$num !== FALSE
AND, &&	Logical and	$num1 AND $num2 $num1 && $num2
OR, ||	Logical or	$num1 OR $num2 $num1 || $num2
XOR	Exclusive or	$num1 XOR $num2
!	Not	! $num

Table 12-1 Comparison operators

In this way the flow of execution can be controlled, depending on user input, events arising or processing of data taking place.

In Listing 12-8 we find another way of controlling the flow of a script, depending on the value contained in a variable. Again, this is exactly the same as described for JavaScript, using the **case** statement and allows a straightforward means of reacting to multiple possibilities. In this example the date is first of all collected and printed out. The date is again collected from the function on its own as a single number and placed in **$diaryDate**. The **case** structure begins with a **switch** statement, followed by the variable you want to check, in this case the **$diaryDate** variable. Within the next block, marked out by curly brackets, is a set of executable lines, each starting with a **case** statement. This contains the choice for that particular response. So, if it was 3 August 2004 then **case 03** would be activated and the code starting at that point executed until it hit the **break** statement at the end. Once the execution has got to this point the code begins executing outside of the code block for the structure.

Finally, if all the cases have been checked and none match the date contained in **$diaryDate**, then it is possible to add in a **default** statement, which starts a section of code to be executed

```
<html>
<head>
<title>listing 12-8</title>
</head>
<body>
<?php
    $Today = date("l F d, Y");
    print("Today is $Today, I will check your
                 diary...<br>\n");

    $diaryDate = date("d");

    switch($diaryDate)
    {
      case 3 : print("you have a dinner date"); break;
      case 10 : print("dentist appointment today"); break;
      case 23 : print("have the day off!"); break;
      case 29 : print("go to conference"); break;
      default : print("You have no booked events today!");
    }


?>
</body></html>
```

Listing 12-8 Using the **switch-case** structure

in that instance. Default means, in this case, if all else fails, run this code. So, if it was 7 August 2004 the default code would run and it would report 'You have no booked events today'.

Now that we have seen how to use both `if` statements and **case** statements it is possible to compare them. In Listing 12-9 there is another version of the same program but using `if else` rather than **case**. While it responds in the same way as the version with **case** it is perhaps a little messier! It is very similar to the **case** version but contains repetition of the check and variable name that it is acting on. Again, there is a default option that is activated should the execution not follow one of the paths above it.

```
<html>
<head>
<title>Listing 12-9</title>
</head>
<body>
<?php
     $Today = date("l F d, Y");
     print("Today is $Today, I will check your
                    diary...<br>\n");

     $diaryDate = date("d");

     if ($diaryDate==3) print("you have a dinner date");
     else
     if ($diaryDate==10) print("dentist appointment
                    today");
     else
     if ($diaryDate==23) print("have the day off!");
     else
     if ($diaryDate==29) print("go to conference");
     else
     print("You have no booked events today!");
?>
</body>
</html>
```

Listing 12-9 Script using the **date** *function*

12.5 **LOOPING**

We may also want a script to repeat a certain number of times. This may be to process data, collect input or output some results, for example.

12.5.1 The for Loop

If you know how many times you'd like a section of code to repeat, you can use a for statement. Listing 12-10 shows how this is done. After an initial piece of code using HTML, the PHP section launches straight into a for loop. A for loop contains the statement itself followed by brackets containing controlling parameters. The first parameter is executed once only before the start of the loop; this is usually a variable that needs initializing. The next parameter is a test that will stop the loop. In this case the test is acting on the $count variable and says 'while the $count variable is less than or equal to 12 then do the following loop'. The final parameter is executed every time the loop has been run through once. Usually this is a statement that will increment the loop counter.

```
<html>
<head>
<title>Listing 12-10</title>
</head>
<body>
<h1>I must learn my 7 times table</h1><br>

<?php
  for($count = 1; $count <= 12; $count++)
  {

    print("7 * $count =".(7*$count)."<br>");
  }
?>
</h1>
</body>
</html>
```

Listing 12-10 Introducing the for loop

So, the idea is:

```
for (INITIALIZE; END CONDITION; UPDATE COUNTER) {
       BODY
}
```

In this program there is some formatting done in HTML, such as the selection of styles, while the rest is done in PHP. In this case we can see that there is a linefeed required to drop down to the next line. As in Listing 12-9 the variable value is included in the actual output string.

When the script executes the loop it runs through each time incrementing (adding 1 to) the $count variable. The first time the loop is entered $count is set at 1 and is printed out and calculated. After one execution $count is incremented again and so on. Finally, the loop completes its twelfth execution and the counter variable becomes 13. At this point the second parameter in the for statement becomes false and the loop is exited.

12.5.2 The while Loop

Another way to do the same thing is to use a while loop. In this approach you have to do more yourself: for example there is only one parameter as opposed to the three in the for statement. The only parameter is the check to see if the counter has reached its limit. When the script in Listing 12-11 is run the counter is set outside the loop to 1. The loop checks the value of $count on entry. If the count is already above 12 then the loop will not be entered at all! In this case the counter has to be incremented within the loop block itself. Note that if the count loop were not altered within the loop block then it would run forever!

```
<html>
<head>
<title>Listing 12-11</title>
</head>
<body>
<h1>I must learn my 7 times table</h1><br>
<?php

    $count=1;

    while( $count<=12 )
    {
        print("7 * $count =".(7*$count)."<br>");

        $count++;

    }


?>
</body>
</html>
```

Listing 12-11 Script using `while`

Listing 12-12 contains yet another way of writing the same program. This time it is made with a do... while loop but what is the difference this time? The difference here is that the loop is *always* executed at least once as the check is at the end rather than the beginning. This can be useful for certain types of problem, so it is worth considering carefully what type of loop is required.

```
<html>
<head>
<title>Listing 12-12</title>
</head>
<body>
<h1>I must learn my 7 times table</h1><br>
<?php

    $count=1;


    do {
       print("7 * $count =".(7*$count)."<br>");

       $count++;

    } while( $count<=12 )



?>
</body>
</html>
```

Listing 12-12 Yet another loop structure

12.5.3 Using break and continue

If you used one of these loops and were processing information – for example inputting data – and wanted to end early (before the natural ending you had set up) how would you do it? Usually, you would have some kind of check or in the case of the for loop, an exact number. In the case of the check you could make the check fall through deliberately early. For example, in the multiplication table script we could have said (although this is not very elegant):

```
if (count==8) count=12;
```

If this was positioned correctly in one of the loops it would have created an early termination before the count had reached 12. Another way to do this is to use the break statement:

```
if (count==8) break;
```

This forces execution to begin again outside the current loop block when 8 has been reached. This may be useful if an abnormal condition came about in the course of data collection, for example. Another interesting inclusion in the PHP language is the `continue` statement.

Listing 12-13 shows the `continue` statement in use. The loop would normally just print out numbers from 0 to 5 but instead misses out 2. This is because the effect of the `continue` statement makes the loop miss out that particular run through of the loop and skip to the next. In this case the print statement is not executed and the loop begins at the top again. If the `continue` statement was swapped for a `break`, the loop would terminate at 2.

```
<html>
<head>
<title>Listing 12-13</title>
</head>
<body>
<h1>Doing the loop</h1><br>

<?php
  for ($i = 0; $i <= 5; $i++) {
      if ($i == 2) continue;
      print "$i<br>";
  }
?>

</body>
</html>
```

Listing 12-13 *Skipping an iteration*

In this section you have seen how to control the flow of your program by making decisions with the `if` statement and repeating with the `for` statement.

Checkpoint!

We now know:

- how to control how a program executes, depending on conditions
- two ways to do this: `if` and `case`
- that there is more than one way to achieve the same result
- how to repeat code a specific number of times.

12.6 CHAPTER SUMMARY

■ PHP can be either embedded in an HTML file or in a separate file.

■ Good programing practice should be maintained by ensuring readability – add structure, spacing and comments.

■ There are lots of in-built functions in PHP; make sure you check them before writing your own to do the same thing!

■ Choose good variable names and remember, in PHP, they begin with the dollar symbol. Also, they are loosely typed.

■ You can access form variables set up in an HTML script from within a separate PHP file.

■ If statements can check that certain conditions are present and then execute appropriate code. They can also have an alternative else block to perform instead.

■ If there are several possible alternatives a switch statement may do the job more elegantly. It also incorporates a default option should the value not be there.

■ Remember that conditions are tested for by a double equals sign and assignment is through a single equals.

■ If you want to repeat (iterate) a known number of times over a section of code, use a for statement.

■ If you want a loop with the check at the start, use a while construction.

■ If you want a loop with the check at the end, use a do... while construction.

■ To break a loop early, use a break statement.

■ To miss a single iteration of a loop but to keep going, use the continue statement.

Chapter Quiz

• Find out what the current version of PHP is, by visiting the Web sites mentioned at the end of the chapter. When this was written, the current version was PHP5.

• Find out where you can read documentation for PHP online.

• What function might you use to see the status of your PHP?

• What is the difference between echo and print? Both can output a string.

Key Words and Phrases

Concatenation Joining together two or more strings. In PHP this is done with the dot character

Increment A variable that increases in value

Iteration Repetition of a section of code

Loosely typed If a language is loosely typed, explicit declaration of a variable's type is not required

Operator A symbol that, when used with values, performs an action and usually produces a result

Recursive Something that refers to itself

Useful Web Addresses

```
http://www.php.net
http://www.w3schools.com/php
http://www.zend.com
http://www.phpfreaks.com
```

13

PHP 2: ARRAYS, FUNCTIONS AND FORMS

Here, you learn how to further manipulate data within PHP and in the process get to grips with new functions, loop structures and the verification of data input through forms. Simple arrays to dynamic structures are discussed, along with the ability to manipulate strings through special functions. Attention is particularly given to how to enlist specific features of PHP when processing data and how these can be used to add security.

This chapter continues our exploration of PHP and we start to meet features that make it such a useful language for the Web. The language also includes aspects that are similar to, if not exactly the same as, a lot of programing languages that went before it and it builds on these. For example, in this chapter there are sections of developing your own functions, string manipulation and arrays. These are further enhanced by realizing features exist to make life a lot easier for programing on the Web.

PHP contains many of the structures and elements that JavaScript does. Another example of this is arrays, although there are some slight differences that you will pick up. Arrays can, for example, be treated in a dynamic sense (if you should wish to), exactly like a stack data structure with the accompanying functionality. Details of the visitor's software can be gathered and the browser controlled. Form information can be gathered easily and processed with advanced string manipulation. Information can be written to local server side files and encrypted if necessary. This kind of built-in functionality makes programing rapid and enjoyable without the need to reinvent the wheel!

13.1 ARRAYS

Arrays, as you may recall from JavaScript, are like variables but instead of just holding a single value they can hold many. To be able to hold more than one value and still be able to access them for changing and reading, you must use an index, with the first index value being 0, rather than 1.

```php
<?php

    $myarray = array( );
    $myarray[0] = "This";
    $myarray[1] = " is ";
    $myarray[2] = " my array";

    echo( $myarray[0].$myarray[1].$myarray[2]);

?>
```

Listing 13-1 *Using an array*

Listing 13-1 shows an array being declared as $myarray, which is then initialized with string values. The contents of the array are then accessed and printed out. Note again that the concatenation (joining) operator is used to add the three strings together for output.

It's also possible to set the values at the start of the program rather than, as above, as separate operations:

```php
$myarray = array("This", " is ", " my array");
```

The array values can be different types; the above values are all strings. You can, for example, mix them quite easily:

```php
$myarray = array("one", 2, 3.5);
```

The last two values in this case are numerical, so you can perform numerical operations with them:

```php
$total = $myarray[1] + $myarray[2];
```

Once you have assigned a value to an array element it's still possible to change it:

```php
$preference = array("red", "white", "blue");

$preference[1] = "green";
```

The array will now contain red at index 0, green at index 1 and blue at index 2.

13.1.1 **Arrays and Loops**

PHP has some clever ways of accessing arrays within loops, so you can visit all or particular members of an array when you need to without complex programing.

```
<html><head></head>
<body><ol>
<?php
    $preferences = array ("red", "white", "blue","silver",
                    "aqua","cyan", "yellow");

    echo("The current preferences are");
    foreach($preferences as $value)
    {
        echo("<li>This preference is: $value </li>");
    }
?>
</ol></body></html>
```

Listing 13-2 The *foreach* loop

Listing 13-2 shows how PHP can be mixed with HTML to produce a fairly simple script. The various preferences are output to the browser, one at a time on a numbered line. The numbering is done using HTML to produce a list. The loop is formed with a `foreach` structure. This works by extracting each value one at a time from the stated array. As the loop progresses, these values are placed in the second variable, `$value`. The echo statement within the loop itself then outputs it. The exact output in this case will be:

1. This preference is: red
2. This preference is: white
3. This preference is: blue
4. This preference is: silver
5. This preference is: aqua
6. This preference is: cyan
7. This preference is: yellow

This is a little easier than using a `for` loop as you don't need to know how big the array is for its end point. If the `for` loop, or any of the other loops such as `while,` were used then you would need this information. This can be gained by using the `sizeof( )` or `count( )` functions on the array.

Listing 13-3 shows the same script but rewritten with the `for` loop. The terminating point is found with `sizeof( )`.

```
<html><head></head>
<body><ol>
<?php
    $preferences = array ("red", "white" , "blue","silver",
                  "aqua","cyan", "yellow");

    echo("The current preferences are");
    for ($i=0; $i<sizeof($preferences); $i++) {
    {
        $value = $preferences[$i];
        echo("<li>This preference is: $value</li>");
    }
?>
</ol></body></html>
```

*Listing 13-3 An equivalent **for** loop*

What if we wanted to add more values to the array? Well, in some languages and traditional static arrays this would not be possible, or at least it would be a little cumbersome to achieve! However, with PHP it is possible to add values to the beginning and end of an array using array_unshift( ) and array_push( ). To add values to the beginning:

```
array_unshift($preferences, "black", "gold");
```

It's possible to add some at the end with:

```
array_push($preferences,"green", "pink");
```

You can probably think of how to remove items from the array; you could delete the item you want rid of and copy the others around it into new positions. PHP makes it easy by including more commands! To remove an item from the start of an array use:

```
array_shift($preferences);
```

To remove items at the end:

```
array_pop($preferences);
```

If you have studied data structures you will notice that PHP is treating the dynamic array as a stack with **pop** and **push**. This can be visualized as a stack of plates: when you want to put a plate (the information) in the stack you place it on top (**push**) and when you want to take an item off you take the top one (**pop**). This is the well-known LIFO (Last In First Out) structure. Of course, the array can be accessed in other ways too, so there is only a similarity with that particular kind of command set.

Arrays can also be sorted using the `sort( )` command, which will order them from lowest to highest:

```
sort($preferences);
```

If there is a set of strings stored in the array they will be sorted alphabetically. The type of sort applied can be chosen with a second optional parameter:
- `SORT_REGULAR` – compare items normally (don't change types)
- `SORT_NUMERIC` – compare items numerically
- `SORT_STRING` – compare items as strings
- `SORT_LOCALE_STRING` – compare items as strings, based on the current locale.

Alternatively, it's possible to mix them up:

```
shuffle($preferences);
```

It's also possible to join two arrays together:

```
$endArray = array_merge($prefs1, $prefs2);
```

Here the end array is made up of the joining of two other arrays, `$prefs1` and `$prefs2`.

An array can also be copied in sections:

```
$endArray = array_slice($prefs, 2, 6);
```

In this case the end array is made up of the `$prefs` array between 2 and 6.

There are a great many different useful functions for manipulating arrays, covering extracting sections of data, sorting, summing, ordering and merging. There is even a function for choosing random data from the array, if you wish!

13.1.2 Keys and Values

An important aspect of using arrays with PHP is the ability to have key–value pairs. This allows you to refer to an element in an array by a name rather than an index, as shown in Listing 13-4.

This shows how easy it is to remember where you put your data held in an array. The points to note here are the difference in quotes used, singular and double, when defining your keys and values along with the special association operator `=>`.

The key–value array format is also used with forms where the input name on the form is the key and the content is the value.

```php
<?php
    $mydata = array ('name'=>"Charles Lutwidge Dodgson",
                     'age'=>28, 'occupation'=>"logician,
                     writer");

    echo("my name is ".$mydata['name']." my age is
        ".$mydata['age']);
?>
```

Listing 13-4 *Using an associative array*

13.1.3 **Forms and Associative Arrays**

Accessing form values is quite easy with PHP and very useful! For example, Listing 13-5 is
an HTML input form that captures data from a user, which it then sends to a PHP script.

```html
<html><head></head>
<body>
<form action="check.php" method="post">
What is your customer number?
<input type="text" size="12" name="customer"><br>
<br>Please select your pizza: <br>
<input type="radio" size="40" name="pizza"
            value="Mushroom">Mushroom<br>
<input type="radio" size="40" name="pizza"
            value="Pepperoni">Pepperoni<br>
<input type="radio" size="40" name="pizza"
            value="Calzone">Calzone<br>
<input type="radio" size="40" name="pizza" value="Four
            Cheeses">Four Cheeses<br>
<input type="radio" size="40" name="pizza" value="Veg
            Special">Veg Special<br>
<input type="radio" size="40" name="pizza" value="Sea Food
            Special">Sea Food Special<br>
<br>Please Select base: <br>
<input type="radio" size="40" name="base"
            value="Thin">Thin<br>
<input type="radio" size="40" name="base"
            value="Crispy">Crispy<br>
<input type="radio" size="40" name="base"
            value="Deep">Deep<br>
<input type="radio" size="40" name="base"
            value="Stuffed">Stuffed<br>
```

```
<br>Extras: <br>
<input type="radio" size="40" name="drink"
            value="Coke">Coke<br>
<input type="radio" size="40" name="drink"
            value="Soda">Soda<br>
<input type="radio" size="40" name="sidedish"
            value="salad">Salad<br><br>
<input type="submit" value="Submit your order!">
</form>
</body></html>
```

Listing 13-5 *HTML input form for PHP processing*

The HTML form is made up of the usual input elements consisting of text input and radio buttons. The difference to JavaScript or other processing is what happens when the submit button is clicked. As you can see from the action property it is sent to a PHP script called check.php via the post method.

Listing 13-6 is the check.php script that processes the HTML form. The first thing that happens in this script is the transfer of content from the form POST array into variables. Notice here, as mentioned, that the input labels become keys for the actual array.

```
<?php
$customer = $_POST['customer'];
$pizza = $_POST['pizza'];
$base  = $_POST['base'];
$drink = $_POST['drink'];
$sidedish = $_POST['sidedish'];

if (empty($customer) || empty($pizza) || empty($base)) {
// stop execution of PHP script using die function!
die("<br>Please fill out the form carefully....<br>");

}

echo("Customer $customer has ordered a $pizza with a $base
            base ");
if (!empty($sidedish)) {
    echo(" they'd also like a $sidedish ");
}
if (!empty($drink)) {
```

```
echo(" and have chosen a $drink drink");
}

?>
```

Listing 13-6 PHP to process the HTML form

Once the information has been transferred for simplified access, the contents can be checked. Here, an initial check is made to see if the form has been filled out reasonably; that there is a customer number, and that a pizza has been chosen as well as a base. If these are not present, then the form stops. After printing out the customer's main details, checks are made on two optional items, the side salad and drink. It only prints these out if selected. You can check your variable contents as usual and verify that they match what you expect them to be. For example, PHP has various ways of doing broader checks on variables. As seen above an initial check may be on whether there is actually any content at all! This is done with the empty( ) function. It is also possible to see whether they have answered with a number with is_numeric( ), although you can check any variable for various types including: is_integer( ), is_bool( ), is_float( ), is_array( ), is_string( ), is_null( ) and is_long( ).

Checkpoint!

- An array has a single variable name but multiple accessible contents.
- Indexing begins at 0.
- Array items can be used in the same way as normal variables, applying various operations such as mathematical or string concatenation.
- An array can be initialized when it is declared.
- Useful structures allow iteration through an array such as **foreach**. Other loop structures can be used to index through the array too.
- Functions enable various operations to be performed on an array, such as **sizeof( )**, **shuffle( )** and **sort( )**.
- An array can also be treated as a dynamic data structure such as a LIFO stack.
- Associative arrays allow access through keys.
- Associative arrays are used to access many important values in PHP, such as values from server (via **$_SERVER**) and forms (via **$_POST**).
- You should verify that returned values from forms are as expected, using PHP functions.

Test Yourself!

- Attempt to use an array to store information (perhaps about a music collection) and output the data to a Web page.
- Try the various functions on this data, for example shuffle( ) and sort( ).
- As a slightly longer exercise, attempt to implement a stack with a Web interface, utilizing the array functions array_pop( ) and array_push( ).

13.2 **FUNCTIONS**

The idea of a function is to separate a section of code that can be used frequently, possibly applied to different data for example. You have already encountered many built-in functions present in PHP. These are recognizable by the rounded brackets after the function name; they can also contain *parameters*. Functions can also be user-made too, using the function keyword:

```
function test1( ) {

    echo("Hey this is inside your function<hr>");

}

function test2($name) {

    echo("Hey, $name, this is the second function");

}

functions test3($num1, $num2, $num3 = 10) {

    $someOp = $num1 + $num2 +num3;
    return $someOp;

}
```

The functions can be placed anywhere in the Web page as long as they are included in the usual <?php ?> brackets. They can then be called just like the internal PHP functions:

```
<?php
    test1( );
    test2("Bert Fry");
    $result = test3(4, 5, 6);
?>
```

In function **test3** there are 3 arguments (or parameters); the last variable has a default value of 10 if the user does not supply one. This function also has a value that is returned, in this case to the result variable.

13.3 BROWSER CONTROL

PHP can control various features of a browser. This is important as often there is a need to reload the same page (maybe if a page form needs re-attempting) or redirect the user to another one.

Some of these features are accessed by controlling the information sent out in the HTTP header to the browser. This uses the **header( )** command such as:

```
header("Location: index.html");
```

In this case there would be a redirection to the index.html page. It's also possible to reload the current page:

```
<?php

header("Cache-Control:no-cache");

$self = $SERVER['PHP_SELF'];
...
<form action = "<?php $self ?>" method ="post">
```

This code fragment shows a common technique where information is processed to some degree on the same page as it is collected. Initially, header information is sent, instructing to always reload the page rather than relying on a cached version. The second part, which sets the $self variable, defines it as having the value of the URL of this page. Later in the script a form can utilize the $self variable to actually point at this page, so the data collected can be checked and, if it is not correct, the form can be re-displayed. This tends to keep the scripting quite compact and together on one page rather than chaining another script.

The main thing to remember when using the **header( )** function is that it should be sent as the first output to a page or an error will be given such as 'headers already sent' which, of course, they would have been!

13.4 BROWSER DETECTION

The range of devices with browsers is increasing so it is becoming more important to know which browser and other details you are dealing with in order to appropriately render the Web page.

The browser that the server is dealing with can be identified using:

```
$browser_ID = $_SERVER['HTTP_USER_AGENT'];
```

$_SERVER is a global array with lots of useful information stored in it about the server's current status. The HTTP_USER_AGENT is an environment variable in the table that contains this information.

Typical responses to querying the variable are as follows:

```
Mozilla/5.0 (Macintosh; U; PPC Mac OS X; en) AppleWebKit/312.1
                (KHTML, like Gecko) Safari/312
```

This shows the Safari browser running on Mac OS X.

```
Mozilla/5.0 (Macintosh; U; PPC Mac OS X Mach-O; en-US; rv:1.7.6)
                Gecko/20050225 Firefox/1.0.1
```

This shows Firefox running on Mac OS X.

```
Mozilla/5.0 (compatible; Konqueror/3.4; Linux) KHTML/3.4.0 (Like
                Gecko)
```

This shows Konqueror running on (Slackware) Linux.

So, all you need to do is check the returned string containing the browser information (and OS if you like!).

13.5 STRING MANIPULATION WITH PHP

A lot of what is done in PHP is based around the manipulation of strings, whether it be input from the user, databases or files that have been written.

To begin with, it's possible to think of a string in PHP as an array of characters so it's possible to say:

```
$mystring = "this is a test";
print $mystring[0]; // which will print 't'
print $mystring[3]; // which will print 's'
```

This uses an index (a number in square brackets) as an offset from the beginning of the string, starting at 0.

Often, there are specific things that need to be done to a string, such as reversing, extracting parts of it, finding a match to part, or changing case. You could do these manually with the aid of loops but, as usual with PHP, many of these things are already done for you in the form of functions.

Table 13-1 shows some of the string functions available within PHP. Often you need to process input from the user and check they have filled a form out correctly. For example, the following code fragments are for the registering of a user to a Web site, which in this case uses a plain text file. A database or *encrypted* file would normally be used.

The first thing you may want to do is strip out leading and trailing spaces to get at the actual string you want to process from the incoming form data:

```
// collect the data from the html form
$name_in  = $_POST[$name1];
$email_in = $_POST[$email1];
$ident_in = $_POST[$ident1];

// check if filled out
if (empty($name_in) || empty($email_in) || empty($ident1)) {
        die("Please fill out all of the required fields");
}

// trim whitespace either end of the string
$name  = $trim($name_in);
$email = $trim($email_in);
$ident = $trim($ident_in);
```

If you wanted to limit their registration to a specific email address group, possibly belonging to a particular organization, you could use a check on the email address supplied:

```
// check contains organization tail
  if (!strstr($email,"@mdx.ac.uk")) {

    die("Must have a valid mdx address!");

  }
```

Notice here, a check is being performed with the strstr( ) function to see if the email part exists in the entered string. Sometimes it's useful to check the length of a string:

```
// check length of id
  if (strlen($ident)!=7) {

    die("Please fill in the correct details");

  }
```

String function	Purpose
strlen($string)	Returns length of string
strstr($string1, $string2)	Finds string 2 inside string 1; if not found returns false, otherwise returns the portion of string 1 that contains it
strpos($string1, $string2)	Finds string 2 inside string 1; if not found returns false, otherwise returns the index position where the substring begins
substr($string, startpos) substr($string, startpos, endpos)	Returns string from either start position to end or the section given by startpos to endpos
strtok($string, $delimiters) strtok($delimiters)	Splits a string up into tokens. Initial call contains both string and delimiters, further calls only require delimiters as string is stored
trim($string) rtrim($string) ltrim($string)	Trims away white space, including tabs, newlines and spaces, from both beginning and end of a string. ltrim is for the start of a string only and rtrim is for the end of a string only
strip_tags($string, $tags)	Strips out HTML tags within a string, leaving only those within $tags intact
substr_replace($string1, $string2, start, end)	Similar to substr but replaces the substring with string 2 at start through to optional end point. Returns transformed string
str_replace($search, $replace, $string, $count)	Looks for $search within $string and replaces with $replace, returning the number of times this is done in $count
strtolower($string)	Converts all characters in $string to lowercase
strtoupper($string)	Converts all characters in $string to uppercase
ucwords($string)	Converts all first letters in a string to uppercase
explode($delimiters, $string)	Similar to strtok but breaks string up into an array at the points marked by the delimiters
stripslashes($string)	Strips out inserted backslashes

Table 13-1 *Some string functions in PHP*

The strlen() function is used to check the length of an identity code that should be a specific length.

Checkpoint!

- ■ It's possible to write your own functions using the **function** keyword.
- ■ The **header()** function allows control over the visitor's browser via the HTTP header information. It is possible to reload or redirect, for example. Make sure that this is the first output to the page though!
- ■ When developing your own applications and Web pages it's important to know what kind of browser your visitor is using, and also the device itself, to render display information correctly. The browser may be one for a mobile device such as pico, for example.
- ■ There are a great many functions built into PHP for the manipulation of strings.

13.6 FILES

If all our checks were okay, so far, we may like to see if that user identity is already in a list we have stored. If we have a list that contains:

```
username: identity : email : other_data
```

the following code fragment could be used to check if the identity is already present:

```
$result = -1;

// reads the members list into an array, $data
$data = file("members.txt");

// iterate through file
foreach ($data as $line)
{
    $arr = explode(":", $line);

    if ($arr[1] == $num)
    {
    $result=1;
    break;
    }
}
```

Firstly, a flag variable is set to -1, and then a text file is read in. The text file is then looped through line by line. When a line is extracted, it is then broken up into an array using the **explode** function, which breaks each part of the line up when it finds a colon. The array entry at position 1 (remembering that arrays begin at 0!) is the identity code. If they match then $result is set to 1, otherwise it will remain at -1 when it comes out of the loop. Also notice here that a **break** command is used to stop the loop going through any more lines of data.

Once the identity number has been checked to see if it is already in the list and is not present, you would probably want to add the new user details in. We know the order of our data is username, identity, email...separated by colons. This is the format that the data needs to follow, and to do this the concatenation operator is needed:

```
$newreg =  $name.":".$ident.":".$email;
```

To write this back into our list of users we could add it to the $data array or append it back to the file:

```
$filename ="members.txt";

// open for read/write, create if doesn't exist
$file = fopen($filename, "a");


$newreg = $student.":".$studid.":".$email."\n";

fwrite($file, $newreg);
fclose($file);
```

The file name is the same as before but this time we are using the **fopen( )** function with an append attribute, ''a'', as the *mode* string. The **fopen( )** function can be used to write, ''w'', read, ''r'' and append, ''a''. Placing a ''+'' with these, such as ''a+'', allows reading and writing to take place. If a file does not exist for a write operation then it is created. It is also possible to specify whether a binary file (such as a gif picture) is being written or a text file (as is here). To do this, include ''b'' for binary or ''t'' for text within the mode string, e.g. ''wb'', write binary. In this case we want to append, or add to the end of the file. The new line is then made up and written. Finally, the file is closed.

13.7 PASSWORDS

A password system can be fairly easy to set up. There are a couple of approaches to this: asking the user for a password and confirming it, or emailing them with an initial password that they can change. The second approach has the benefit of checking their email address is valid as they won't be able to log in if they have given someone else's address.

If passwords are involved then it is not a good idea to have them just written clearly in plain text; luckily PHP has a good choice of mechanisms to encrypt. Probably the easiest way is the crypt( ) function:

```
$encrypted = crypt($password);
```

This is a one–way process because the original password cannot be derived, even if given the encrypted password, which could be stored in a file. To authorize a person to access the Web site using a password encrypted in this way:

```
// $passwd = encrypted password from file
// $tstpass = incoming password attempt from user input
result = -1;
if (crypt($tstpass,$passwd) == $passwd) {
        // there is a match!
    $result = 1
}
```

This simply tests the encrypted, stored password against the user input from a form. If there is a match then the result variable is changed. Other encryption options exist such as md5( ).

13.8 EMAIL

An email can be sent to the address the user supplies to verify the user's desire to sign up to a Web site or newsletter; it could, after all, be a bogus registration. In PHP this is quite easy to do, although there must be a mail server running on the host! Here is an example code fragment of how to send an email:

```
#recipient's email address
$to = $email;

#subject of the message
$re = "Purr-fect Cats Web Registration";

#message from the feedback form
$msg = "Hello, you are now registered to the Purr-fect
        Cats Website.\nInitial password: $passwd\n\n";

#set the From header
$headers = "From: webmaster@Purr-fect-Cats.co.uk";
```

```
       #send the email now...
       mail($to,$re,$msg, $headers);
```

13.9 UPLOADING

Once you have a site up and running you may like to have the capability for files to be uploaded. The first stage of this could be a simple HTML form:

```
<form name="subform" action="upload.php" method="post"
               enctype="multipart/form-data">
<input type="hidden" name="max_file_size" value="40000">
<br><br>Select the file to upload:<br>
<input type="file" name="file" size=50> <br>
<input type="submit" value="Upload File">
</form>
```

This form attempts to set a maximum file size but this technique should not be relied on, as it is fairly easy to bypass, it being only HTML! The input type of file enables a file to be selected. Once the submit button is clicked on, the file is copied up to the server. The PHP can then process it further before it is copied from a temporary upload area into wherever the PHP may want it. This is a good time to check that it's the kind of file you want uploading to the server so make sure your various checks are done, such as file extension/type and size. Here is the basic fragment for uploading:

```
// checks if upload via POST
if (is_uploaded_file($_FILES['file']['tmp_name']))
{

  //Get the Size of the File
  $size = $_FILES['file']['size'];

  //Make sure that $size is not too big
  if ($size > 1000000)
  {
     echo 'File Too Large.';
     exit();
  }


  if($file_name !="")
  {
    $tot_name = "uploads/$file_name";

    // actually put the file in the correct place
```

```
                 // from the temporary upload area
                 copy ("$file",$tot_name ) or die("Could not copy file");

             }
             else
             {
                 die("No file specified");
             }

         } else {
             die("File upload error");
     }
```

Note how the initial name of the file and file size are taken from an associative array (with key–value) $_FILE. The actual upload is completed when the copy statement has been successfully executed. Three variables are created by the HTML form when a file is submitted: file_name; file_size and file_type. These are accessible in your PHP by the same names with the usual dollar sign in front.

What if the person uploading the file actually sends a server side script? They could execute it and possibly gain access to all of your system. For example, it's relatively easy to write a script that will display all the files in the Web area and delete or modify them if they want! There are a few things you can do to help stop any uploading data being executed with evil intent:

- Don't let anonymous people upload at all; make people have an account or register and keep a log of activities/uploads.
- Allow only certain kinds of specific file, check file extensions and run special functions to disable any script that may be present.
- Load files to a non-obvious named directory, hopefully inaccessible from the outside world (unless that's what you want!).
- Check the size of the file being uploaded.

Checking file extensions is fairly simple:

```
         if (strstr($file_name, ".exe")) {
             die("Not accepted: must not be an exe file");
         }
```

Using the function strip_tags, as described in Table 13-1, will delete any embedded HTML code, such as that which allows script to be embedded. You may like to add other ways of checking any uploaded code, especially if it can be viewed afterwards.

Checkpoint!

■ Always verify and process incoming data from a user. Check for white space around the information or simply use trim. Does it conform to the data you expect – if you are expecting an email address does it look like one? If it is an identity code is it the right length and does it consist of the correct characters?

■ PHP allows file handling and manipulation.

■ If you are using a file, remember to maintain the order of data.

■ Any security-critical information stored in such a file should be encrypted using PHP's various functions such as **crypt( )** or **md5( )**.

■ It's possible to communicate with a visitor through email within PHP as long as a mail server is set up on the same host.

■ PHP will control file uploads from a user. As with any information being uploaded or passed to the server this should be carefully processed to check it is what you expect. Simple checking may include file size restrictions, format and type.

■ The variables **$file_name**, **$file_size** and **$file_type** are automatically created when you upload a file.

Test Yourself!

• Attempt to develop a registration page for a Web site that allows a user to enter their details, process them and write details to a file.

• Look in one of the PHP online manuals and find out how to use encryption such as md5( ).

• Add a password and use appropriate encryption.

• Add a log-in page that verifies a user by simply checking the name and password.

• Finally, add the ability to upload '.txt' files only.

13.10 **CHAPTER SUMMARY**

■ Arrays are very useful data structures and are made even more so in PHP by the ability to use associative arrays with key–values.

■ There are several useful functions available to manipulate arrays, which include the ability to treat the structure as a stack.

■ Loop structures exist, such as foreach, which allow iteration through arrays.

■ Form information is easy to access, process and verify.

■ User-made functions can be made using the function keyword.

■ Mechanisms exist for browser recognition such as $_SERVER['HTTP_USER_AGENT'].

■ Browsers can be controlled through the header( ) function.

■ A great many string functions exist to allow manipulation.

■ Specialized functions exist, such as encrypt( ) and md5( ), for encryption.

■ It is possible to allow files to be uploaded from the user but, as with any incoming information, they should be carefully verified to check they are what is expected.

Chapter Quiz

• You may like to investigate and experiment with how to identify or control visitors' browsers. Write some scripts that will output the type of browser currently in use, then redirect it, after a while, to another page.

• Develop a script to allow input from a user in a text area that is then output to another page through PHP. What are the dangers here? What if the user adds script to the input field – how could this be stopped? Are there any characters that cause problems?

• Develop a number-guessing game that works all within one page or script. A clue here is to use page reloading so the script recalls itself...

Key Words and Phrases

Associative array An array that utilizes keys (names) to access values rather than index numbers, making it more friendly to a user

Encryption The process of obscuring (or making hidden) information to make it unreadable without special knowledge

Function A section of script made separate to the main code, which can be called whenever is required. It may have a list of arguments in its function header and a return value

Keys and values These are used in associative arrays to make them more user friendly and accessibly

LIFO Last In First Out, a data structure in which items are organized so that the last data added will be the first data to be output

Redirection In PHP a page can be redirected to another using the `header( )` function

Reload The loading up of the same page from the Web rather than from the cache, for example in PHP with the `header( )` function

Stack A LIFO data structure that usually has various functions (or methods) attached to it, allowing `push` (add an item) or `pop` (remove an item)

Useful Web Addresses

`http://uk.php.net/`

`http://www.php.net/docs.php`

14

MORE ADVANCED PHP

The aim here is to provide a glimpse of the further possibilities within PHP, including cookies, sessions, objects and more advanced file handling.

There are lots of amazing features in PHP that make it a very simple to use and a rapid development language. Some of the more useful features are explored here. Often when developing a Web application or site you want to manipulate files or write new ones, so in this chapter this is explored and the basics studied. To keep a site secure, it's necessary, sometimes, to encrypt any data that is stored in such files or create ways of enabling one user to access data over the site. In this chapter some encryption methods are noted and cookies or sessions suggested as a means of maintaining data persistence over several pages.

The final part of this chapter looks at how to use object-oriented programing with your PHP scripts and Web applications!

14.1 FURTHER FILE HANDLING

So far we have seen two ways of accessing and altering files. The first was to read in the contents of a text file to an array:

```
$data = file("members.txt");
```

The second was using fopen( ) to append to a file:

```
$file = fopen($filename, "a");
```

To read the contents of a file into a variable, use:

```
$file = fopen($filename, "r");

$fsize = filesize($filename);

$text = fread($file, $fsize);

fclose($file);
```

The first thing that happens here is that the fopen opens the file for reading and returns something (a pointer!) to reference it with. The next step is to get the actual size of the file (in bytes), which is then read into the $text variable. The fread( ) function does the actual work of reading the file into the appropriate size. Finally, as with all file operations, the file should be closed with fclose( ).

Writing to a file is similar, except the write mode is chosen:

```
$file = fopen($filename, "w");

fwrite($file, "Akhenaten Amarna Letters\n\n");

fclose($file);
```

This would overwrite a file with the same name, rather than adding to it. To check if the file already exists before using a write statement it's possible to use:

```
if (file_exists($filename))) {

// script here


}
```

There are several other file functions that are useful. These include the ability to delete and copy files, as well as reading directory contents. Copying a file is fairly simple:

```
copy($source, $destination);
```

The two parameters here must be the name of the file and path; for example the file could be signin.php and the path to it could be /myweb/admin/. So, the total source could be /myweb/admin/signin.php. Note here that forward slashes are used to describe paths for Unix, whereas Windows uses backslashes! A similar command is for renaming files:

```
rename($oldname, $newname);
```

It's sometimes necessary to delete files. These may be ones you have written to or uploaded:

```
if (unlink($filename)) {

    echo("file has been deleted<br>");

} else {

    echo("sorry, could not delete file<br>");

}
```

Again, the $filename contains the path and filename. If the unlink command has been successful then it will return true and the appropriate message will be displayed.

Reading directories to find out what is contained in them is a useful function, particularly if you are giving a user some Web space, for example.

```
// Careful here, backslashes for Microsoft OS;
// Unix or Linux needs a forward slash!
$dir = "\php\mydir\";

if (is_dir($dir)) {
    if ($dirref = opendir($dir)) {
        while (($file = readdir($dirref)) !== false) {
            echo "filename: $file : filetype: " . filetype($dir
                        . $file) . "\n";
        }
        closedir($dirref);
    }
}
```

The is_dir() function checks that it is really a directory and not a file. Just as when a file is opened, opendir makes a directory accessible and returns a reference to it. The loop will read the files in the directory until there are no more. Each of these is printed out, together with its file type as provided by a function with the same name. As usual, the file is closed, but this time it is done with closedir().

If you try this fragment out in a program you will notice a couple of odd entries in the file list it prints out. These are a single dot, which is a pointer (or reference) to the current directory, and a double dot, which is a pointer to the parent directory. It is a simple matter to stop these printing by adding a conditional statement.

14.1.1 Building a Visitor Log

One of the more interesting things you can do is add a log of visitor details to a Web site. While you may find some of the details from your server log files, it is possible to build a log in the format you want with any other details of that particular visit, such as file uploads and pages visited.

The way to get basic information about your user is to use the $_SERVER array:

```
$IPaddress = $_SERVER['REMOTE_ADDR'];
$referer   = $_SERVER['HTTP_REFERER'];
$browser   = $_SERVER['HTTP_USER_AGENT'];
```

You may like to add time and date information too:

```
$time = date("H:i dS F");
```

Test Yourself!

- If you have an active Web site, try adding the ability to log incoming details of visitors to a text file with a date stamp.
- Try developing a simple Web site that registers users, complete with a password that is then stored in a text file.
- Alter the above so that passwords and any other important details are encrypted.

Checkpoint!

■ Read, write and append operations are all available for manipulating and accessing your own files.

- Files can also be deleted and copied.
- Directories can be read.
- Visitor details can be accessed using the $_SERVER array.

14.2 COOKIES

A cookie is a piece of information, stored as a small text file on the visiting computer to a Web site. Although it can vary it is possible to store up to 4000 characters in a cookie and up to 20 can be stored for a single Web site. Limits are also imposed on how many cookies can be stored on a computer, usually around 300 in total. These limits can usually be controlled by options in a browser, which maintain a cache for such files.

Cookies allow information from a Web site to be stored but as they can be opened by a simple editor and inspected, any passwords or sensitive data should be encrypted, or some other method should be used that allows indirect identification, such as an ID code.

Typically, a cookie is used to identify or store options about a visitor. For example, once a user has logged in they can be greeted by name or have a particular Web site configuration selected, including graphics, fonts and colors.

Using PHP, cookies can be set up with the setcookie( ) function, which should be used like header( ) before any other output, including <html> and <head> tags as well as any white space! When setcookie( ) has been successful and creates a cookie it returns true otherwise it fails with a boolean false being returned.

The setcookie( ) function contains quite a few parameters; all except the name are optional. To skip over an argument and supply another later in the list simply replace it with an empty string or in the case of the integer expire parameter, use a 0. Usually, to set up a simple cookie the parameters would be:

```
setcookie(name, value, expire);
```

So, you could have:

```
setcookie("user","ralph",time( )+1800);
```

A more complex cookie is made up of:

```
setcookie(name, value, expire, path, domain, secure);
```

The various parameters are explained in Table 14-1.

Parameter	Description	Examples
name	The name of the cookie	`'cookiename'` is called as `$_COOKIE['cookiename']`
value	The value of the cookie	`value` is retrieved through `$_COOKIE['cookiename']`
expire	The time the cookie expires	`time( )+60*60*24*30` will set the cookie to expire in 30 days. If not set, the cookie will expire at the end of the session (or when the browser closes)
path	The path on the server on which the cookie will be available	If set to `'/'`, the cookie will be available within the entire domain. If set to `'/test/'`, the cookie will only be available within the /test/ directory and all sub-directories, such as /test/exam/, of the domain. The default value is the current directory that the cookie is being set in
domain	The domain on which the cookie is available	To make the cookie available on all sub-domains of example.com, set it to `'.example.com'`. The is not required but makes it compatible with more browsers. Setting it to http://www.example.com will make the cookie only available in the www sub-domain
secure	Whether or not a cookie should use a secure HTTPS connection.	0 (FALSE) or 1 (TRUE), the default is 0

Table 14-1 *Cookies with PHP*

If all the options but the name are absent, then the cookie will be deleted from the visitor's computer. Another way to do this is to set the expiry time to a negative value, which will make the browser remove it. To normally use the expiry option, a time can be set using the current time and then adding on a set required period. For example:

```
$value = 'some value';

setcookie("MyCookie", $value);
setcookie("MyCookie", $value, time( )+3600);  /* expire in 1 hour
          */
setcookie("MyCookie", $value, time( )+3600, "/~richard/",
          ".example.com", 1);
```

A cookie can be viewed in several ways:

```
// Print an individual cookie
echo $_COOKIE["MyCookie"];
echo $HTTP_COOKIE_VARS["MyCookie"];
```

Another way to see all the cookies is use a special version of print that outputs information about a variable in human-readable form:

```
print_r($_COOKIE);
```

This will show all cookies currently contained in the $_COOKIE array.

Listing 14-1 shows how a cookie can be used for authentication.

```php
<?php
    // This is script login.php
    $user = $_POST['user']; $pass = $_POST['pass'];
    $self = $_SERVER['PHP_SELF'];

    if( ( $user != null ) and ( $pass != null ) )
    {
      if ($pass=="mypassword") {
         setcookie( "checkpass","okay" );
         header( "Location:loggedin.php" );
         exit( );
      } else {
         setcookie("checkpass");
      }
    }
?>
<html>
<body>
  <form action="<?php echo( $self ); ?>" method="post">
  Please enter your details for access:<br>
  Name: <input type="text" name="user" size="10">
  Password: <input type="text" name="pass"
                 size="10"><br><br>
  <input type="submit" value="Log in">
  </form>
  </body>
</html>
```

Listing 14-1 *Using cookies for passwords*

The first thing that Listing 14-1 does is collect input from the HTML form that it holds; however, if it has not been executed the variables will not exist! The $self variable is then made to point at this page. The form data is then checked to see if it is empty; if not, then it is checked to see if it matches the 'hardwired' password. This is probably not the most secure of options but for the purposes of this example it is good enough. If it does match then a cookie is set to say the authentication is okay, and a new page is loaded. If there is no match then the cookie is deleted, should it already exist. Note how this page uses the self-calling mechanism by placing the reference to its own page's URL in the form action part.

```php
<?php
    // This is script loggedin.php
    $check = $_COOKIE['checkpass'];
    header("Cache-Control:no-cache");

    if( !$check == "okay" )
    {
        header("Location:login.php" );
        exit( );
    }
?>
<html>
 <body>
 Welcome to the Web site!
 </body>
</html>
```

Listing 14-2 *Checking the cookie password*

The next listing, 14-2, is the one that is chained after the cookie is set and authentication has gone okay. This script gets the value of the cookie, checks it is okay; if not, it recalls the log-in script.

14.3 SESSIONS

Another method exists for maintaining persistence of data between pages throughout a Web site, and this is called sessions.

When a PHP script starts a session, a special file is created in a temporary directory on the server; this is where the registered session variables and values are stored. The information stored here is then available during the entire visit to the Web site.

As with many of the default settings of PHP, the actual location of the temporary directory where such session files are stored is determined by a file named `php.ini` in the `session.save_path`. This can be changed to a more convenient location if desired.

When a session is started, a unique identifier for that session is generated randomly, composed of 32 hexadecimal numbers such as `1a7723b8d8e32568bdf418ca8b4e2901`. It's this number that ties a user to their data. A cookie called `PHPSESSID` is then sent to the user, containing the session identification. The session file in the temporary directory is then created with the session identification, prefixed with the word "`sess_`", so for the above session it would be `sess_1a7723b8d8e32568bdf418ca8b4e2901`.

When a session variable needs to be accessed, the identity number is retrieved from the `PHPSESSID` cookie and the temporary directory is looked in for the file that has this name. The required variable is then found and the value extracted, ready for use.

To start a session using PHP, the `session_start( )` function is used. When this is used, a check is performed to see if a session is already active and, if none is current, then one is started up. The other action it performs is to alert the PHP engine to expect session variables to be used during the script, so it is wise to use this function at the start of a page.

Session variables are accessed using the `$_SESSION` array; for example, a session variable called `total` would be accessed with `$_SESSION['total']`

Listing 14-3 is a script that shows how sessions and session variables work. When the script initially runs, the `session_start( )` function creates a new session. If the `total` variable doesn't exist as a session variable then it is initialized and set to 1. The HTML code then outputs the value of `total`. The next time the page is loaded (for example, when the page reload button is clicked) the session variable, rather than being initialized, is incremented and so on.

Sessions like this are very useful for carrying data over several pages on a Web site, so you can log a user in after verifying their identity, and maintain their preferences or user options.

A problem still remains – what if the user has turned off their cookies in the browser? The answer to this is to use the URL to pass the session ID to the next page rather than the cookie:

```
<a href="somewebpage.php?<?php echo(SID); ?>">PageLink.html</a>
```

Here, there is the normal URL link but embedded is a PHP command that outputs the session ID. This is passed on to the next page, making the session persistent across the pages and therefore access to variables available.

```php
<?php
    // start up a session if not active
    session_start( );

    //
    if ( !isset( $_SESSION['total'] ) )
        $_SESSION['total'] = 1;
    else
        $_SESSION['total']++;
?>
<html>
<body>
<h2><?php echo( $_SESSION['total'] ); ?> visits to this
            page  times during this session</h2>

</body></html>
```

Listing 14-3 Starting a session

Listing 14-4 starts a session if one is not active, then outputs the session ID string. A link to the next page is given, which the user can click on. Within this link is the mechanism for passing on the ID of the session using the URL. Once the link is selected the next page is loaded up and the session is maintained as can be seen from the identical hex string that is output.

```php
<?php
    session_start( );
?>
<html>

 <body>
 Session ID =
 <?php
 // get the session ID
  echo(session_id( ));
 ?>
 <br><br>
 <a href="next.php?<?php echo(SID); ?>">Go to next page</a>
 </body>
</html>
```

Listing 14-4 Session continuation [1]

```php
<?php
    session_start( );

    if ( !isset( $_SESSION['total'] ) )
        $_SESSION['total'] = 1;
    else
        $_SESSION['total']++;
?>

<html>
 <body>
 Session ID = <?php echo session_id( ); ?>
 <br>
 <?php echo( $_SESSION['total'] ); ?> visits to this
             page!<br><br>
 <a href="session_start.php?<?php echo( SID ); ?>">Go to
             previous page</a>
 </body>
</html>
```

Listing 14-5 *Sessions with visit count [2]*

The second page, Listing 14-5, also keeps a running total of the number of visits of the current session and supplies a link to the previous page. Again, to keep the current session active the session ID is sent back via the URL. This shows that between pages, information can be used and not lost.

Both cookies and sessions can be used to carry information throughout a Web site about a particular visitor. Cookies are a very simple method to store information but do have problems in that they can be switched off by the user, or accessed and therefore interfered with. Another problem exists in that newer devices, some of them mobile, do not have the capacity to store cookies.

Sessions do not have to use cookies but do require that the session ID is passed with the URL if they are not available. The function `session_start( )` is also required at the beginning of each script, although this can be resolved by altering the `session.auto_start`, which is usually set to 'off' by default. To alter this, find the `php.ini` file and load it into an editor. Change the entry for `session.auto_start` from 0 to 1, which will turn this feature on.

Sessions are probably safer and more reliable to use on Web sites, particularly for e-commerce, to ensure information is available across the pages without relying on the visitor's browser.

Test Yourself!

- Check you know the features of the browser you are using; what security level is active – does it allow cookies? How do you adjust the various options in your browser?
- Try writing a few Web pages that utilize cookies by storing information about the user at one point and adjusting a page, depending on preferences that are held.
- Write the same few Web pages as above but using sessions to store the preferences between pages.
- After allowing pages to store preferences using sessions, alter them so they work even if cookies are not active!

Checkpoint!

- Cookies are a small text file stored on the visiting computer to a Web site.
- Browsers have a feature that allows the cookies to be disabled and therefore not saved; this must be allowed for by a programer.
- Cookies are typically used to store user preferences or authorization strings, which must be encrypted as they could be viewed on the visiting computer.
- Cookies have several features such as an expiration time and security.
- PHP can use cookies with the `setcookie` command.
- Sessions are an alternative method of making data persistent between Web pages.
- Sessions can be used without cookies, using the URL to pass a session ID.
- A check should be made at the start of scripts that the present session is still current and active. This can be done automatically by changing the default setting in the configuration file `php.ini`.

14.4 MOBILE TECHNOLOGIES

There are a number of mobile devices becoming available with the ability to connect to the Web in one way or another. These include mobile phones, PDAs and other hybrids. These smaller devices are becoming more compatible with standard browsers and applications but software that is specialized for this small equipment is still around. This means that when you do send information to this type of device it needs to be in the right format, for example to match a small screen. There are several micro- or mini-browsers:

Default browsers used by mobile phone vendors

- NetFront by Access Co. Ltd
- Nokia Series 40 Browser by Nokia
- Nokia Series 60 Browser by Nokia
- Obigo by Obigo AB (Sweden), owned by Teleca Systems AB
- Openwave
- Opera by Opera Software ASA
- Pocket Internet Explorer by Microsoft Inc.

User-installable microbrowsers

- Andromeda
- Bluelark Bluelark bought by Handspring Inc.
- Doris by Anygraaf Oy
- NicheView by Interniche Technologies Inc.
- Minimo by Mozilla Foundation
- Palm™ Web Browser Pro by PalmOne, Inc.
- Picsel by Picsel Technologies Ltd
- Pixo by Sun Microsystems
- RocketBrowser Rocket Mobile, Inc.
- SAS
- Skweezer by Greenlight Wireless Corporation
- Thunderhawk by Bitstream Inc.
- Wapaka
- WebViewer by Reqwireless
- Novarra.

Microbrowsers generally accept a combination of languages, including WCSS, XHTML, WAP and MHTML, intending to deal with the more minimal resources of the device such as low memory capacity, low bandwidth and smaller screen size. The newer microbrowsers are closer to larger full-featured computer applications in that they will accept normal HTML along with WAP, CSS, JavaScript and plug-ins such as Macromedia Flash.

14.4.1 Browser Check

To check for which browser using PHP, search the HTTP_USER_AGENT environment variable:

```
$browser = $_SERVER['HTTP_USER_AGENT'];

if (strstr($browser, "Pixo")) {

// output small images for microbrowser
```

```
} else {
    // normal output
}
```

14.4.2 WAP and WML

Wireless Application Protocol (WAP) is an open international standard for applications that use wireless connections such as mobile phones and PDAs. WAP contains its own protocol suite, which enables devices to communicate with gateways into the Internet. After the initial media hype, WAP interest seemed to wane, only taking off in particular areas of the world with manufacturers developing and favoring their own in-house systems. WAP has, however, made something of a return to the marketplace more recently with many services, such as travel updates and useful resources, being offered to mobile phone networks.

The markup language used with WAP is Wireless Markup Language (WML), which is based on XML. A simple example is given in Listing 14-6.

```
<?xml version="1.0"?>
<!DOCTYPE wml PUBLIC "-//WAPFORUM//DTD WML 1.1//EN"
"http://www.wapforum.org/DTD/wml_1.1.xml">
<wml>
<card id="Card1" title="Do some WML!">
<p>
Hello WAP World!
</p>
</card>
</wml>
```

Listing 14-6 *A simple WML script*

Just like any other Web page you want to view, these WML scripts are placed on a server that must be enabled for WML in its list of acceptable MIME types. This is usually done within its configuration scripts or as a **.htaccess** file. Using your WAP mobile phone you can then view the page, which should be named something like `hello.wml`.

To develop with WAP and WML it's probably a good idea to use a special online application to view your pages, rather than viewing with a mobile device that may cost more in terms of connection time! One such service is Wapsilon (`http://wapsilon.com/`).

WML is a very simple language and many tutorials exist such as the w3schools site (`http://www.w3schools.com/wap/`).

14.4.3 PHP, WAP and WML

Just like HTML, PHP can also output WML successfully as long as the correct headers are sent and the server is set up with the right configuration, particularly the MIME types mentioned above. An example is shown in Listing 14-7.

```php
<?php
// send wml headers
header("Content-type: text/vnd.wap.wml");
 echo "<?xml version=\"1.0\"?>";
 echo "<!DOCTYPE wml PUBLIC \"-
//WAPFORUM//DTD WML 1.1//EN\""
    . " \"http://www.wapforum.org/DTD/wml_1.1.xml\">";
?>

<wml>
<card id="card1" title="Example 1">
  <p>
    <?php
    // format and output date
    $curr_date = date("M d Y");
    print $curr_date;
    print "<br/>PHP and WML together!";
    ?>
  </p>
</card>
</wml>
```

Listing 14-7 Using PHP and WML together

14.5 OTHER ADVANCED PHP FEATURES

So far this chapter has covered some of the more advanced features of PHP but there are so many more that you probably could do with a book on each! Whether you are interested in networks, XML, file transfer, encryption, databases or data archiving there are features built in for the task you have in mind, so it's always worth looking through the online manual or tutorials to check, before starting out. The following list gives some idea of the scope of PHP's ability:

* network connections (socket, FTP, ping...)
* graphics manipulation
* zip file handling
* encryption
* parsing tools.

14.6 OBJECT-ORIENTED PROGRAMING

All computer languages are based on some kind of philosophy or view of the world. There are several of these paradigms including structured and object-oriented (OO) models. In many languages you don't have a choice of which model because they are entirely based on that particular viewpoint. Java, for example, has an OO view only. PHP, however, has some degree of flexibility in that you can easily follow a structured or OO approach if you like. This section will provide a brief introduction to using objects with PHP but there are many sources on this particular type of programing if further study is required.

PHP 4 and PHP 5 (and no doubt PHP 6!) are object oriented although there have been some changes in the model used, which will be looked at. Make sure you know which version of PHP you are working with.

14.6.1 What Is an Object?

The object-oriented paradigm has particular ideas and philosophy.

Encapsulation

An object contains data, as properties and methods (a similar idea to functions), which add behavior. Although in PHP these are written in as functions, within the OO paradigm they are known as methods.

Polymorphism

This means that, depending on the circumstances, an object acts in different ways. In some OO languages, for example, an object will act differently if supplied with a string to a method rather than a numeric value. In PHP this is slightly unusual anyway, as it is loosely typed and will allow a string or a numeric value for an argument to a method!

Inheritance

The idea here is that an object can be passed along and inherited by another object. For example, if you wanted to make a top model HIFI tape recorder you could make it straight off in a special factory or you could begin with a basic model that was already in production and add to that design. In this way you have the basic functionality available and hopefully this will take less time than producing the new model from scratch.

```
<?php

class Cat {

    var $name;

    function Cat() {

    $this->name="sid";

    }

}
$myCat = new Cat();
print "the cats name is ";
print $myCat->name;
?>
```

Listing 14-8 *OO PHP 4 with constructor*

Listing 14-8 shows a script written for PHP 4, which is object oriented. It contains a class (the template for an object) with a property (name) and a constructor that has the same name as the class itself. The constructor is a special function that is called when the object is being made and is usually used to set up properties with default values. In this case, the Cat class is always initially set up with the name of sid. The way the name property is accessed is by using a special variable or reference that points at that particular object, using this. Basically, a new Cat object is made and referenced with $myCat. Anything you want to access inside that object, such as properties or functions, can be done using ->, which links such items to their object.

This is done slightly differently in PHP 5, as can be seen in Listing 14-9. The first thing you may notice is how PHP 5 uses public to define scope for both its variables and functions. The next thing is that the constructor now no longer shares its name with the class but has a special keyword, __constructor; that is, two underscores then the constructor keyword.

In the above example, there is direct access to a property; generally this is not a good idea as it more properly should have an indirect access method.

Listing 14-10 shows the idea behind access methods for a property. There are two methods that allow the name property to be either called up or actually set to a new value. This mechanism allows a certain amount of buffering between the programer and the class. For example, you could include mechanisms within the set method to stop certain values

```php
<?php

class Cat {

    public $name;

    function __construct() {

    $this->name="furball";

    }

}

$myCat = new Cat();

print "the cats name is ";
print $myCat->name;
?>
```

Listing 14-9 *OO PHP 5 with constructor*

```php
<?php

class Cat {

     public $name;

    function __construct() {

    $this->name="snowball";

    }

    function getName() {

        return $this->name;
    }

    function setName($freshName) {
            $this->name = $freshName;

    }
```

```
    }

    $myCat = new Cat();

    print "The initial cats name is $myCat->name<br><br>";

    $myCat->setName("fleabag");

    print "The cats new name is $myCat->name!";


?>
```

Listing 14-10 *Access methods*

occurring if you wished, perhaps a blank string or a numeric property that only has values within a certain range.

In the PHP 5 scripts there are visibility indicators attached to properties, which control the extent to which both properties and methods can be manipulated by the caller. This defines how open or closed a class is and gives three levels of visibility ranging from the most open public, through protected to the most closed, which is private. Methods and properties are by default public, giving full access to them within the class.

The private visibility will not allow manipulation outside of the class definition, giving protection from an object instance intruding on the internal workings of a class. Protected visibility limits access to the class that defines the item and inherited classes.

Access methods can be made to manipulate items at any of these visibility levels safely and are the best way to approach the altering of values.

14.6.2 **Inheritance**

To stop you having to reinvent the wheel, OO programing allows a basic object to be built on by inheriting its various properties and behaviors.

Listing 14-11 shows an OO version of a script that models a HIFI tape recorder (HIFI). As you can see, there is a class that defines the basic setup of a HIFI, including the functions of play, rewind, fast forward and stop. A further class, super_HIFI, takes this and builds on it using inheritance. The extends keyword enables you to do this at the class declaration header. In this case, more functionality is added, including search and mark, to give it a kind of memory for tape positions. Several things are worth noticing about the script, such as

```php
<?php
    class HIFI {
        public $tape_pos;
        public $mode;
        public function __construct() {
            $this->mode = "stand by";
            $this->tape_pos = 0;
        }
        public function play() {
            $this->mode = "play";
        }
        public function ffwd() {
            $this->mode = "fast forward";
            $this->tape_pos++;
        }
public function rwnd() {
            $this->mode = "rewind";
            $this->$tape_pos--;
        }
        public function stop() {
            $this->mode="stopped";
        }
        public function mode() {
            return $this->mode;
        }
    } // class HIFI

class super_HIFI extends HIFI {
        public $tape_memory;
        public function __construct() {
            parent::__construct();
            $this->tape_memory=0;

        }
        public function search($position) {
            $this->mode = "search";
            $this->tape_pos=$position;
        }
        public function mark() {
            $this->tape_memory = $this->tape_position;
        }
    } // class super_HIFI
```

```
$myHIFI = new super_HIFI;

    $myHIFI->play( );

    print $myHIFI->mode( );

    $myHIFI->search(210);

    print $myHIFI->mode( );

?>
```

Listing 14-11 *Inheritance using OO PHP*

the way the constructor in the extension object calls on the parent constructor to build this object first and the way you can still use all the features of the parent class such as properties and methods.

As well as providing constructors, PHP also has destructors! These methods are used when an object is no longer in use and all references to it in the memory are destroyed. They are only available in PHP 5 and are similar to constructors in the way they are set up:

```
public function __destruct( ) {
        echo ("This object is now destroyed!");
    }
```

Hopefully, this section will have interested you in OO programing with PHP. If you want to study this in more depth, there are lots of sources about it on the Web and in books, both generally and particularly for PHP.

Test Yourself!

- To experiment with OO programing, develop your own `animal` object with properties like weight, fur color, energy level, and methods that allow these to alter such as `feed( )` and `sleep( )`.
- Try adding some form of inheritance to `animal` so other types of animal are based on this one but have new features.
- Add a destructor to the `super_HIFI` script.

Checkpoint!

- There are several types of programing; usually the language you use is based on a particular type.
- PHP is (as usual) fairly easy going as to your approach to programing, even allowing an OO approach.
- OO programing has three main ideas: encapsulation, polymorphism and inheritance. Encapsulation means that data and methods are captured within an object. Polymorphism means that an object can act differently, depending on the supplied data. Inheritance is the idea that features from one object can be made to persist through to other objects that are built upon it.
- Objects can contain properties (data) and methods (in PHP as functions), which are also called behaviors.
- A class is the template for an object.
- An object is created with the new keyword.
- Objects can contain constructors and destructors. Constructors are called when an object is first made or instantiated and can initialize values. Destructors are called when there are no more references to an object in a script.

14.7 CHAPTER SUMMARY

- PHP offers some good features for file manipulation so data can be written, read and appended to.
- File manipulation (such as copying and deleting) is also available, along with the ability to read and traverse directories.
- Information on a visitor can be retrieved via the $_SERVER array.
- Cookies can be used to make information persist over many pages on a Web site but they must be enabled on the visitor's browser.
- Sessions also allow information to persist over pages; they do not have to rely on cookies and, therefore, whether they are enabled on a browser.
- PHP has many features that simplify common tasks that are encountered while building Web applications and sites. It is a good idea to check online information sources, tutorials and manuals for the latest updates.
- PHP can also be programed in an OO manner, using all the usual features available in such languages as Java.

Chapter Quiz

- How secure can you make a Web site using PHP and what would be the best way to implement it?
- What is the best way to validate that a user is who they say they are when registering them on a Web site?
- Why are cookies not the most secure way of keeping information available?

Key Words and Phrases

Class A template for an object

Constructor The first method to be called when a object is instantiated

Cookie A small text file saved on the client, allowing information to be present over several pages of a Web site or to persist for a set period. Needs the client's browser to be cookie enabled to use them

Destructor The last method to be called when an object is finally terminated, usually when there are no more references to it within a script or program

Encapsulation The idea of containing data and methods within an object

Inheritance The building of a new object based on an initial starting set of attributes and behaviors gained from another object

Object The principal idea behind the object oriented programing paradigm; an encapsulation of properties (data) and behaviors (methods)

OO, OOP Object-oriented programing is a particular model or paradigm, containing a specific approach and philosophy to coding

Session A way of making data persist over an entire Web site or several pages, which does not have to reply on cookies

WAP Wireless Application Protocol, a protocol suite developed for the communication of wireless devices such as cell phones and PDAs

WML Wireless Markup Language, the scripting language based on XML and used with WAP to create information pages similar to HTML

Useful Web Addresses

http://en.wikipedia.org/wiki/Php

http://www.php.net/

http://www.phpbuilder.com/

http://www.zend.com/

http://wapsilon.com/

http://www.w3schools.com/wap/

http://www.zend.com/zend/tut/wap.php

15

NETWORK AND WEB SECURITY

The aim of this chapter is to make you aware of threats to online security that you and your users must guard against. The most common forms of attack are studied, such as viruses and worms, cross site scripting, email problems, Trojan horses, phishing and many other mechanisms.

Possible solutions are also looked into, including firewalls and anti-virus software.

Writing applications, developing Web sites and sometimes just surfing the net can have security implications. In this chapter we encounter how hackers can attack computers and thieves can collect enough information to perpetrate crime in their victims' names. Knowing the mechanisms involved allows more secure applications to be written because you are aware of the issues involved.

Viruses and worms are looked at in some detail, showing how they have evolved over time and how the techniques employed have developed from fairly simple to multi-functional, multi-payload attacks. For example, it is now possible for both viruses and worms to attempt to avoid detection by anti-virus software.

There are brief introductions to many areas of security here; phishing, key logging, email attacks, cross site scripting and spoofing. All these issues are important whether you be a developer, Web master or a user of the Internet.

15.1 **INTRODUCTION**

An increasing array of sophisticated attacks by hackers and viruses mean that even the average user of the Internet must make use of certain precautions and defenses.

A budding Web master or developer of applications has to take an even wider appreciation of the security situation into view. This is a large and complicated subject but the basics will be provided here to stimulate interest in the right areas.

15.2 **HOW HACKING BEGAN**

Before the Internet was established, computer and electronics enthusiasts set up bulletin board services (BBS), which were connected to via standard telephone lines and acoustic modems. BBS were similar to Web sites and forums that exist now, allowing hobbyists and academics to swap ideas and keep in touch with each other. The only problem with this was that the technologies involved only allowed very slow transfer of information and this meant using the telephone lines for long periods, possibly over long distances. This meant high costs so many of the people, whose interest was in computer communications and electronics in any case, learnt ways of controlling the telecommunications system to allow themselves free calls. This activity was known as phone phreaking. This kind of hacking involved a mixture of techniques from electronics through to social engineering. It involved sending signals down phone lines to activate special circuits, normally only known to telephone engineers, or tricking operators to make connections on their behalf. Programs were written that allowed a hacker to scan through lots of telephone numbers, looking for lines with a modem that they could connect to, and then probe to find out who it belonged to and how to access it. This could be viewed as the precursor to modern hacking of IP and port scanners.

Hackers also turned their attention to breaking into voicemail systems, not only raiding other people's messages but also embedding their own accounts within the systems.

With the invention of other technologies, hacking has gone across to other forms; cellular networks, satellite television and wireless computer networks. Cellular hacking involves using radio scanners to steal a phone's electronic serial number (ESN) and mobile identification number (MIN), which are transmitted periodically so that the network knows where to send an incoming call. These can be stolen and reprogramed into a phone to intercept or make calls for which the other person is billed. Satellite and cable TV also suffer from hacking in the form of descramblers being made available for people to decode broadcasts.

Wireless computer networks have more recently come under attack from a variety of techniques that lay systems open to abuse. Due to lack of understanding or awareness many people still set up their wireless networks incorrectly with insufficient security. This not only allows someone nearby to hack into their computers but also to access the Internet. For example, it is possible to drive around in a car looking for hot spots and to sit with a laptop and hack into such a system. This activity, known as *war driving*, relies on many ready-made software tools that allow the detection and measurement of signal strength; the probing of the security at such a location; and finally, the penetration of the network via password or encryption code cracking. It is often the case that such systems have been set up incorrectly, so no great amount of sophistication or force is required.

15.3 WHO IS HACKING NOW?

There are some strong trends implying that security threats aren't going away:

- Nearly 75% of companies cited employees as a source of hacking attacks.
- 45% of businesses had reported unauthorized access by insiders.
- 80% of Instant Messaging in companies is done over public IM services such as AOL, MSN and Yahoo, thus exposing them to security risks.
- 45% of executable files downloaded through Kazaa contain malicious code.
- 88% of business professionals have detected spyware on their networks in the past 12 months.
- Although 99% of companies use anti-virus software, 82% of them were hit by viruses and worms.
- Blended (multiple technique) threats made up 60% of the top 50 malicious code submissions during the first six months of 2005, an increase of 9% from one year ago.
- The number of malicious code attacks with backdoors, which are often used to steal confidential data, rose nearly 37% in the last year.

Sources: Websense uk, CSI/FBI, Trusecure, Symantec Security Report, 2005.

Various security reports are available for download from the Internet. Symantec publish regular, current reports on threats in their press pages.

15.3.1 Motivations

There are a wide range of reasons behind hacking:

- Beating the system – proving yourself. This plays on the ideas of fitting into a group and feelings of self-worth, being better than those around you who may reject you for some reason (possibly for being a geek!).
- Disgruntled employee – vengeance. Who knows a company's system and weaknesses better than those who formally worked there? They have the opportunity to compromise a system before actually leaving the place of work.

- Special Interest Groups. This includes people who derive the motivation for hacking from interests they have, including sexual orientation, political biases, racial and religious activism. They may focus their attacks on other groups with pro-active hacking by defacing Web sites or they may simply maintain Web sites declaring their particular viewpoint. Cyber-terrorism is a real threat of the future that may target the economic and industrial infrastructure of a country with possible loss of life. For example, it may be possible to hack into an airline system's computer, power supply companies or food processing plants.
- Industrial espionage. People can deliberately hack into a rival company's system, or be paid to do so, in order to figure out or ruin business plans.
- Warfare. With a large number of military systems completely computer based, from communications to weapons systems, the frontline of the future may see hackers who belong to military campaigns attempting to disrupt the other side's capabilities.
- Censorship. Where ideologies differ there are, and will be, attempts to hide information from people, or to filter it, even where the Web sites in question are usually freely open. This may be done to prevent exposure to other political, religious or ideological viewpoints.

Checkpoint!

■ Hacking is not a recent development and tends to match new technologies as they arrive.

■ The motivations are many, including ego and the interests of an individual, group or nation.

■ Insecure activities by employees threaten a company's network.

■ The future will see the development of larger-scale attacks of cyber-terrorism and cyber-warfare, aimed at disabling a country's economic, industrial or military capabilities.

15.4 TYPES OF ATTACK AND INTRUSION

This section gives some idea of the kinds of technique available to hackers and the mechanisms involved in such attempts.

15.4.1 Denial of Service (DoS)

This is an attack on a computer system that consumes resources so that users experience loss of service. The attacks are typically aimed at routers, Web, email and DNS servers. The kinds of technique used are as follows:

- overloading or consumption of system or network resources such as CPU, network bandwidth or disk space
- disrupting physical network components
- disrupting configuration information such as routing information
- disrupting OS functionality by exploiting software vulnerabilities.

A common form of attack is to flood a network with bogus packets that prevent normal network traffic. The source address of such traffic is usually spoofed to hide the origin of the attack. This makes these kinds of attack particularly hard to guard against as it is difficult to build a set of rules that will guard against an ongoing assault. It is particularly hard to defend against a distributed attack coming from many computers. This can be done by utilizing computers that have been compromised by viruses or Trojan horses, turning them into *zombie* or slave machines that are capable of being controlled for an attack. An array of computers set up in this way is known as a *botnet*.

15.4.2 **Cross Site Scripting (XSS)**

This technique involves a usually trusted site running scripts that are placed there by another party with malicious intent, such as the capturing of bank or credit card details. For example, a user may trust a site, buythis.com, but another user has found a way to embed JavaScript in the site possibly by placing it in entries on a notice board. The user that trusts the site enters their details in it, not realizing that it is actually running script by a third party that is not connected with the actual site itself. Another way that this may be achieved is by using the maliciously embedded code to capture the session ID and access the user's account. The name 'cross site' comes from the way the attack is directed 'across' the Web site, from the attacking data source to the attacked browser.

15.4.3 **Spam**

Spamming is the sending of unsolicited messages, usually in bulk, to lots of email addresses. The name derives from the Spam Monty Python sketch, which involves the meat product of the same name. Spamming is usually not classed as targeted mail messages in any sense, although it could represent this too. It is usually commercial advertising, although it has been used for other purposes.

As well as email spam, other variations have appeared such as instant message spam, newsgroup spam, search engine spam, weblogs spam and more recently mobile phone spam!

Email addresses are harvested from Web sites and mailing lists. There are programs that crawl the Web looking for email addresses that are likely to be valid. These can then be mailed with spam or used as illegitimate return addresses.

Spamming has been the subject of legislation in some areas, including the United States and various solutions have been sought and suggested as a way of discouraging this activity.

15.4.4 **Email Bomb**

An email bomb is a way of targeting either an individual inbox or mail server and overwhelming it to such an extent that it becomes unusable. Shutting off a mail server that is under attack is of little use as such messages will simply wait for it to come back on line, due to the way such systems work. Scripts exist that will automate the process of an attack; or simply subscribing the victim to many mailing lists will achieve a similar effect. It is difficult to protect against this kind of attack, although easier than it was in the past. Email boxes are now larger and it is possible to filter mail or subscribe to a service that will do this for you. IP addresses are also usually available belonging to the person who subscribed to a service, although this may be spoofed and may not be their own! ISPs may also be able to help block mail.

15.4.5 **Spoofing**

The idea behind spoofing is to pass off oneself as someone else. This can take many forms. For example, it may be as simple as using someone's identity in terms of username and password. It can also mean that someone is managing to use an IP address that is not their own, more specifically known as IP spoofing. In a *man in the middle attack* two people communicating do not realize that there is someone pretending to be the other party in the conversation. So, if Andrew and Simon are using IRC to chat, Alex sits between them, listening to Andrew and pretending to be Simon while Simon's conversation is likewise being intercepted and responded to by Alex.

15.4.6 **Phishing**

Like spoofing, phishing is the art of masquerading. It can also be known as Web page spoofing. A typical way of applying this particular technique is the replication of a Web site down to the last detail, including graphics and input forms, which the visitor thinks is the real thing. The user can then be tricked into giving away their bank details, for example. In a similar way, an email can be sent, purporting to be from a bank, which directs the user via an embedded link to a replicated site where again the details can be extracted from the victim.

15.4.7 **CGI Insecurities**

Before PHP and a lot of other Web scripting languages, one of the choices for processing user input via HTML forms was the Common Gateway Interface (CGI). The form input information could be passed to a program existing in a special CGI directory on the server for further processing. The only problem here was that the language could be any normal programing language that would run on the server. This was usually C, which is not specifically a Web-oriented language with all the features that are useful for security. It became obvious to hackers that any input passed to such a program could sometimes be made to either crash the program or, even worse, execute commands on the server. This was done by overloading the input buffer. Once commands can be run, security on the server can be compromised and special hacking tools (called *rootkits*, from being the root user) can be installed to gain control of the computer.

15.4.8 Session Hijacking

When a user is legitimately logged into a system it is possible for the session to be taken over by another party; this is known as session hijacking. This is done is by taking over a session's IDs in order to seize control of the user's Web application session. The ID codes are either captured or seized in some way, such as using brute force techniques. Typically, this is aimed at retrieving the session cookie or URL containing the ID string.

15.4.9 Key Logging

This can also be called keystroke logging or other variations although the idea is the same. Key logging involves installing an invisible (to the user) piece of software that captures information typed by the user, which it then records or sends over a network. This interception of what the user types allows passwords to be found out or whole documents to be viewed. It has been also used for law enforcement and espionage. There are both hardware and software versions of key loggers. Hardware can rely on a connection to the keyboard, while the software version can be written and installed quite easily. Some key loggers can be active with viruses and worms, or as a part of a Trojan horse.

15.4.10 Identity Theft and Stalking

An increasingly bad trend is that of identity theft. This involves collecting details that belong to someone else and then using them to gain credit or buy goods or services. It may be as simple as intercepting credit details on insecure e-commerce links with hacking tools, or it may be more complicated and involve raking through rubbish bags for thrown-out bank statements and receipts.

Usually a computer only needs bank details, or social security/national insurance number, to establish a user's identity. Once the details have been captured, a variety of activities can be instigated in the victim's name. For example, thieves have opened credit card accounts and built up huge debts in other people's names; they have also bought cars, set up mobile phone accounts and taken out large loans. This has the effect of destroying the victim's credit rating and forcing them to pay off debts, as well as legal bills.

Thieves can do this for years without raising any suspicion of what is going on, and can then move on to yet another stolen identity.

Obviously stealing your wallet has the effect of giving some details to such a thief, so it is wise not to carry all your personal information with credit cards. You should also be aware of who you give details to, and what you are placing in your rubbish bin without shredding!

To limit the threat of identity theft, you can do the following:

- Carry limited details in your wallet.
- Shred personal documents before throwing them out.
- Be aware of what details you place on the Internet, on Web sites, blogs, forums and chat rooms (they can stay online for years!).
- Be careful what information you give out directly, on the telephone and in emails to people.
- Check a Web site's authenticity before entering details.
- Check how secure a Web site is before entering details. Does it use secure pages (https) or some other technique?

There are also organizations that help in both the recovery after an identity theft and the protection of identity itself.

It's probably worth noting here that the collection of information about a person is not always used for identity theft but instead for electronic stalking. The large number of databases and information sources on the Web make it possible to gather an amazing amount of data about a person. Using free services, it is possible to find a person's address, business details, family history (including births, marriages and deaths) and even who they live next door to! Subscribing to special services allows even more detail to become apparent.

15.4.11 Trojan Horse

A Trojan, or more correctly, Trojan horse in a computer context is a malicious piece of software that is masquerading as a legitimate program. The name is derived from the classical myth of the siege of Troy in which the Greeks left a large wooden horse outside the gates of the city. The Trojans, believing that this was a gift, brought the horse inside the city walls. When night fell, soldiers who had been hiding inside the hollow wooden horse crept out and opened the gates, allowing the Greek army into the city! The idea with computer software is the same, in that someone may send out an email with a program attached. People believe the program is legitimate software and run it, only to find out that they have been taken in by the 'gift'!

The idea here is not that such a program replicates itself, as with viruses and worms, but simply that the user is tricked into running it, at which point the program can damage or modify the system in some way. These programs can also be used to open backdoors for access to the computer resources or perform spying functions.

The answer to Trojan horses is that users should be made aware of the likelihood of this kind of attack, both from email attachments and software downloads from Web sites. Emails with attachments from unknown sources should simply be deleted. Anti-virus software and services can usually be configured to scan incoming mail so that attachments are removed or made safe.

15.4.12 **Social Engineering**

The idea behind social engineering has a slightly different slant to how you would normally attempt to break into a system. It does not involve sitting at a computer for hours and applying brute force techniques or sophisticated probes; instead the target is the human user of such a system. After all, there may be all kinds of defense strategies but the weakest link may be that the users are the easiest target due to their gullibility.

While it may prove difficult for the hacker to actually ask for a username and/or password from the systems admin., it may be easier to retrieve details from the user. This may be in the form of an email or a telephone call in which the hacker calls upon the sympathies of the user to supply login details, made more convincing by knowledge of a few company executives' names or details about company strategies. This is the main idea behind social engineering, the convincing of a user to give away information. The hacker in this case can also try many people in an organization, if one should fail.

Another technique may involve disrupting a service in some small way, then posing as a technician to fix this kind of fault. Here the user may be only too happy to give away their username and password.

Yet another way to approach social engineering is actually in person, rather than on the phone or by email. It is possible, for example, for the hacker to masquerade as a consultant or technician and to enter a building where they are free to either ask people for various details or view written-down passwords and, finally, to access a system directly. Other on-site jobs, such as a cleaner, make it equally easy to access a system in person.

15.4.13 **Spyware/Malware/Adware and Popups**

Software from Web sites may be instantly downloadable and free but there may be a hidden cost. Some software can act as a way of capturing your activities or information while others will either bombard you with adverts for products or open up ways for other Web applications to do so. *Popups* are simple browser windows that can be made to display adverts. Many more up-to-date browsers allow popups to be blocked if required.

15.4.14 **Viruses and Worms**

Viruses and worms have been around for some time now, at least since the 1980s. Some viruses are not destructive and are created out of fun and for the challenge in itself. These may do nothing more then print annoying messages or lock a computer up for periods of time. However, there are now many viruses that are destructive and will happily destroy all data on a system. Both types of virus, whether damaging or not, are unwelcome and steps should be taken to guard against them.

A virus is a program that can replicate itself. This could be across program files, by corrupting or adding data to them, infecting a memory disk directly, possibly in the boot sector, or by using macro capabilities built into word processing or spreadsheet documents. A virus that is at large on the Internet is said to be *in the wild!*

File-infecting viruses can use macro-enabled documents and spread by email or removable disks such as floppy disks, although they can also spread just as easily via other media types such as Zip or CDs. Macro viruses work by infecting similar types of document with their own code, written in the macro language of the specific program that created them, such as Microsoft Word or Microsoft Excel. The main macro language used is Visual Basic for Applications (VBA), although others have been used too. As macros usually play a role in defining the templates that make up documents, it is these that viruses infect and are passed on by. Possibly the first kind of virus of this type was named the Concept virus, which can infect Microsoft Word documents on both Windows- and Macintosh-based computers. It was originally written using the macro language in Microsoft Word Version 6.0 although it can infect other versions. It seems that its main purpose was to prove that it is possible to write viruses in macro languages. There is no effect on files; its only action is to display a dialog box.

A virus has a choice as to how it attaches itself to programs or files, and this could be at the start of a program, the middle or the end. Viruses linking to the front or back end do not usually destroy the file and it may be possible to recover it. However, an overwriting virus will replace some of the program's code with its own so it is harder to deal with and it may not be possible to recover. Also, because these viruses may simply replace some of the current code with their own, they will not alter the size of the file, so become harder to detect!

A boot virus works by infecting the boot sector, an important area that tells the computer how to deal with the disk. It spreads when you access or boot from the disk as it is on the first sector that is looked at. Infection then spreads to any other disk that is inserted.

Some viruses, known as multipartite viruses, have now combined the various techniques of spreading, and use boot and file infection to increase their chances of replicating. By doing this, however, they make themselves a target for anti-virus programs, which can find them more easily, due to the large number of places they are hiding. An example of this type of virus is Natas (Satan written backwards!). This can infect both files and boot sectors on hard disks and floppies, while also changing its appearance to avoid detection.

Worms, like viruses, are capable of self-replication but do not attach themselves to executable programs or require such a file to propagate themselves. They are self-contained and generally exploit the file transmission process itself. The first worm was probably implemented by researchers as far back as 1978, although the first one to attract media attention was the Morris worm, released in November 1988. This quickly infected a large number of computers linked to the Internet relying on bugs in the BSD Unix system.

A worm can have many tasks built into it, known as *payloads*, including deleting files, carrying messages and sending documents via email. A worm can also open backdoors on computers, allowing hackers to enter such systems or make the machine become a zombie for use by spammers. A worm with more than one payload is also known as being *multi-headed*. Even simple worms can create a slow down on an infected network just through their reproductive methods.

A history of computer viruses is given in Table 15-1.

Anti-virus software allows the control and destruction of viruses, worms and other types of unwanted software, such as spyware. It scans for viruses through the computer memory and disk storage, looking for matches within its virus dictionary or identifying suspicious behavior by applications that are running. Anti-virus software allows the control and destruction of viruses, worms and other types of unwanted software, such as spyware. It scans for viruses through the computer memory and disk storage, looking for matches within its virus dictionary or identifying suspicious behavior by applications that are running. Once the anti-virus program finds a virus it will attempt to remove and fix any files it is attached to. The user can be offered the chance of quarantining or deleting the infected files, depending on the situation. Anti-virus software, in order to be effective, needs to have its dictionary of virus definitions kept up to date, usually by a connection with the software manufacturer over the Internet.

More comprehensive anti-virus software will also scan incoming email and may have firewall facilities.

Checkpoint!

- A large number of threats exist, targeting various points of weakness.
- These weaknesses include the OS, the applications software, the network software, the server systems and scripts, as well as the people themselves!
- Viruses, worms and Trojan horses present a persistent and dangerous threat to computer systems. They are likely to keep evolving throughout new technologies.
- Users and staff should be briefed or trained and made aware of security matters.

Year	Name	Description
1986	Brain	First computer virus in the wild
1986	PC–Write	First Trojan horse program disguised as shareware
1988	MacMag	First Macintosh virus
1988	Scores	Major Macintosh virus
1988	Internet Worm	First worm to cause major havoc on the Internet
1989	AIDS Trojan	Trojan horse that held a user's data hostage until a fee was paid
1991	Tequila	Polymorphic virus
1992	Michelangelo	Major media interest
1996	Boza	First Windows 95 virus
1996	Concept	First macro virus infects Word documents
1996	Laroux	Virus that infects Excel documents
1996	Staog	First Linux virus
1998	Strange Brew	First Java virus
1998	Back Orifice	Trojan horse, providing remote access to computer
1999	Melissa	First virus to spread using Outlook and Outlook Express email
1999	Tristate	First virus to infect Word, Excel and PowerPoint
2000	DoS	Not so much a virus or worm, but large-scale denial of service attacks on major Web sites
2000	Love Bug Worm	Fastest-infecting worm so far
2000	Timofonica Worm	First mobile phone worm
2000	Life Stages Worm	First worm to appear as a simple text file
2000	Phage	First Palm OS virus
2000	Liberty	First Palm OS Trojan horse

Table 15-1 *A history of computer viruses*

Year	Name	Description
2000	WebTV/Flood	First virus affecting WebTV users
2000	Hybris Worm	First self-updating worm
2001	Klez Worm	Worm that mails itself and also infects with the virus ElKern
2001	Rans	First virus infecting Perl files
2001	Peachy Worm	First worm infecting Adobe Acrobat PDF files
2001	MTX	First combination virus/worm/Trojan horse
2002	SWF.LFM	First virus infecting Shockwave Flash files
2002	Myparty Worm	Worm that installs a Trojan horse backdoor then contacts the author who can gain access
2002	Scalper	First worm infecting Apache Web servers
2003	Slammer (Sapphire) Worm	Fastest-spreading worm to date
2003	Sobig Worm	Spread by network shares
2004	MyDoom/Novarg	Spread through email and file-sharing software; faster than any previous virus or worm
2005	Zotob Worm	Exploits various vulnerabilities in Microsoft OS such as plug-and-play
2006	Nyxem Worm	Spread by mass-mailing. Attempts to disable security-related and file-sharing software.

Table 15-1 *(continued)*

15.5 FIREWALLS

For both the average user and the Web server site, the first line of defense against attack is often the firewall.

A firewall shuts down access points, or ports, which may be normally open for communication. A lot of ports have associated applications or uses, as was shown in Chapter 1. Often if a service or application is active it will be listening for communication with an appropriate protocol on a given port number. For example, the standard FTP port is 21, so an FTP server would be listening on this particular port number.

Basically, the more ports you have open and active, the more open a computer is to attack. It is possible for a hacker to probe a machine's ports using either manual tools or automated scripts/programs over the Internet.

A normal computer user is likely to want several ports open, otherwise they would have a very limited experience online! For example, there should be an accessible port 80 for Web browsing. Other services that are used should also have the correct port available such as FTP, SMTP and possibly any chat or message services such as mIRC or ICQ.

Firewalls will block ports either outward or inward, so, for example, you may browse on the Web with outward HTTP requests but not have incoming requests on that port taken up by your machine, even if a Web server is running. This may be useful if Web applications are being developed locally but you do not want them publishing yet.

With so many ports available on a computer it would be a lengthy task to say for each one whether you want it completely shut down and open or closed for inward or outward requests. However, most firewalls have default settings and levels of security that can be customized to your particular requirements.

Many intelligent firewalls will not only watch for external activity on ports but will also report or block an application's access to the Internet unless it has been cleared to do so before.

15.6 **PASSWORDS**

The password is often the most important defense in the security of a system. There are several ways to improve the way it is chosen and supported:

- Encourage the use of long passwords (> eight characters).
- Do not echo the password to the screen.
- After a period of inactivity, require the password to be re-entered.
- Request a change of password after a given time period (e.g. three weeks).
- Use secure encryption methods on transmitted passwords.
- Use password policy to ensure a strong password.
- Use methods of entry other than the keyboard (e.g. a USB or biometric device).

An interesting point should be made here – that the harder a security is and the more measures it supports, the more likely users are to be alienated and therefore become a risk in themselves. They may, for example, write down a hard to remember password, or one that changes frequently.

15.6.1 **Password Policy**

A password should be made sufficiently hard to guess, or otherwise acquire, by applying an appropriate level of security:

- password length – imposing a specific or minimum length
- password formation – imposing requirements on how a password is composed. For example, mixing of upper- and lowercase letters, inclusion of numerical digits, inclusion of special characters, stopping of dictionary or other words, stopping of calendar dates or license plate numbers, which may be guessed. The system may also suggest password formations, which the user selects
- password longevity – changing the password frequently (may also check whether the passwords are too similar)
- password hygiene – not sharing an account, not using the same password for more than one account, not revealing the password to anyone directly or via email or telephone, not writing it down, logging off when leaving a computer unattended, changing the password if someone may know it.

Any policy should also deal with how many attempts can be made at a password before the account is frozen.

15.7 **DEFENSE!**

With so many means of attack, one would think there was not much you could do in defense of such an onslaught! We have seen that the most important things you can do are as follows:

- Keep your firewall settings configured correctly.
- Keep your anti-virus software up to date.
- Ensure your OS is sufficiently secure and hardened to an appropriate level for its position in your network. This may mean only having necessary ports open for communication, for example.
- Ensure you have the latest security updates for your OS.
- Make your wireless system secure by using the correct security level and encryption.
- Configure your server correctly with the proper user permissions. Look into 'jailing' your users and limiting access as much as possible.
- Limit the amount of information you give away about your system and how it is configured. For example, the option `ServerTokens Minimal` will stop the Apache server giving away too much about itself! If users don't need to know something, don't tell them!
- Watch logs for odd behavior. Monitor users with your own scripts that write traces of people's behavior across your site – it's surprising what people get up to! Don't forget also, when it comes to logging IP addresses, that it is possible to anonymize your IP, using special services and proxies so it doesn't have to be correct. See the *Tor project* for details: `http://tor.eff.org`.

Checkpoint!

- There are many ways of protecting a computer system and network.
- User and staff training to raise awareness of issues is a good idea.
- Firewalls and anti-virus software should be used and correctly configured.
- Password policies should be enforced.
- OS, servers and system software should be hardened; this may mean simply correct configuration, minimal port access and logging of activity. Ensure permissions are correctly set for user accounts.

15.8 CHAPTER SUMMARY

- Hacking tends to adapt to technologies.
- Hacking exploits weaknesses in the security of an OS, server or other devices. Employees or other system users should also be made aware of giving information away and being targeted themselves.
- There are many reasons for such attacks, varying from an individual's feelings of self-worth, through to their allegiances to organizations, groups and nations.
- Certain computer activities within companies by employees pose a threat to whole networks, usually already behind firewalls.
- As there are so many methods of attack against a system, a comprehensive security policy must be adopted by companies.
- Software and applications must be rigorously checked for security implications.
- It is possible to harden software and systems against attack by configuring them correctly and limiting users' access as far as possible.

Chapter Quiz

- There are various sites with security announcements on about the latest threats. Try visiting these and find out what the newest are for your particular system (a good starting point may be Symantec at http://www.symantec.com).
- Possibly the most secure OS available is OpenBSD, a version of Unix. What makes it so special?
- Build your own timeline of viruses – what are the more complex viruses capable of doing and how?

Key Words and Phrases

Cross site scripting A type of exploit in which information from one context, where it is not trusted, is inserted into another, where it is, and thereby produces an attack

Firewall A piece of hardware or software that prevents unauthorized use of the network by limiting access

Hacker A person who exploits a system's weaknesses in order gain entry

Phishing The act of fraudulently trying to acquire sensitive information such as passwords or personal details

Spoofing The masquerading of a person or IP address to avoid identification

Trojan horse A piece of software that enters a system by stealth and deposits or executes a piece of destructive code

Virus A self-replicating program that spreads by inserting copies of itself into code or documents

Worm A self-replicating program, similar to a virus, which is self-contained

Zombie computer (abbreviated to Zombie) A computer that has been compromised by a hacker, virus or other source so that it can perform tasks on behalf of the hacker

Useful Web Addresses

http://www.symantec.com/

http://tor.eff.org/

http://www.openbsd.org/

http://en.wikipedia.org/wiki/Notable_computer_viruses_and_worms

16

The aim of this chapter is to help you understand databases so that they can easily be utilized in your Web applications and sites. The basic idea of the database is explored, together with how well it can be linked in with server side scripting. All the basic functions are studied, together with how these can be communicated directly to the database server.

While information can be stored in files using PHP, this is in some ways a difficult approach to storing data. There is much more handling and formatting required than using a database and, because it is quite a complex task, there is more chance of error.

Databases allow large amounts of information to be securely and efficiently kept. As well as storing textual information, such as names and addresses, it is possible to store entire files and binary executables!

A lot of packages that contain Apache and PHP also contain MySQL, which is an extremely popular choice of database engine. It can easily be used with PHP and often you simply submit queries to it in exactly the same format as if you were communicating with it directly via a monitor program or command line shell.

16.1 **INTRODUCTION**

Any Web site that requires users to register and log in needs a way of storing the information that is collected in that initial session. This may be as simple as the visitor selecting a username and password, plus maybe adding password hints. The more secure you want it to be, the more detail you add, especially for banking Web sites. As has been shown previously, it's possible to store these details in a file on the server that you write with PHP commands such as fopen and fwrite, although you would probably want to encrypt any sensitive details such as passwords. This file takes the place of a database because, like a database, it is a container and, hopefully, a structure that orders the data for easy retrieval later on.

A database then is a container for information that orders the information and allows ways of manipulating and updating the data. It should also have mechanisms to make stored information secure. The difference between this and keeping a file with the data stored in an ordered way yourself is that much of the hard work is done for you! The Database Management System (DBMS) looks after all the housekeeping tasks and manipulation of data; all the programer has to do is ask questions to retrieve any information or use simple statements and commands to update, delete or append the stored data.

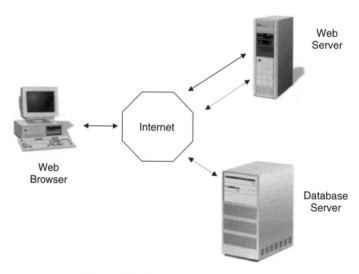

Figure 16-1 Communications with a DBMS

Figure 16-1 shows the idea behind a DBMS connected to a network such as the Internet, but equally applies to a business-based LAN. In this diagram the visitor is connected to the

Internet and logged onto a site and is therefore in communication with the Web server. Any access to the related database on the DBMS server is also passed over the network (shown in the diagram as a dashed line). This might be, for example, when the user initially logs on and the Web server wants to check the entered details or later, if information is being accessed.

While you are developing, or for small databases, there is no reason why your Web and database server shouldn't be on the same physical machine.

16.2 **RELATIONAL DATABASES**

Relational databases store data in tables. A table is divided by columns with labels to identify the stored data.

A few definitions are necessary here, as sometimes database terms can be confusing between different sources! As you can see from Table 16-1, the whole information set is called a table. A single row, of one particular individual, is known as a record or tuple. A downward column is a field or attribute; so in this example it could be firstname or password.

member_id	firstname	lastname	email	password
001	Lynda	Snell	lsnell@hayfever.com	lama123
002	Bert	Fry	bfry@yahoo.com	birdy2
003	Emma	Grundy	EmmaG@yahoo.co.uk	willOrEd4me
004	Neil	Carter	pigman@gmail.co.uk	wotnopigs1
005	Ruth	Archer	ruthybabe@farmers.com	ooodavid1
006	Kenton	Archer	Kenton@jackscafe.co.uk	Meriel4
007	Brian	Aldridge	moneybags@czechfarm.com	siobhan33
008	Pip	Archer	musicalme@borchester.co.uk	eee3k
009	Roy	Tucker	roytuck@businessweek.co.uk	bizzybee2

Table 16-1 A database table

As data is entered into a table the rows are not ordered in any way, so a way of identifying a single record is needed. In the table shown here there is a member_id field for this purpose. Usually you can get the database system to do this automatically and it becomes what is known as the *primary key*, although it can also be specified if there is already a suitable uniquely identifying field.

A database may consist of many tables or related items of data. For example, Table 16-2 could form the basis of a membership list for a library, which could be called `member`. We might have another table, called `book`, containing the names of books as shown in Table 16-3.

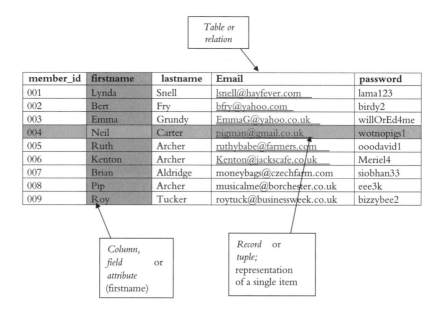

member_id	firstname	lastname	Email	password
001	Lynda	Snell	lsnell@hayfever.com	lama123
002	Bert	Fry	bfry@yahoo.com	birdy2
003	Emma	Grundy	EmmaG@yahoo.co.uk	willOrEd4me
004	Neil	Carter	pigman@gmail.co.uk	wotnopigs1
005	Ruth	Archer	ruthybabe@farmers.com	ooodavid1
006	Kenton	Archer	Kenton@jackscafe.co.uk	Meriel4
007	Brian	Aldridge	moneybags@czechfarm.com	siobhan33
008	Pip	Archer	musicalme@borchester.co.uk	eee3k
009	Roy	Tucker	roytuck@businessweek.co.uk	bizzybee2

Table or relation

Column, field or attribute (firstname)

Record or tuple; representation of a single item

Table 16-2 *Parts of a database table*

book_id	ISBN	title	author
001	0006280609	*The Screwtape Letters*	C.S.Lewis
002	0340830409	*Seven Ages of Britain*	J.Pollard
003	0450547426	*Stranger in a Strange Land*	R.A.Heinlen
004	0954732405	*Alice Through the Looking Glass*	L.Carrol
005	1563892499	*Flash: Terminal Velocity*	M.Waid

Table 16-3 *The* book *table*

How do we connect the two tables if member 001 borrows book 003? Well, one way of doing this would be to create yet another table! This would contain both the members' IDs and the books they borrow, as shown in Table 16-4.

member_id	book_id
008	002
003	001
005	004
006	005

Table 16-4 *The* `borrows` *table*

Here we see that member 008 (Pip Archer) has borrowed 002 (*Seven Ages of Britain*) and member 003 (Emma Grundy) has borrowed 001 (*The Screwtape Letters*) and so on.

16.2.1 Design and Modeling

An essential first step to constructing a database is to analyze the requirements carefully by studying the data involved. To design a database it is possible to use specific methodologies and visualization tools. One of these is called entity-relationship (ER) modeling, which is a clear and simple method of expressing the design of a database. Using this approach the various attributes, entities and relationships are captured in diagram form, which resembles a flowchart.

Figure 16-2 is an entity-relationship diagram describing the book library database used earlier. There are two entities (represented by the table itself), `Member` and `Book,` which contain the various attributes attached to them such as `firstname`, `lastname`, `password`, `email`, `member_id` and `title`, `author`, `ISBN`, `book_id`. Note here that the primary key is usually underlined. A relationship between two entities is usually expressed using a diamond shape,

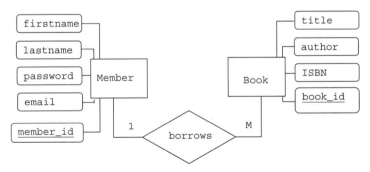

Figure 16-2 *An entity-relationship diagram*

which connects the entities involved. A word suitably describing the relationship is placed in the diamond. The M describes the *degree* or *cardinality* of the relationship, which in this case is 1 to many (M meaning multiple) – a member may borrow many books. There are other kinds of relation although this is the most common. There are also one to one and many to many. There are quite a few ways of showing the same thing but the idea remains the same with these three basic ways of showing cardinality.

Rectangles represent entities, the objects being modeled, and are labeled with a meaningful title. Diamonds represent relationships between entities and have a descriptive title. Rounds rectangles, or ellipses, represent attributes that describe an entity. Lines that are used to connect relationships and entities can be annotated to reflect the cardinality of that relationship. This may be one to one, one to many or many to many. These are usually shown as 1 to 1, 1 to M (or N) and M to M. Lines also link attributes to entities but are not labeled.

16.2.2 What is Normalization?

Normalization is a process of optimization in which the potential for redundancy is removed. If this is not done the following happens:

- Any repetition of data throughout the database makes it much bigger.
- More occurrences of the same data make maintaining the database harder and can create anomalies. An example of an anomaly is the update of a customer address; multiple entries of the same data will require all of them being changed with the possibility of a mistake taking place.

Normalization usually follows a series of stages, called normal forms (NF):

- first normal form (1NF)
- second normal form (2NF)
- third normal form (3NF)
- Boyce Codd normal form (BCNF)
- fourth normal form (4NF)
- fifth normal form (5NF).

The stage that the process begins at is un-normalized normal form (UNF)! The first three normal forms are usually enough to remove any anomalies, as further stages remove problems that occur only rarely.

For first normal form the database must conform to two rules:

- **All attributes (columns) must be atomic**. This means that information should be broken up into its most minimal but important form and not embedded within other data.

- **There should be no repeating groups**. This means that there shouldn't be columns that contain the same type of data, for example different kinds of car spread across three columns. Instead, a new relation should be made called `cars`.

The second normal form has only one rule:

- **All non-key attributes must be dependent** *on the whole key* **and not just one attribute of the key.** When a composite key is present, this means that attributes in that relation must be dependent on all of the key otherwise they are in the wrong relation. For example, if our database consisted of motorbike owners and their respective bike purchases we could make a composite key that was made of customer ID and model but information about the motorbike could be derived from only part of that key and so isn't dependent on the whole key. However, if we wanted to find out the color of the bike the customer bought, then we could search for the customer and this would give us the color – assuming they only bought one bike. But what if the customer has ordered two bikes, of different models and different colors? In order to find the color of a specific bike we would need to know the `CustomerID` and the model number. Therefore, color is dependent on the *whole* primary key and not just a part of it. This means that color is in the correct relation as it is specific to the customer and the model, whereas information about the bike, which is dependent upon the model alone, should be in a different table.

The third normal form also has only one rule:

- **No attribute must be dependent on a non-key attribute.** This means that every attribute must be directly dependent on the primary key and not on any other column. If there is no direct dependency then the attribute is stripped off to its own relation.

Database design and normalization is worthy of an entire book but hopefully this section has made you interested enough to have a look into this further, especially if you are considering implementing databases in your application or Web site.

Checkpoint!

- Databases provide a useful function for use in Web sites.
- They can store a lot of information in a secure and structured way.
- The DBMS does not have to be on the same physical machine as the Web server but uses the network.
- Relational databases have a particular architecture and methodology attached to them.
- These databases contain tables as relations made up of attributes and records.

■ Databases should usually begin with careful analysis of requirements and the development of a model, possibly using entity–relationship diagrams.

■ Normalization is a way of optimizing a database so the potential for redundancy is removed. It consists of different stages (or forms) that are reached by applying specific rules.

Test Yourself!

- Check your installation package for MySQL and phpMyAdmin.
- Find the appropriate documentation, either in the package itself or the Web site associated with it.
- You can install MySQL as a stand-alone application, if all else fails!
- Familiarize yourself with how to start and stop the MySQL server.
- How do you start the MySQL monitor?

16.3 SQL

Structured Query Language (SQL) allows you to manipulate a relational database's structure and content.

16.3.1 MySQL

MySQL is a very popular DBMS with over six million installations. It is open source but, unlike other projects such as Apache, is owned and sponsored by a *for-profit* company, MySQL AB. This Swedish company develops and maintains the software and sells both support and service contracts.

MySQL can be used by many programing languages including C#, C, C++, Eiffel, Java, Smalltalk, Lisp, Perl, PHP, Python, Ruby, REALbasic and Tcl. Any language supporting the open database connectivity (ODBC) interface should be able to use MySQL too. MySQL's native language is C.

Probably the most popular pairing for languages and database systems is PHP and MySQL, particularly for Web applications. It is easy to use and has various ways of interacting. For example, besides being able to run your PHP scripts, you can use the MySQL monitor to talk directly to the server with SQL or use several tools to manage it, such as phpMyAdmin, or the GUI applications MySQL Administrator or MySQL Query Browser.

16.3.2 **Starting, Stopping and Checking MySQL Server**

Just like the Apache Web server or any other server, you need to start it up. Different computer systems require different ways of doing this so you should refer to the install documentation. For XAMPP on Windows this is usually done with a batch file under the main directory called `start_mysql.bat`. This file can be clicked on to get it going although if it does fail for any reason you may not see any error messages because it will close straight away! To get around this, open a command prompt and change to the directory it's in and execute it by typing its name; you will then see any messages. In Windows the command prompt will stay on the screen while the server is active – don't close it! On a Mac installation of XAMPP (well, MAMPP!) you can start everything (Apache, MySQL etc.) by simply typing:

```
/usr/local/xampp/mampp start
```

If you do get a problem it can be the same as starting any other server software in that other applications may have grabbed some of the required resources such as ports. Check that your system isn't running another server on the same port or clashing in some other way. Another possible problem may occur if you are running security software that blocks access to ports or keeps an eye on activities in your machine in a bid to stop spyware. If this is the case it may inform you when your server does start and ask you if it is okay for that program to proceed. Of course, you could just disable your security but that's not advisable unless you are having real problems and need to see what is causing clashing or blocking of resources.

Once you think you have the MySQL server running it can be checked to see if it is functioning and everything is okay. To do this using XAMPP, simply go to the main server home page on `http://localhost/` and click on 'status'. This should show which servers are currently active on your computer, which includes MySQL and Apache.

To stop your MySQL server using the XAMPP installation on Windows, click on the `mysql_stop.bat` batch file. Using the Mac version send the instruction `stop` via the `mampp` command:

```
/usr/local/xampp/mampp stop
```

16.3.3 **The MySQL Monitor**

The MySQL software comes with a special program that allows you to talk directly to the MySQL server through SQL commands. Start up your Web server and MySQL server in the way that is described in your documentation and then try and locate the MySQL monitor, which should have a file name such as `mysql`. Once you have located it, execute it in a command line, or shell window:

```
mysql -u root
```

If a password has already been set up for the root user, it will need to be included too:

```
mysql -u root -p password
```

For example:

```
mysql -u root -p letmein4
```

Figure 16-3 shows the kind of display you get when the monitor is up and running. If you type show databases; as above you may get a different result set but you should get test which is usually set up for everyone initially. The mysql database is used by the MySQL system itself. Note that all SQL commands end with a semicolon; this is so you can break a long query up over many lines and it will only be processed when the semicolon is reached.

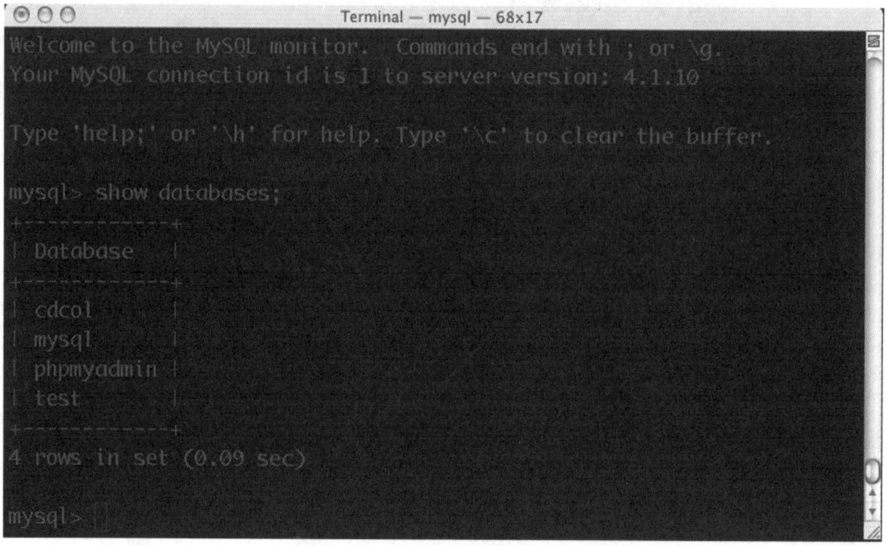

Figure 16-3 *The MySQL monitor*

To actually access a database that is listed with show databases, type use and the database name. So, if you type use mysql, then type show tables it's possible to see what tables are in that particular database. To see how a table is actually constructed type explain followed by the table name.

There are certain housekeeping tasks you need to do, particularly when working in the MySQL monitor; for example, you may wish to add users or add a password for the root user:

```
grant all privileges on *.* to username@domain
identified by "password" with grant option;
```

So, for user `bill` it could be:

```
grant all privileges on *.* to bill@localhost
identified by "letmein4" with grant option;
```

As with a lot of SQL commands there are lots of options so check the documentation!

When you have finished in the monitor, type either `exit` or `quit`.

16.4 BASIC COMMANDS WITH PHP EXAMPLES

To utilize the MySQL system queries are submitted via a string in PHP and directly if using the MySQL monitor.

16.4.1 Connection to the Server

To connect with PHP the `mysql_connect` command can be used:

```
mysql_connect(server, username, password);
```

You may use the code fragment:

```
$connect = mysql_connect("localhost", "sid", "sesame");
```

If you are using the monitor in a shell or command line you don't need to connect, as you are already!

16.4.2 Creating a Database

To create a database, use the SQL command:

```
create table tablename
```

This can be done directly in the monitor, or in PHP as:

```
mysql_connect ("localhost","$user","$password")
$sqlstr = 'CREATE DATABASE '.$dbname;
mysql_query($sqlstr);
```

where `$dbname` is the name of the database you want to create. Note when sending queries in this way through PHP, do not add a semicolon to the end of the string.

16.4.3 **Selecting a Database**

Before you can actually use a database you need to select it as shown above if in a MySQL monitor with **use**. In PHP:

```
$result = mysql_select_db("library", $connect) or die("Error
                selecting db");
```

The **die** command stops further script processing with an error message if the database cannot be selected.

16.4.4 **Listing Databases**

In SQL **show databases** will display all the current databases. One way to do the same thing in PHP is:

```
$result = mysql_list_dbs($connect);
for ($row =0; $row < mysql_num_rows($result); $row++) {
        $dbases .= mysql_tablename($result, $row) . "<br>";
}

echo($dbases);
```

The **$connect** variable is the connection you opened with your **mysql_connect**. The **$result** variable contains the actual databases but they still need to be extracted and formatted, which is what the loop does.

The **mysql_tablename** function is now deprecated and instead you could simply send **show databases** via a query string.

16.4.5 **Listing Table Names**

To see what tables exist within a database using PHP:

```
$result = mysql_list_tables($db);
$rcount = mysql_num_rows($result);

for ($i=0;$i<$rcount;$i++) {
  $tabname = mysql_tablename($result, $i);
  tablist .= $tabname . "<br>";
}

echo($tabname);
```

Again, it's possible to use a query string to say **show tables [from db_name] [like 'pattern']**. Or use it within the MySQL monitor.

16.4.6 Creating a Database Table

A database table is made in both PHP and directly with the monitor using basically the same command: create database. This is followed by a list that makes up the structure of the database table. In the case of PHP the command is actually made up as a string and then submitted using the mysql_query command.

```
// first of all create the database
$query  = 'create database people';
$result = mysql_query($query);

// select the database
mysql_select_db('people') or die('Error: cannot select
                database!');

// make up the query
$query = 'create table contact( '.
        'pid INT NOT NULL AUTO_INCREMENT, '.
        'pname VARCHAR(25) NOT NULL, '.
        'pemail VARCHAR(54) NOT NULL, '.
        'psubject VARCHAR(32) NOT NULL, '.
        'pmessage TEXT NOT NULL, '.
        'PRIMARY KEY(pid))';
//submit the create table as a SQL query
 $result = mysql_query($query);
```

Note the various types available for fields. These can be broken into text and numeric types with some for special cases, such as dates.

As you can see in Table 16-5 there are a number of different types covering most eventualities! In addition to the type in the create table command, there are optional field modifiers. These add even more control over what can happen in that particular column. The various modifiers available are as follows:

- not null – meaning that this field must not be empty
- unique – the entry must not be duplicated anywhere in this column
- primary key – specifies a column to be used as the primary key
- auto_increment – generates a number one greater than the previous one in this column (and therefore there must be numeric data in this field!).

16.4.7 Inserting Data

Data is inserted into a database table in the MySQL monitor using insert:

```
insert into tablename (field1, field2, field3,... ) values
                (value1, value2, value3,... )
```

CHAR( )	A string of defined and fixed length from 0 to 255 characters long
VARCHAR( )	A string of defined but variable length from 0 to 255 characters long
TINYTEXT	A string with a maximum length of 255 characters
TEXT	A string with a maximum length of 65535 characters
BLOB	A string with a maximum length of 65535 characters
MEDIUMTEXT	A string with a maximum length of 16777215 characters
MEDIUMBLOB	A string with a maximum length of 16777215 characters
LONGTEXT	A string with a maximum length of 4294967295 characters
LONGBLOB	A string with a maximum length of 4294967295 characters
TINYINT( )	−128 to 127 normal 0 to 255 UNSIGNED
SMALLINT( )	−32768 to 32767 normal 0 to 65535 UNSIGNED
MEDIUMINT( )	−8388608 to 8388607 normal 0 to 16777215 UNSIGNED
INT( )	−2147483648 to 2147483647 normal 0 to 4294967295 UNSIGNED
BIGINT( )	−9223372036854775808 to 9223372036854775807 normal 0 to 18446744073709551615 UNSIGNED
FLOAT	A small number with a floating decimal point
DOUBLE(,)	A large number with a floating decimal point
DECIMAL(,)	A DOUBLE stored as a string, allowing for a fixed decimal point
DATE	YYYY-MM-DD
DATETIME	YYYY-MM-DD HH:MM:SS
TIMESTAMP	YYYYMMDDHHMMSS
TIME	HH:MM:SS

Table 16-5 *Data types in MySQL*

For example:

```
insert into people (id, firstname, lastname) values (1234, Sid,
                    Perks);
```

In PHP, after connecting to the server and selecting the database, build the query in a string and then submit it:

```
$query = "insert into people (id, firstname, lastname) values
                ($id, \"$firstname\", \"$lastname\" )";

$result = mysql_query($query, $connect);
```

An important thing to note here is that, when using PHP for the insertion query, the quotes must have a backslash in front of them to make the system interpret the line correctly!

16.4.8 Altering Tables

Sometimes it is necessary to slightly adjust a table once it's set up. For example, you may want to change the limit on the number of digits or characters on a given field.

To do this in the monitor, the following SQL code could be used:

```
alter table tablename modify fieldname char(28);
```

e.g.:

```
alter table people modify fieldname char(28);
```

which, in PHP, could be submitted via:

```
$query = " alter table people modify fieldname char(28)";
$result = mysql_query($query, $connect);
```

16.4.9 Queries

Once you have set up a database with your information, queries can be applied to actually find information. To do this, queries are built up as a string:

```
$sql = "select * from contact where pid>10";
$result = mysql_query($sql, $connect);
```

The result is stored in the result string which can be retrieved:

```
while ($row = mysql_fetch_array($result))
{
    echo(row["book"]."-".row["ISBN"]);
}
```

16.4.10 Deleting Databases

To remove a database, simply use a `drop database` command, followed by the name of the one you want to get rid of. In PHP use:

```
$query  = 'drop database people';
$result = mysql_query($query);
```

16.4.11 Deleting Data and Tables

SQL contains commands for removing data from a database. Simply use:

```
delete from tablename where field=x
```

e.g.

```
delete from people where pid=10;
```

To do this in PHP add the query to a string and submit it via `mysql_query`.

The structure of tables can also be altered by deletion. For example, if you suddenly realize that you don't actually need a particular column:

```
alter table contact drop pemail;
```

To destroy a whole table:

```
drop table contact;
```

Checkpoint!

- SQL provides a way of manipulating a relational database's structure and content.
- MySQL is a popular DBMS that is usable in many languages.
- It provides a way of directly communicating with the server or through other languages.
- There are many SQL commands for accessing, manipulating and updating your database. Query commands allow complex questions about your data to be resolved and output.

16.5 **PHPMYADMIN**

This is a very useful piece of open source software that is sometimes included with packages that have both PHP and MySQL. It can also be downloaded separately (from `http://www.phpmyadmin.net`) and consists of a set of PHP scripts that act as a front-end to your MySQL DBMS. It's really useful as a tool to see what your PHP scripts are doing while developing!

The easy way to access phpMyAdmin is through the initial startup screen on your server home page if you installed via XAMPP; if not, check your documentation. The first screen you are presented with should be similar to Figure 16-4. This allows you to view the status of your MySQL server and alter basic aspects of both its and phpMyAdmin's operation.

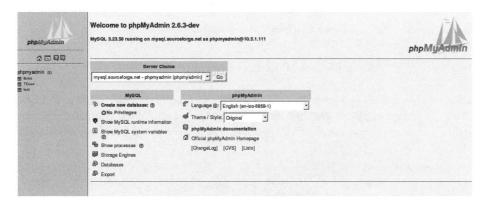

Figure 16-4 *phpMyAdmin initial screen*

phpMyAdmin will let you see every aspect of your MySQL server, including statistics on runtime information. This is shown in Figure 16-5.

To return to the main screen at any time, go to the left-hand menu and click on the 'home' button.

To make a simple database, place a name in the 'create text' input window and click 'create'. For this example, let's enter 'bookcase'. The next page allows you to make a table for the selected, new database. At any time, you can start working with another database by selecting one with the drop-down list on the left-hand menu.

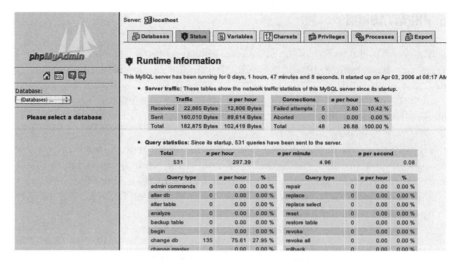

Figure 16-5 *phpMyAdmin runtime information*

To create a table, enter 'books' and '4' for the number of fields.

In the simple example in Figure 16-6, we can fill out the fields (Title, Author, Publisher, ISBN) and leave the type to VARCHAR with a length field of 50. When you make your own database you can set these however you feel suits the database you are making, of course!

Figure 16-6 *phpMyAdmin creating a table*

Figure 16-7 shows the page directly after a table is created; notice how you are shown the actual query that was used to make it. This is what you would have used if you typed it in to the MySQL monitor or as a string if you used PHP scripting.

Hit the insert icon to enter data into the database table, as shown in Figure 16-7. When you click on 'go' the next page will allow you to generate a PHP string for that particular data. The ability to see SQL queries being generated or even PHP code for a script is particularly useful for the beginner!

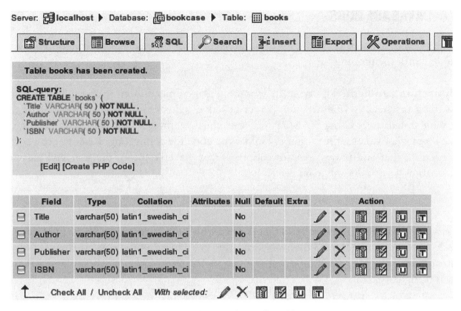

Figure 16-7 *phpMyAdmin after table creation*

As you can see from Figure 16-8 there are a number of functions available. These include: structure for building tables and suchlike; browse for looking through data; SQL for executing queries; search for finding specific items; insert for entering more rows of data; export for dumping the database to files of different formats; operations for performing various admin tasks such as renaming or restructuring tables; empty for emptying the database; and drop for deleting a given table.

Field	Type	Function	Null	Value
Title	varchar(50)			Developing Web Applications
Author	varchar(50)			Ralph Moseley
Publisher	varchar(50)			Wiley
ISBN	varchar(50)			0470017198

Figure 16-8 *phpMyAdmin insert data*

When you first start experimenting with PHP a tool such as phpMyAdmin allows you to check on what exactly is happening or to correct any mistakes that have been caused by bugs in your program.

16.6 **DATABASE BUGS**

There are several common problems that can occur with PHP database scripting. Here are a couple worth mentioning.

Connection problem. This typically comes up as a connection error on the browser. The first thing to check is whether your server is active! Check using the appropriate method for your installation. Using XAMPP you can check with the Web server home page on localhost via status. If it is online, look at the code for connecting: has it got the correct connection, user and password information? If you haven't set up the user and password information you could only connect with:

```
$connect = mysql_connect("localhost", "root", "");
```

Password problem. The error says that the password is incorrect. The first thing to do is to check whether you encrypted the password prior to saving it in the database (or text file for that matter!). if so, you need to repeat the same encryption function on any user password that is being checked!

16.7 **EXAMPLES**

Open either phpMyAdmin or the MySQL monitor and create a new database called myusers. Then make a table within that database that is called userdb and has the following fields:

> id_code type INT (you can make this field auto-increment and primary key)
> user_name VARCHAR of length 50
> password VARCHAR of length 20
> age   INT

So, the SQL would be something like:

```
CREATE  TABLE 'userdb'  (
'id_code' INT NOT  NULL  AUTO_INCREMENT ,
'user_name' VARCHAR( 50  )  NOT  NULL ,
'password' VARCHAR( 20  )  NOT  NULL ,
'age' INT NOT  NULL ,
PRIMARY  KEY ( 'id_code'  )
);
```

You can then insert some data using PHP, the MySQL monitor or phpMyAdmin; here is the SQL query:

```
INSERT  INTO 'userdb' ( 'id_code','user_name','password', 'age')
VALUES ('1','bertfry','anchoves','32');
```

Add some more users with your chosen method then write a login script like Listing 16-1.

```html
<html><head><title>Log-In</title></head>

<body>
Please enter details:<br><br>

<form action = "login.php" method = "post">

What is your user name:<br>
<input type = "text" name = "username"> <br><br>

What is your password:<br>
<input type = "text" name = "password"><br><br>

<input type = "submit" value = "Go!">
</form>

</body>
</html>
```

Listing 16-1 *HTML form for login*

The things to remember with Listing 16-1 are that you must connect the script to process by placing its name in the form action attribute. In this case this is login.php. This script (shown in Listing 16-2) will take the data entered via the form input and check that it has been entered (just a basic test for whether anything is entered) then connect to the database and query the relevant fields. Notice here that the data is passed into variables within the program. Another variable is also used to store the name of the calling page so, if anything should go wrong such as the data not being correct or simply not being entered, the page can be reloaded.

```php
<?php
// login.php script to process log-in details
$username = $_POST['username'];
$password = $_POST['password'];
$login =  $_SERVER['HTTP_REFERER'];

// check if filled out correctly, return if not!
if( ( !$username ) or ( !$password ) )
{ header( "Location:$login" ); exit(); }

// make the connection, place in your own
```

```
//username and password here if changed
$conn=@mysql_connect( "localhost", "root", "" )
        or die( "Cannot connect!" );

// select the database to access
$rs = @mysql_select_db( "myusers", $conn )
        or die( "Database problem!" );

// build a query
$sql = "select * from userdb where user_name=\"$username\"
            and password = \"$password\" ";

// send the query
$rs = mysql_query( $sql, $conn )
        or die( "Could not execute query" );

// how many rows have come back in response?
$rows = mysql_numrows( $rs );

// if there is a row present then everything okay!
if( $rows != 0 )
{
  echo ("<h2>$username Okay - !Welcome!</h2>");
}
else
{
  header( "Location:$login" ); exit();
}
 ?>
```

Listing 16-2 Script to process login details

Checkpoint!

■ A useful application exists called phpMyAdmin. It consists of a set of PHP scripts. Sometimes this software is included with installations of Apache.

■ This software allows you to interact with any of your current databases and creates a fairly simple interface to your MySQL.

■ It can be useful to check on databases you have developed in others ways, such as PHP, and are maybe having problems with.

■ A database can be selected to work with or a new one created. It is then possible to create and edit tables.

- Data can be inserted, altered or appended.
- SQL scripts for operations are shown as the user presses buttons to do the task.
- PHP scripts can be generated.
- Databases can then be exported as files or in other formats.

Test Yourself!

- Find and review the online MySQL documentation.
- Start up the MySQL monitor.
- Set the password for root (important!).
- Experiment with some basic commands such as `show databases` and `show tables`.
- Try and design a library for the loan of DVDs, making sure you capture all the relevant information about the DVDs themselves, members and the process of the loan. Finally, when satisfied, add the ability to show details of current fines for overdue discs.
- Implement the database using the MySQL monitor.
- Install phpMyAdmin and study the database you have created.
- Consider how you would add a Web site front-end to the DVD library.
- Write some scripts to interact with your database and build up to a full interface with it.

16.8 CHAPTER SUMMARY

- Web sites are enhanced by using databases to store collected information.
- They make data manipulation very simple and secure.
- The DBMS can be network linked rather than sharing resources with a Web server or other applications.
- Relational databases are easy to understand and implement.
- Relational databases consist of tables (relations), attributes (columns) and records or tuples (rows).
- It's important to carefully analyze the database requirements before beginning any programing work, possibly employing entity–relationship (ER) diagrams to model it.
- Normalization can be used to reduce the possibility of redundancy and therefore anomalies.
- A popular DBMS for use with Web sites and PHP is MySQL.

- Communicating with the database server in MySQL is fairly simple and possible in many languages.
- The SQL language allows you to access and manipulate your data. It contains many commands for various operations on the information you have stored, allowing complex queries to be developed.
- Tools exist to act as a front-end to the MySQL server; this allows you to check on the structure of databases or update them. One of the more popular is phpMyAdmin.

Chapter Quiz

- Find some more online information sources for Web databases using PHP. Start by looking at the Web sites given below.
- Attempt to design a database for a car dealer, initially using ER diagrams.
- Continue with your design and apply normalization techniques as described in this chapter.
- Finally, implement these designs as an online database only utilizing HTML, CSS and PHP.

Key Words and Phrases

Data type Like variables in programing and scripting, every field has an associated type that declares it to be numeric, string information or some other form of data

DBMS Database Management System, the actual engine that handles queries and organizes the data

Entity This represents a class of objects such as people, cars or library. It possesses properties and is usually represented in the database as a table

Entity-relationship (ER) diagram A data model or diagram of high-level descriptions

MySQL A DBMS that is based on SQL and is multi threaded/multi user

Primary key A value that is used to uniquely identify a particular row or tuple in a table

Query A specification of a problem to be calculated by a database

SQL Structured Query Language, the most popular database language used to retrieve and manipulate data in a relational DBMS

Table The basic component of a relational database, containing a number of rows (records) and fields (columns). Another name for table in this context is a relation

Useful Web Addresses

```
http://www.mysql.com/
http://dev.mysql.com/tech-resources/articles/ddws/
http://uk.php.net/mysql/
http://www.phpmyadmin.net/
```

17

ALTERNATIVE SCRIPTING LANGUAGES

The aim of this chapter is to have a look at the various technologies available for developing Web applications. This can be useful to familiarize you with legacy code that may be met while maintaining older applications and Web sites.

No one book can describe all the Web development languages in sufficient depth for the novice programer. However, in this book there has been a focus on HTML, JavaScript, XML, PHP and a few more. Here, we give a brief overview of those other technologies that can be met *in the wild!*

A brief description is given of each, with a few appropriate examples to emphasize the style or brevity of a language. As well as this, Web links are given to the main source for that language, the community that supports it or an initial information point. Some links are also given to general Web technologies reference sites.

17.1 LEGACY CODE AND APPLICATION DEVELOPMENT CHOICES

At some point you may have to maintain someone else's code, or simply be interested in what else is out there. This may come as a shock but PHP is not the only Web development language!!

17.1.1 CGI

Common Gateway Interface (CGI) was invented by NCSA in 1993 to allow their Web server to store parameters passed from the server environment to the shell where a CGI program can be spawned as a separate process.

CGI raises security issues due to the way it passes information over to any type of program outside of a secure Web environment. It is a lot safer to use languages with Web-specific features that enable more secure data transfer.

A popular language used with CGI is Perl and this will be looked at next.

Web pages:

```
http://hoohoo.ncsa.uiuc.edu/cgi/
http://www.w3.org/CGI/
```

17.1.2 Perl

Practical Extraction and Report Language (Perl) was originally developed for text manipulation, roughly following the structure of the C programing language. It is a procedural-based language (with support for object-oriented programing too in Perl 5), which is interpreted as opposed to compiled, with an emphasis on being efficient, easy to use and practical. Perl tends to look difficult to follow and has a reputation for being less than elegant! Perl does, however, have a large support base and third-party library.

It is now used for network programing, Web and graphical user interface (GUI) development as well as many other areas.

A Hello World! program in Perl simply consists of the lines:

```
#!/usr/local/bin/perl
 print "Hello world!\n";
```

The first line specifies the location of the Perl interpreter, usually in this location, on Unix systems. The second line outputs the phrase. Note the use of the backslash n for dropping down a line, which is similar to several languages based on C.

Web pages:

```
http://www.perl.com/
http://www.perl.org/
```

17.1.3 **ASP**

Active Server Pages is a Microsoft technology on the server side for generating Web pages and is marketed as an add-on for the Internet Information Services (IIS). ASP pages are generally written in VBScript although other languages are selectable using special directives.

The Hello World! program for ASP is shown in Listing 17-1.

```
<html>
<body>

<%
response.write("Hello World!")
%>

</body>
</html>
```

Listing 17-1 Simple Hello World! *script for ASP*

Just like in PHP you are free to use HTML tags within the output string to format the page being written in the HTML browser. If you choose to use VBScript for ASP pages you have access to its functions too, such as WeekdayName as shown in Listing 17-2.

```
<html>
<body>

The day is
<%response.write(WeekdayName(weekday(date)))%>,
in the month of
<%response.write(MonthName(month(date)))%>

</body>
</html>
```

Listing 17-2 Using VBScript built-in functions for ASP

Ready-made objects are available that make programing easier; for example, for maintaining cookie-based sessions there is the Session object. The main objects are as follows:

- **Session** This is used to access information and manipulate a session. It stores variables about the user within a session and there is one **Session** object created for each user.
- **Application** This gathers together all the information for one page, and is used much like the **Session** object but there is only one **Application** object for all users rather than one for each.
- **Request** This is used to access the user's HTTP request header and body, as well as to read cookies and retrieve HTML form information.
- **Response** This gives control over data being sent to the client. This usually relates to setting up cookies and control over caching of pages.
- **Server** This object is used to access properties and methods on the server.
- **ASPError** This allows you to view information about the last error in the current session.

To show how these objects are used and the various similarities in functionality to PHP, there follow several examples.

Listing 17-3 shows how it is possible to access various useful variables using the **Request** object. In this case they are part of the server variables collection. A sample output from such a script might be:

```
<html>
<body>

<p> Your browser is:
<%Response.Write(Request.ServerVariables("http_user_
          agent"))%>
</p>

<p> Your IP address is:
<%Response.Write(Request.ServerVariables("remote_addr"))%>
</p>

<p> DNS lookup is:
<%Response.Write(Request.ServerVariables("remote_host"))%>
</p>

<p> The method used is:
<%Response.Write(Request.ServerVariables("request_
          method"))%>
</p>

<p> Server Domain Name is:
<%Response.Write(Request.ServerVariables("server_name"))%>
</p>
```

```
<p> Server Domain Name is:
<%Response.Write(Request.ServerVariables("server_port"))%>
</p>

<p> Server Port is:
<%Response.Write(Request.ServerVariables("server_
            software"))%>
</p>

</body>
</html>
```

Listing 17-3 *Using the built-in* **Request** *and* **Response** *objects*

```
Your browser is: Mozilla/4.0 (compatible; MSIE 6.0; Windows NT
            5.1)
Your IP address is: 163.12.13.140
DNS lookup is: 163.12.13.140
The method used is: GET
Server Domain Name is: www.cs.mdx.ac.uk
Server Port is: 80
Server Software: Microsoft-IIS/5.0
```

The Request object can also be used in the collection of data from the user via a form. Just like in PHP there is a choice of using the GET or POST method for data transfer.

```
<html>
<body>

<form action="http://www.mdx.ac.uk/StudentApp.asp"
            method="get">
First name: <input type="text" name="first_name"
            size="30"><br>
Last name: <input type="text" name="last_name"
            size="30"><br>
<input type="submit" value="Request an Application">
<input type="reset" value="Clear form">
</form>
<%
dim first_name
first_name= Request.QueryString("first_name")
If fname<>"" Then
Response.Write ("Thank you " & first_name & "!<br/>")
```

```
Response.Write("Your request has been received")
End If
%>

</body>
</html>
```

Listing 17-4 Collecting and using information from a form using *GET*

In Listing 17-4 the GET method is used to access information from a user's Web form:

• The QueryString collection is used to get information from the user's form.
• The Write method is used to pass information back to the user's browser.

In Listing 17-5 the POST method is used in the form and the data is actually accessed in the ASP script with Request.Form.

```
<html>
<body>

<form action="http://www.mdx.ac.uk/StudentApp.asp"
            method="post">
First name: <input type="text" name="first_name"
            size="30"><br>
Last name: <input type="text" name="last_name"
            size="30"><br>
<input type="submit" value=" Request an Application ">
<input type="reset" value=" Clear form ">
</form>

<%
dim first_name
first_name=Request.Form("first_name")
If fname<>"" Then
Response.Write ("Thank you " & first_name & "!<br/>")
Response.Write("Your request has been received")
End If
%>

</body>
</html>
```

Listing 17-5 Collecting and using information from a form using *POST*

Other types of form can be used for input. Listing 17-6 shows how radio buttons can be used to select options then processed using ASP.

```
<html>

<% dim course
course=Request.Form("course")
%>

<body>
<form action="course.asp" method="post">
<p> Select desired course:</p>

<input type="radio" name="course"
<%if course="Multimedia" then Response.Write("checked")%>
value="Multimedia">Multimedia</input><br />

<input type="radio" name="course"
<%if course="Networks" then Response.Write("checked")%>
value="Networks">Networks</input><br />

<input type="radio" name="course"
<%if course="IT" then Response.Write("checked")%>
value="IT">IT</input><br /><br />

<input type="submit" value="Submit" />
</form>

<% if course<>"" then
Response.Write("<p>Your choice is: " & course & "</p>")
end if
%>

</body>
</html>
```

Listing 17-6 Using HTML radio buttons with ASP

Just like using PHP, it is possible to redirect users to new pages. PHP does this using the header function, such as:

```
header("Location: reg.html");
```

ASP can do the same thing with:

```
<%
Response.Redirect " http://www.cs.mdx.cs.uk "
%>
```

Listing 17-7 shows how this can be used within a page with the option to redirect to a specific page left to the user.

```
<%
if Request.Form("select")<>"" then
Response.Redirect(Request.Form("select"))
end if
%>

<html>
<body>

<form action="Application.asp" method="post">
<input type="radio" name="select"
            value="Application1.asp"> Application 1<br>
<input type="radio" name="select"
            value="Application2.asp"> Application
            2<br><br>
<input type="submit" value="Submit!">
</form>

</body>
</html>
```

Listing 17-7 *Using redirection in ASP*

You can, of course, combine features of the language you are using with ASP (in this case VBScript!) to come up with some novel ideas. Listing 17-8 shows how you could make a random redirection script using `randomize`, `rnd` and the redirection function within ASP.

```
<html>
<body>

<%
randomize()
r=rnd()
```

```
if r>0.5 then
response.write("<a href='http://www.mdx.ac.uk'>
            mdx.ac.uk</a>")

else
response.write("<a href='http://www.cs.mdx.ac.uk'>
            cs.mdx.ac.uk</a>")

end if
%>

<p>
Every Time you Refresh or Reload the page, it will display
            one of the following 2 links:
mdx.ac.uk or cs.mdx.ac.uk Chances are 50/50 for each.
</p>

</body>
</html>
```

Listing 17-8 *Random redirection*

The amount of actual data sent by a user can be checked using the **Request** object. Listing 17-9 shows how the number of bytes can be accessed.

```
<html>
 <body>

 <form action="question.asp" method="post">
 Type your question here:
 <input type="text" name="txt"><br><br>
 <input type="submit" value="Submit">
 </form>

 <%
 If Request.Form("txt")<>"" Then
 Response.Write("Your question is: " & Request.Form & "
            with a total bytes of: " &
            Request.Totalbytes)
 End If
 %>

 </body>
 </html>
```

Listing 17-9 *Finding the amount of data passed through a form*

The `Response` object can be used to manipulate cookies. This is shown in Listing 17-10.

```
<%
dim numvisits
response.cookies("NumVisits").Expires=date+30
numvisits=request.cookies("NumVisits")

if numvisits="" then
response.cookies("NumVisits")=1
response.write("Hello! This is your first time at our Web
          site.")

else
response.cookies("NumVisits")=numvisits+1
response.write("Hello again, the number of times you
          visited our Web site is" & numvisits)

end if
%>

<html>
<body>

</body>
</html>
```

Listing 17-10 *Using cookies with ASP*

Listing 17-10 demonstrates the creation of a welcome cookie using the Cookies collection.

When you run the above code for the first time, the following will appear in your browser:

```
Hello! This is your first time at our Web site
```

When you run the code for the second time you get a slightly different message:

```
Hello again, the number of times you visited our Web site is 2
```

Every time you run the script it will increase the number by 1.

As you have seen, ASP can be used in much the same way as PHP. It has many of the same features, which are just done in slightly different ways.

Web page:

```
http://www.w3schools.com/asp/asp_intro.asp
```

Checkpoint!

- Although you may like a particular scripting (or programing!) language, the chances are, if you started working professionally, you would have to look at someone else's code and even have to maintain it!
- Some alternatives to PHP are CGI, Perl and ASP.
- CGI needs special security considerations.
- Perl can be hard to follow but is similar to C. It was originally developed for text processing.
- ASP is a Microsoft technology for server side scripting, with similar ideas to PHP.

Test Yourself!

- If you have a suitable installation that includes either Perl or ASP, try out some of the example scripts.
- Can you take one of the PHP scripts in this book and convert it to the Perl or ASP equivalent?

17.1.4 Java

Although not strictly a Web development language, it's probable you will come across object-oriented Java being used somewhere! It's very useful for various tasks involving network and Web technologies as it has libraries and classes for most eventualities whether it is XML, Web services, databases, servlets, applets or writing full-blown servers.

Java normally uses a virtual machine to run its semi-compiled code, making it platform independent. However, there are now several virtual machines available as well as a native code compiler in the public domain called GCJ as part of the GNU project.

Listing 17-11 shows a simple Java program that, when compiled for its virtual machine, will run and output the `Hello World!` statement. This language can be used on the server or client side. It can also be used to write whole servers or mini-server applications as it has libraries with all the required network tools.

You may also have learnt of one way in which Java can be used with Web pages; that is, applets. Applets allow you to use the power of Java by being embedded within an HTML page.

```
class myHelloWorld
{
        public static void main(String args[])
        {
            System.out.println("Hello World!");
        }
}
```

Listing 17-11 *A first Java program*

To actually use an applet, like the one in Listing 17-12, you need to compile it with the Java compiler. In this case, because the class is called HelloApp, the file it is in should be called HelloApp.java and it should be compiled as:

```
javac HelloApp.java
```

```
// You need this for making an applet
import java.applet.*;
// This is for drawing
import java.awt.*;

// HelloApp is the the executable class
// Extends applet means that you will build the  code on
                the
// standard Applet class
public class HelloApp extends Applet
{

// This method is called when the applet is started
    public void init()
    {
    // nothing needed for this example
    }

// This method is called when the applet is finished
// For example, when the user goes to another page or exits
            the browser
    public void stop()
    {
        // nothing needed for this example
    }
```

```
// To actually draw on screen
// Overrides the empty Applet method so you couldn't call
            it
// "drawMessage" for example.

    public void paint(Graphics g)
    {
    //method to draw text on screen
    // The string is followed by x and y coordinates
        g.drawString("Hello Everybody!",10,20);
        g.drawString("Hello World!",10,40);

    }
}
```

Listing 17-12 A simple Java applet

The Java compiler then outputs a file, in this case called `HelloApp.class,` which can be kept with the HTML page that it is used with.

Listing 17-13 shows a simple HTML page that could have the embedded applet within it. This is a good way of harnessing the power of a full-blown programing language. The Java applet is downloaded by the client browser and run using a Java virtual machine, which is a plug-in to the browser. Usually, the code is kept in a 'sandbox' or separate area so that it cannot access local files and data, although full access can be granted if the user agrees. It can be kept in a cache so that when the page is revisited it can run immediately rather than being downloaded again.

```
<html>
<head>
    <title>My Hello World Applet</title>
</head>
<body>

<applet width=300 height=300 code="HelloApp.class">

</applet>

</body>
</html>
```

Listing 17-13 An HTML page for embedding the applet

Obviously, there are a few disadvantages to using applets:

- They have to be downloaded as separate byte code.
- The browser needs to have the Java virtual machine plug-in.
- The virtual machine needs to start running before code is executed.
- Code that is not granted the trust of the user can have limited use.

Web pages:

```
http://java.sun.com/
http://gcc.gnu.org/java/
http://www.javaworld.com/
```

17.1.5 JSP

JavaServer Pages is another means of generating Web-based content on a server system. This content could be HTML or XML for example. The technology itself allows Java code and pre-defined actions to be embedded into such content. XML tags, called JSP actions, exist that can be used to invoke built-in functionality. Interestingly, JSP is compiled into servlets by a JSP compiler, which can then additionally be compiled by a Java compiler or simply generate byte code for the servlet.

Web page:

```
http://java.sun.com/products/jsp/
```

17.1.6 The .NET Framework

This Microsoft system encompasses many different programing languages, providing a Web services strategy that can connect information, people, systems, and devices through software. In short, it integrates the Microsoft platform, providing a means to quickly develop secure software that has Web services capability for communicating across systems.

As we have seen, Web services utilize industry standard protocols such as XML and SOAP, the XML-based messaging service standardized by the W3C.

There are several key factors in the .NET framework:

- **Common Language Infrastructure (CLI)** This is a set of specifications for a runtime environment, including a type system, a base class library and a machine-independent intermediate code known as the Common Intermediate Language (CIL).
- **Common Language Runtime (CLR)** This provides a platform for running code that conforms to the CLI. Before CIL can be executed the CLR has to translate it usually via Just-In-Time compilation into native code.

The development languages included within the .NET framework are as follows:

- **C#** (C Sharp) This is the prime language of the .NET framework in that it reflects the underlying ideas most strictly. These include: managed code, primitives correspond directly to .NET types, garbage collection and many other features (classes, delegates etc.) also correspond to the .NET runtime.
- **C++** This is an upgrade from Microsoft Visual C++ 6.0 and includes much of the functionality, development tools such as the IDE and the use of libraries such as the Active Template Library (ATL) and Microsoft Foundation Class (MFC) libraries. As well as targeting the framework intermediate code it is possible to output native code.
- **Visual Basic .NET** (VB.NET) This is the development of Microsoft's popular Visual Basic into the .NET framework, although it is not backward compatible. It is a fully object-oriented version of the BASIC language.
- **J#** (J Sharp) This is based on a Java-type syntax and much of the functionality is provided by Visual J++ 6.0, although it is not targeted at a Java virtual machine. Instead programs that are developed use the .NET framework.
- **ASP .NET** This is a version of Active Server Pages that is based on the .NET framework. It varies significantly from the original ASP.

The .NET framework includes garbage collection capability and managed code, which helps to protect against such problems as memory leaks.

Web pages:

```
http://www.microsoft.com/net/
http://www.gotdotnet.com/
http://www.asp.net/
http://www.codeproject.com
```

17.1.7 C#

For a closer look at one of the main languages within the .NET framework a few examples are included here. In true computer science style let's begin with a `Hello World!` program!

```
public class HelloClass
{
    public static void Main( )
    {
        System.Console.WriteLine("Hello world!");
    }
}
```

Listing 17-14 C# `Hello World!` *program*

Listing 17-14 shows the simple `Hello World!` program written for C#. This program works on the command line and outputs the message. If you are familiar with Java you will notice the similarities!

```
<%@ WebService Language="C#" class="HelloService" %>
using System;
using System.Web.Services;
public class HelloService
{
[WebMethod]
public string SayHi(string Person)
{
    return "Hello, " + Person;
}
}
```

Listing 17-15 Simple Web service implementation

Listing 17-15 shows how easy it is to develop a Web service using C#. This particular Web service only returns a string but complex types can also be handled. These services are quite easy to set up and the methods used are handled as if they are local to the machine. SOAP, XML and HTTP are used in this process to transport information to the remote Web service.

Web pages:

```
http://www.c-sharpcorner.com/
http://www.csharphelp.com/
http://www.csharp-station.com/
```

17.1.8 Mono

Mono is an open source project from Novell. It intends to create an ECMA-compliant and .NET-compatible framework that includes tools, languages and support modules. These include C# and CLR. Mono is targeted at GNU/Linux, UNIX, Mac OS X and Windows-based systems. Although Mono includes much of the functionality of .NET and has been seen as its direct replacement in some cases this is not the entire truth as Mono functionality goes beyond this. It contains a large suite of software and tools for development as well as the MonoDevelop IDE as a front-end that ties together all the various features.

Web pages:

```
http://www.mono-project.com/
http://www.gotmono.com/
```

17.1.9 **IKVM**

A Java compiler exists for Mono and the .NET platform called IKVM (sometimes IKVM.NET). It contains a Java virtual machine implemented on .NET as well as Java class libraries and tools that enable Java and .NET interoperability. IKVM runs Java byte code directly on the Microsoft .NET framework or Mono unlike J#, which is just a Java-like syntax on. NET.

Web page:

http://www.ikvm.net/

Checkpoint!

- Java, although not strictly a scripting language, can still be very useful for Web applications – you could go as far as writing your own server!
- Java can actually be embedded in Web pages, as an applet.
- An applet is a good way of capturing the power of a full-blown programing language within a Web page.
- JavaServer Pages, like PHP and ASP, is a choice for scripting that you may wish to consider learning.
- The .NET framework is a Microsoft technology for providing a Web services strategy that can connect information, people, systems, and devices.
- One of the more interesting developments within the .NET framework is the language C#, which is useful for the rapid development of Web services.
- Mono is an open source project that attempts to create a .NET-compatible framework targeted at GNU/Linux, UNIX, Mac OS X and Windows-based systems.

Test Yourself!

- If you have Java installed on your machine, try out the example applet in this chapter by embedding it in a Web page.
- Using the Web links available, look into how useful C# would be for your Web application development.
- Consider installing .NET or Mono and experimenting with C#.

17.2 **CHAPTER SUMMARY**

- **Although you may prefer one language to work in, it's usually better to be aware and have experience of many.**
- **It's possible you may have to maintain or update a site that uses an unfamiliar technology.**
- **There are a number of languages that have made a mark on Web history and many are still around or evolving.**
- **These include CGI, Perl, ASP, Java, JSP and the .NET platform with its associated languages.**

Chapter Quiz

- The Wikipedia online encyclopaedia is a good first stop for most of the languages mentioned here and will include links and up-to-date history. Try looking up Perl and CGI and find the various support communities.
- Find out which languages are set up on your computer. It may be that if you installed a package such as XAMPP, you already have Perl included!
- If you prefer working with one language, why? There are online debates that point out the merits of one over another. See if you can find one and study what the various programmers think about their favorite!

Key Words and Phrases

.NET A Microsoft platform for software development

ASP Active Server Pages, a Web scripting language usually using VBScript

C# (C Sharp) One of the important languages available for .NET and Mono

CGI Common Gateway Interface

IKVM A Java compiler for the .NET and Mono platforms

J# (J Sharp) A Java-syntax-like language for the .NET platform

Java A notable object-oriented language with classes and functionality for Web development

JSP JavaServer Pages, a Web scripting language based around Java

Mono An open source software development platform compatible with .NET, available for many OS

Perl Practical Extraction and Report Language, a popular interpreted shell scripted language used for many types of application including CGI, Web and network

Useful Web Addresses

http://webref.info/

http://webreference.com/

18

This chapter's main focus is to acquaint the reader with the leading edge of Internet and Web technology, to give some idea of the currently active research areas and inspire interest for future study.

Here the use of the Internet and Web in the near future is looked at, using current research areas and directions as guidance. Several of these stand out as potential for study and are useful insights into just what could happen in our lifetimes.

Breakthroughs in electronics and commercial and military pressures drive the onward progression to astonishing speed, storage and processing power of modern systems. What was not possible only a few years ago has become within the reach of the average consumer.

While speculation about the future can sometimes be unhelpful, inspiration from current research trends can be useful to drive interest and study.

18.1 **INTRODUCTION**

There are many companies and universities with research departments that are investing large amounts of money into new areas of Web technology. It is sometimes hard to see what the future may hold in terms of development and direction, the reason being that sometimes advances come in unexpected areas that, in turn, lead to changes and improvements in others.

Necessity drives change and leads to advancement; for example, think how the speed of communication over the Internet has improved in only a short period. Whereas in 1998 you may have been using a 56 K dial-up modem with your computer, the norm is now likely to be a 2 Mbs broadband connection with up to 24 Mbs available in some places.

Figure 18-1 (data source: `http://www.zakon.org/robert/internet/timeline/`) shows the amazing pace of the growth of the Internet from the early 1990s to the start of the 21st century.

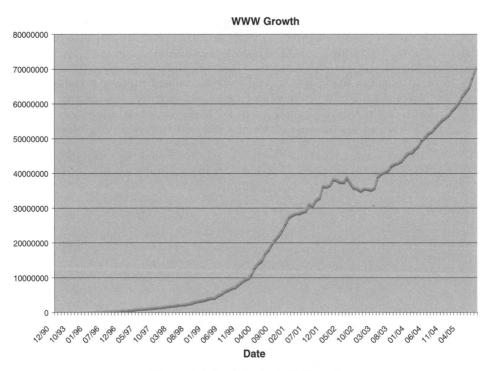

Figure 18-1   Graph showing WWW growth

This growth is expected to continue with the introduction of even faster communication methods such as the replacement of old cables with fiber optics and faster multiplexing techniques being employed.

18.2 LOOKING BACK: TIMELINE

1836 Telegraph patented by Cooke and Wheatstone

1858–1866 Transatlantic cable

1876 Telephone Alexander Graham Bell

1957 Sputnik launched by USSR

1962–1968 Packet-switched (PS) telephony networks

1969 Birth of the Internet First node at UCLA followed by Stanford Research Institute (Santa Barbara) and the University of Utah containing four nodes

1971 People communicate over networks Fifteen nodes present over 23 hosts on ARPANET. Email also invented

1972 Computer communications improved Public demonstration of ARPANET over 40 machines. The Internetworking Working Group (INWG) created to address need for establishing agreed protocols

1973 Global networking takes place International connections established to ARPANET: UCL (England) and Royal Radar Establishment (Norway). Ethernet ideas established, the basis of current LANs. Internet ideas come to light. Gateway architectures ideas developed, defining how large networks, sometimes containing different architectures, can be connected together

1974 Mode of transfer established as packets Transmission Control Program (TCP) specified. Packet networking becomes basis of Internet communication

1976 Networking becomes more accessible Queen Elizabeth sends out an email. Unix over network copy tools are developed and distributed with Unix

1977 Email in use, Internet established Number of hosts over 100. Email system THEORYNET provides mail to over 100 researchers in computer science

1979 Newsgroups USENET established, which is a collection of newsgroups, first Multi-User Dungeons and interactive adventure games

1982 TCP/IP DCA and ARPA establish TCP/IP for ARPANET

1983 Name server developed Name servers required as Internet gets larger and desktop workstations developed

1984 Internet continues to grow Number of hosts increases beyond 1000. Domain Name Servers introduced, allowing use of host names rather than numeric IP addresses

1986 Growth continues 5000 hosts, 241 newsgroups

1987 Further growth 28 000 hosts. Internet Relay Chat (IRC) developed

1989 Still increasing More than 100 000 hosts. First commercial electronic mail carrier. Internet Engineering Task Force (IETF) and Internet Research Task Force (IRTF) established

1990 Expansion of Internet continues 300 000 hosts, 1000 newsgroups. ARPANET ceases to exist. The World comes online (`http://www.world.std.com`), becoming first commercial provider of Internet dial-up access

1991 Modernization begins Commercial Internet eXchange (CIX) Association, Inc. formed after NSF lifts restrictions on commercial use of Net. Wide Area Information Servers (WAIS). Friendly User Interface to WWW established. World Wide Web (WWW) released by CERN (developed by Tim Berners-Lee)

1992 Multimedia changes face of Internet Number of hosts breaks 1 million. Newsgroups 4000. Term 'surfing the Internet' is coined by Jean Armour Polly

1993 WWW revolution begins 2 million hosts, 600 WWW sites. Business and media really take notice of Internet. US White House and United Nations (UN) come online. Mosaic browser takes Internet by storm

1994 Commercialization begins 3 million hosts, 10 000 WWW sites, 10 000 newsgroups

1995 Commercialization continues 6.5 million hosts, 100 000 WWW sites. New WWW technologies emerge: mobile code (Java, JavaScript, ActiveX), virtual environments (VRML)

1996 Browser Wars 12.8 million hosts, 0.5 million WWW sites. WWW Browser Wars begin, fought primarily between Netscape and Microsoft

1997 Further expansion 19.5 million hosts, 1 million WWW sites, 71 618 newsgroups

1998 E-commerce becomes established technology, together with electronic auctions. XML being developed

1999 Country domains continue to be registered; this year, Bangladesh (BD) and Palestine (PS). Balkans conflict creates first large-scale cyber-war

2000 Year 2000 problem affects some systems available through the Internet such as the US timekeeper. Internet infrastructure grows, IPv6 deployed and developed further

2001 Napster embroiled in litigation Radio stations broadcasting on Net face legal problems. Grid computing becomes newly emerging technology

2002 Blogs well established and commonplace. Broadband technology begins to take over from dial-up as means of connection from households

2003 SQL Slammer worm causes havoc and becomes fastest-spreading DoS attack ever. Followed by Sobig.F virus, fastest-spreading virus ever, and Blaster (MSBlast), probably most destructive so far

2004 Speed of transfer rate on Internet is broken with transfer of data at 7.57 Gbps between University of Tokyo and CERN center in Switzerland over a single TCP/IP link. Given this speed, it would be possible to send the contents of a complete DVD anywhere in the world in five seconds! Firefox browser version 1.0 is released

2005 74 million user sites reported online by Netcraft (compared with only 130 in 1993!)

2006 Data transmission speed over a 160 km link taken to 2.56 terabits per second by German and Japanese scientists. Fastest high-speed links, in comparison, carry data at 40 Gbits per second, which is about 50 times slower

Checkpoint!

- The Internet began in 1969.
- It initially started as a small research and academic network, known as ARPANET.
- It rapidly grew in node size and by 1973 global networking was taking place.
- 1977 saw emailing taking place and 1979 saw newsgroup servers established.
- 1982 saw the specification of TCP/IP for ARPANET and in 1983 name servers were developed.

- IRC was developed in 1987, and the WWW was established in 1991 by CERN.
- Multimedia and commerce developed beside the rapid growth of the Internet and WWW usage during the 1990s.
- The Browser Wars took place in the mid-1990s.
- Virus and hacking attacks increased in same period.
- Broadband steadily taking over from dial up during 2000 onwards.

Test Yourself!

- What is the fastest current broadband speed available for the Internet and how does it depend on location?
- What other methods of connection exist besides cable? How fast are they?
- What problems can you predict for continued expansion of the Internet? These could be economic, technical or social.

18.3 LOOKING FORWARD: THEMES FOR THE FUTURE

Below are several areas that will become even more prominent over the next few years:
- speed: faster and faster!
- Universal Access (UA)
- adaptability, reconfiguration and autonomic systems
- wireless
- computers in disguise
- biological and medical
- joined-up computing: converged databases and information; Grid computing
- multimedia.

18.3.1 Speed

At the top of the list is the continuing speed increase, which has already been mentioned.

18.3.2 Universal Access

The next item is Universal Access, the development of technologies to allow everyone to be enabled to use computers and the Internet to their fullest extent. Of course these technologies enhance our ability to gain information and, in the case of some disablement, this may help with the quality of life of an individual. There will be developments in Web adaptation technology, software that dynamically adapts Web pages to meet the needs of individuals with visual, motor, and print limitations.

18.3.3 Autonomic and Adaptable Systems

The field of autonomic systems is steadily becoming realized and applied to many applications. This area is involved with the development of systems that enable applications, systems, and entire networks to become more self-managing. Self-management involves four qualities: self-configuration, self-healing, self-optimization and self-protection. These attributes apply equally at the hardware and software levels, with electronic systems that are capable of reconfiguring their circuits under self- or programmable control.

In an age of viruses and other security concerns the ability to reconfigure, and in some sense to become polymorphic, means that a system can quickly adapt and respond to a threat.

18.3.4 Unwired

In recent years the usage of wireless computing has expanded and will continue to do so with many new ways of linking devices and systems. On a large scale, satellite-based Internet broadband connections are available now with speeds up to 2 Mbps. In the home and office, wireless LANs can be set up quite easily and Bluetooth allows links between device components at small distances. Wireless USB (WUSB) promises to unwire the remaining USB-connected devices such as printers, cameras, scanners and external hard drives with an initial target speed of 480 Mbps – the same as the USB 2.0 standard although, in theory, greater speeds of up to 1 Gbps should be possible.

Mobile devices can currently connect to the Internet using cell net services with WAP and GPRS.

Other embedded devices are likely to start using wireless technologies, particularly in consumer and industrial applications, in a similar way to how wired devices do at present for updating their software or passing on collected information.

18.3.5 Computers in Disguise?

Computers may become harder to actually label as such, as they become embedded into houses, goods and possibly clothing. The easiest way to link such devices into networks would be to use wireless links built into the circuits.

Radio Frequency Identification (RFID) allows goods, such as military items, library books or items in transit to sale points, to be tracked efficiently. It does this by becoming active when its built-in antenna picks up a specific frequency signal and then producing identification data.

18.3.6 **Biological and Medical**

Over the next few years there will be great advancements in biological and medical technologies, both genetically and through the interface of cybernetic implants. Even now various implants, such as pacemakers, can be communicated with over networks to reset them or alter their configurations. Just as for household goods, it will be possible to communicate with biologically embedded equipment to collect information about a patient or adjust settings for treatment application.

18.3.7 **Convergence**

As the amount of information stored about people increases, so does concern about the availability of that data to various parties for whom the information was not originally intended. The joining up of information sources allows tremendous power. For example, police and security services can use a wide range of information sources to track an individual, including cell phone communication, financial transactions, CCTV coverage, Internet-based communication and travel details (trains, planes, car parks...). Commercial organizations may share information about your purchasing habits, travel preferences and leisure interests or viewing/listening details to build a complete profile and therefore target you with appropriate advertising. The problem with all the sources mentioned is how secure they are as single sources, and even more importantly when they converge and become a threat to privacy.

Convergence also plays a role in the merging of server power as Grid computing. The major purpose of a Grid is to make efficient use of resources in order to solve problems. In essence, Grid computing allows you to unite pools of servers, storage systems, and networks into a single large system so you can deliver the power of multiple-systems resources to a single user point for a specific purpose. To a user, data file or application, the system appears to be a single, enormous computing system.

Another term you may hear of is Web 2.0, which generally refers to services that let people share information and collaborate online. The idea is that there is a more dynamic flow of information than in ordinary Web pages, similar to a desktop application. Examples of this kind of technology usually include RSS, Wikis and blogs, which all, to some extent, have the idea of convergence of information behind them. A lot of these new applications have a social aspect to them, binding together communities that share a common interest. The Wiki allows visitors to sites to add or edit information that is held there, in some cases without even the need to be a member! This becomes then a tool for collaborative writing. One of the problems of such an enterprise is the possibility of vandalism, the deliberate destruction of the content or twisting of the content toward some particular point of view. There are many issues that are controversial or divisive and therefore more subject to this kind of attention than others. Such vandalism can be quickly repaired by reverting to earlier edits and banning offenders' IP addresses.

Blogs provide the means for a person to write about their daily life; usually with a special interest slant from their occupation or interest. For example, a cyclist may write about their rides, equipment or exercise regime and another person may write about their passion for reptiles. This, again, tends to bind groups together and to converge not just the information, but the people themselves.

18.3.8 Multimedia

The speed increase of the Internet will lead to greater multimedia possibilities. TV will be broadcast over the Net, complete with more interactive services that allow the choice of programs and other streamed products. Vast TV archives will allow the selection of materials. Gaming is likely to improve and become even more of a networked phenomenon, with increasingly hyper-realistic worlds delivered to the computer user to interact with.

It will become normal to learn through electronic means, for example online classes and virtual environments for study.

18.3.9 Military

Virtual technologies will also play a role in the battle zone of the future for both the preparation of soldiers for conflict and, during such skirmishes, for the quick visualization of incoming information that needs to be acted on immediately. This may be the threat of incoming missiles, data retrieved from networked drones over the battlefield or current enemy (and friendly!) positions. With such information being vital to the modern military machine, computer and network systems around the conflict zone will be the direct target of attack too. This will occur through the enemy's own hackers, and weapons that destroy, or disrupt, such systems with electromagnetic pulses.

Conflicts around the world will create simultaneous wars within the Internet too. This has already been seen in several wars, such as the Iraq and Balkans conflicts. The Internet becomes a place not only where viewpoints can be aired, for example in the blogs of civilians caught in these zones, but where pro-active disinformation or disruption of enemy services can occur. Tactics can be used to target leaders within fighting nations, to discredit them and cripple finances.

Whole countries with particular policies and ideologies can also decide to filter and block information transfer with the outside world. This form of censorship has occurred in China where a firewall system has been erected. This blocks the flow of particular information, and is known as the Great Firewall of China.

Checkpoint!

- There are several main areas or themes that will touch the Internet; these include speed of transfer, Universal Access, adaptability, reconfiguration and autonomic systems, wireless, visibility and integration of systems, biological and medical, joined-up computing: converged databases and information; Grid computing and multimedia.
- Convergence of systems and information will lead to privacy and security implications.
- Computer systems will become more integrated into everyday appliances and less visible. Such systems will be able to connect to networks wirelessly.
- The Internet will continue to make an impact on social lives as well as political systems and conflicts.

Test Yourself!

- Look up the following phrases and terms, using a search engine or Wikipedia, and find out the latest advances: Wet wiring cybernetics, cyber-warfare, Grid computing, Universal Access HCI, reconfigurable networks, reconfigurable systems.

18.4 CHAPTER SUMMARY

- The Internet originated in academic research that involved the communication of computers between universities with only a very small number of nodes.
- The Internet has rapidly evolved and expanded with several successful offshoots and technologies.
- The Internet will continue to grow and get faster.
- Research will expand the Internet's and Web's capabilities into new areas.
- Several areas that will be expanded into are: Universal Access, autonomic and adaptive systems, embedded and Internet-connected systems (in devices, wearable and biological implants).
- Wireless technology will allow devices to become unwired at various levels, right down to single chip and small circuits.

■ Networks allow the convergence of information and databases, which can be construed as both a benefit and a hazard (to the individual's privacy).

■ Multimedia will be enhanced by fast networks that allow new levels of interactivity and a blurring of boundaries between real and computer-generated content.

■ Wars and conflicts will spill over into the Internet with battles over information, and disruption of electronic systems. Virtual and expert technologies will allow the assessment of complex situations that require immediate response.

Chapter Quiz

• Find some research groups on the Web that look at the future of Web technology and follow up on a thread of their ideas (such as Grid computing). How viable do think it is and what applications could it be put to?

• Find a Wiki site (for example Wikipedia) and study entries that people have made. If you find an entry on a current news item you may actually catch it in the process of being updated!

Key Words and Phrases

Adaptable/Adaptive The ability to adapt to a given situation

Autonomic The ability to self-manage or self-configure in some way

Bluetooth An industrial specification for wireless personal area networks (PANs)

Broadband Generally refers to data transmission where multiple pieces of data are sent simultaneously to increase the effective rate of transmission

Convergence The bringing together of two or more sources of information

Cybernetic Deals with investigating signal processing, decision making and control structures

Dial-up access An inexpensive but slow method of Internet access

Electromagnetic pulse The disruptive electromagnetic radiation from an explosion, especially nuclear, which results in damaging currents and voltage spikes in electronic systems

Embedded system A special-purpose computer system that is completely encapsulated within the device it controls

Expert system A program that contain rules that analyze information, allowing a recommended course of action to be chosen

GPRS General Packet Radio Service, a mobile data service available to users of mobile phones, providing data services at a moderate speed

Grid computing This is the usage of resources of many separate computers, connected by a network (usually the Internet), to solve large-scale computation problems

Reconfigurable A system that can alter the way its components or resources are used; this may be in terms of software, hardware or both

RFID Radio Frequency Identification, a way of tagging an object with a label that becomes active at specific times to impart its description

Universal Access The idea and research area of making information technology accessible to anyone, anytime and anywhere through inclusive design, customization, adaptation and adaptive systems

Virtual An item or complete world can be made to exist in software form. This virtual representation of an object can enhance or simplify a user's view of it

WAP Wireless Application Protocol, an open, international standard for applications that use wireless communication, for example Internet access from a mobile phone

Wiki A type of Web site that allows anyone visiting to edit, or add content, sometimes without the need to register

Useful Web Addresses

http://www.irtf.org/

http://www.alphaworks.ibm.com/

http://en.wikipedia.org/wiki/Internet

http://ieet.org/

http://www.cordis.lu/ist/fet/home.html

Glossary

.NET A Microsoft platform for software development

Absolute When applied to CSS positioning, refers to the specifying of exact coordinates for an element

Adaptable/Adaptive The ability to adapt to a given situation

Aggregator A type of software that retrieves syndicated Web feeds according to the preferred desires of its user. It can also be applied to Web sites or portals that offer this service

Animation The process of producing the illusion of motion, usually by flicking between image frames

Apache HTTPd A popular open source Web server for many platforms

Array In JavaScript, an object that contains data and has properties and useful methods such as pop, push and join. The data can be of mixed type

ASP Active Server Pages, a Web scripting language usually using VBScript

Assignment Variables take on a value

Associative array An array that utilizes keys (names) to access values rather than index numbers, making it more friendly to a user

Atom A file format based on XML and used for various tasks such as Web feeds and blogs

Attribute An optional item added to an HTML element tag that alters specific features

Autonomic The ability to self-manage or self-configure in some way

Blog A web-based publication of periodic articles that are updated on a regular basis

Bluetooth An industrial specification for wireless personal area networks (PANs)

Border Defines all aspects of a border

Broadband Generally refers to data transmission where multiple pieces of data are sent simultaneously to increase the effective rate of transmission

Browser Wars A name given to the competition between Web browsers for dominance in the marketplace, particularly in the late 1990s

C# (C Sharp) One of the important languages available for .NET and Mono

Cache A memory store that can hold frequently requested Web pages

CGI Common Gateway Interface

Character entity Certain characters can be encoded as HTML entities that can take their place. For example, '<' can be encoded as <

Class A template for an object

Client–server A model for network application architecture in which there are defined clients and separate servers

Client side Refers to operations that are performed by the client in a client–server relationship; in this context the side that has the browser operating

Concatenation Joining together two or more strings. In PHP this is done with the dot character

Constructor A method that is used to initialize an object

Convergence The bringing together of two or more sources of information

Cookie A small text file saved on the client, allowing information to be present over several pages of a Web site or to persist for a set period. Needs the client's browser to be cookie enabled to use them

Cross site scripting A type of exploit in which information from one context, where it is not trusted, is inserted into another, where it is, and thereby produces an attack

CSS Cascading Style Sheets, a language used to describe the presentation of structured documents in HTML and XHTML

Cybernetic Deals with investigating signal processing, decision making and control structures

Data islands A way of including information stored in an XML file inside an HTML page

Data type Like variables in programing and scripting, every field has an associated type that declares it to be numeric, string information or some other form of data

DBMS Database Management System, the actual engine that handles queries and organizes the data

Decrement To reduce a variable by a specific amount

Deprecated A feature of software or programing language is said to be deprecated when it is phased out or made obsolete

Destructor The last method to be called when an object is finally terminated, usually when there are no more references to it within a script or program

DHTML Dynamic HTML, the combination of HTML, CSS and JavaScript to enrich a Web site

Dial-up access An inexpensive but slow method of Internet access

Distro An abbreviation of distribution, usually applied to versions of Linux

Div Divides a page into logical sections

DOM Document Object Model, a standardized hierarchy for accessing parts of an HTML document

Driver A software component that provides an interface between different levels in a computer system, usually between software and hardware

DTD Document Type Definition, a document containing a set of rules that determine how an XML file should be structured. Can be inadequate for some XML documents, the alternative being the schema

Dynamic DNS service A service that keeps the DNS up to date with changes in a dynamic IP address that is associated with a server

Dynamic IP An IP that changes from time to time, due to the ISP

Dynamic Web page A page that reacts to events or user input and alters its output accordingly

Electromagnetic pulse (EMP) The disruptive electromagnetic radiation from an explosion, especially nuclear, which results in damaging currents and voltage spikes in electronic systems

Element An HTML tag usually comprises an opening tag, consisting of optional parameters/content, and a closing tag, which is not always required. An empty element contains no content or end tag but may still have attributes

Embedded system A special-purpose computer system that is completely encapsulated within the device it controls

Emphasis A way of adding a degree of impact to some text, such as making it bold or italic

Encapsulation The idea of containing data and methods within an object

Encryption The process of obscuring (or making hidden) information to make it unreadable without special knowledge

Entity This represents a class of objects such as people, cars or library. It possesses properties and is usually represented in the database as a table

Entity-relationship (ER) diagram A data model or diagram of high-level descriptions

Enumerated An ordered sequence, or list, of information

Escape sequence When special characters are included within a string a backslash is required before it, to enable it to be output. An example is the single quote

Event driven Using events to trigger execution of specific code

Expert system A program that contain rules that analyze information, allowing a recommended course of action to be chosen

Firewall A piece of hardware or software that prevents unauthorized use of the network by limiting access

Font A member of a typeface, a coordinated set of character designs, usually comprising an alphabet, a set of numerals and punctuation, although may also contains symbols too

Form A data collection mechanism within HTML that allows the design of various styles of input to suit most types of information

Frame A feature of HTML that allows layout to be broken into separate areas

FTP File Transfer Protocol is a standard for transferring files between computers

FTPS File Transfer Protocol over SSL, another version of FTP running over SSL/TLS for security

Function A section of script made separate to the main code, which can be called whenever is required. It may have a list of arguments in its function header and a return value

GPRS General Packet Radio Service, a mobile data service available to users of mobile phones, providing data services at a moderate speed

Grid computing This is the usage of resources of many separate computers, connected by a network (usually the Internet), to solve large-scale computation problems

Hacker A person who exploits a system's weaknesses in order gain entry

Heading A set of tags that specify font size and emphasis for different levels within a document

Horizontal rule A horizontal line that runs across the page; different types can be selected

HTML HyperText Markup Language, a markup language designed for the development of Web pages and other information viewable within a browser

HTTP HyperText Transfer Protocol, the main method of transferring information on the WWW, using a request/response mechanism

Hyperlink A reference to another document or resource

ID For giving a unique name to a particular division

IKVM A Java compiler for the .NET and Mono platforms

Image caching A technique for improving animation by loading and storing the images to be used ahead of the time of use

Increment To increase a variable by a specific amount

Inheritance The building of a new object based on an initial starting set of attributes and behaviors gained from another object

Inline frame A frame that can be set out with other text and graphics

Internet When written with a capital 'I', refers to the publicly available system of interconnected networks that communicate standardized protocols such as IP

Interpreter A software component that analyzes a script and acts on the commands given

Invoke To start, or call, a function to enable it to execute

IP Internet Protocol, one of the main protocols used on the Internet

Iterate To repeat a section of code

Iteration Repetition of a section of code

J# (J Sharp) A Java-syntax-like language for the .NET platform

Java A notable object-oriented language with classes and functionality for Web development

JSP JavaServer Pages, a Web scripting language based around Java

Keys and values These are used in associative arrays to make them more user friendly and accessible

LIFO Last In First Out, a data structure in which items are organized so that the last data added will be the first data to be output

Line break A formatting term that relates to where a sentence or paragraph is dropped to the next line down. In HTML this can occur when a <br> element is used

List An HTML element that allows the simple presentation of lists of information in unordered or ordered (enumerated) forms

Loop A section of code that is repeated

Loosely typed If a language is loosely typed, explicit declaration of a variable's type is not required

Margin For setting the amount of space between sides of an element's border and the parent element

Meta tag Gives information about the page rather than its content

Method An associated piece of code that, in JavaScript, is actually a function, attached to an object

Mono An open source software development platform compatible with .NET, available for many OS

MySQL A DBMS that is based on SQL and is multi threaded/multi user

Object [1] A collection of data and methods

Object [2] The principal idea behind the object-oriented programing paradigm; an encapsulation of properties (data) and behaviors (methods)

Object based/Object oriented A programing language that uses objects

OO/OOP Object-oriented programing is a particular model or paradigm, containing a specific approach and philosophy to coding

Operating system (OS) The system software responsible for management and interaction between applications and hardware

Operator A symbol that, when used with values, performs an action and usually produces a result

Padding For specifying the distance between sides of an element's content area and the border

Peer-to-peer A model for network application architecture in which each node can equally function as client or server

Perl Practical Extraction and Report Language, a popular interpreted shell scripted language used for many types of application including CGI, Web and network

Phishing The act of fraudulently trying to acquire sensitive information such as passwords or personal details

Plug-ins Additional software components that extend a browser's capability

Point size A relative measure of the size of a font, which used to have a more concrete meaning

Port An interface for communicating with a computer program over a network

Primary key A value that is used to uniquely identify a particular row or tuple in a table

Property A piece of data attached to an object

Protocol A standard, or set of rules and conventions, that enables communication between two systems. A protocol can exist in hardware terms as well as software

Query A specification of a problem to be calculated by a database

Radio button A type of input mechanism on an HTML form that usually selects one item from many others

Reconfigurable A system that can alter the way its components or resources are used; this may be in terms of software, hardware or both

Recursive Something that refers to itself

Redirection In PHP, a page can be redirected to another using the header( ) function

Regular expression A string that describes or matches a set of strings according to specific syntax rules

Relative When applied to CSS positioning, refers to specifying coordinates that are relative to the natural positioning of an element within a Web page

Reload The loading up of the same page from the Web rather than from the cache, for example in PHP with the header( ) function

RFID Radio Frequency Identification, a way of tagging an object with a label that becomes active at specific times to impart its description

RGB Red, green, blue, a model used for color definition

RPC Remote Procedure Call, a protocol that allows software on one machine to cause code to run on another

RSS Really Simple Syndication, a name for a group of file formats, based in XML, which are used for Web feeds and blogs

Schema Another way of providing a description for an XML document so it can be checked

Scope The containment of a variable within a specific area of code

Script Usually a program that is interpreted by a browser, e.g. JavaScript

Server An application that responds to requests; in the case of a Web server using HTTP protocol

Server side Refers to operations that are performed by the server in the client–server relationship. Typically the machine that runs the Web server or other server software

Session A way of making data persist over an entire Web site or several pages, which does not have to reply on cookies

SFTP Secure Shell (SSH) File Transfer Protocol, a more secure protocol for transfer of files

SMTP Simple Mail Transfer Protocol, the standard text-based method for transferring email

SOAP Simple Object Access Protocol, a standard for exchanging XML messages over a network

Spoofing The masquerading of a person or IP address to avoid identification

SQL Structured Query Language, the most popular database language used to retrieve and manipulate data in a relational DBMS

SSH Secure Shell, both a protocol and a command line program for connecting to remote computers

SSL Secure Sockets Layer, a secure protocol with encryption

Stack A LIFO data structure that usually has various functions (or methods) attached to it, allowing `push` (add an item) or `pop` (remove an item)

Static Web page A page that simply formats its output without change or reaction to the user or other information

String An object that is a collection of characters wrapped by quotes and also has properties and methods

Table [1] An HTML element that allows layout and data to be structured

Table [2] The basic component of a relational database, containing a number of rows (records) and fields (columns). Another name for a table in this context is a relation

Tag Part of an element in HTML, comprising `<tagname attributes>`; that is, a triangular less than, the tag name and a list of optional attributes. Usually, there is a closing tag such as `</tagname>` but it is not always required

TCP Transmission Control Protocol, a connection-oriented protocol with reliability, working at the transport layer level

Template In XSLT a template is a set of rules that activate when a specific node is matched

Text area An input area on an HTML form that can be sized as required

TLS Transport Layer Security, the successor to SSL with few differences between SSL 3.0 and TLS 1.0

Trojan horse A piece of software that enters a system by stealth and deposits or executes a piece of destructive code

TTL Time To Live, the length of time before a page expires

UDP User Datagram Protocol, a fairly minimal message-oriented transport layer protocol providing no guarantee for message delivery

Universal Access The idea and research area of making information technology accessible to anyone, anytime and anywhere through inclusive design, customization, adaptation and adaptive systems

Untyped Variables are untyped when they do not declare their type before use

Upload To copy or move files to the server from the client. Usually done as part of the development cycle of producing a Web site or application

URI Uniform Resource Indicator, an Internet protocol element that consists of a string of characters that indicate a name or address referring to a resource

URL Uniform Resource Locator, a standardized address for some resource on the Internet or elsewhere; it is a type of URI

Validate A process by which information is checked to determine its correctness

Virtual An item or complete world can be made to exist in software form. This virtual representation of an object can enhance or simplify a user's view of it

Virus A self-replicating program that spreads by inserting copies of itself into code or documents

WAP Wireless Application Protocol, an open, international standard for applications that use wireless communication; for example Internet access from a mobile phone

Web feed A periodically updated document that can contain summaries, blogs and links to longer articles

Web service A collection of protocols and standards used for exchanging data between applications

Wiki A type of Web site that allows anyone visiting to edit, or add content, sometimes without the need to register

WML Wireless Markup Language, the scripting language based on XML and used with WAP to create information pages similar to HTML

Worm A self-replicating program, similar to a virus, which is self-contained

WWW Refers to the World Wide Web, an information space and large subset of the Internet, where items (known as resources) are accessible via links

XHTML Extensible HyperText Markup Language, which has the same capabilities as HTML in terms of expression but is much more strict in syntax

XML Extensible Markup Language, a markup language that can be used to define other markup languages. Used to give meaning and a description of data rather than providing formatting as HTML would

XPath Used to address parts of an XML document by XSLT

XSL:FO XSL Formatting Objects, another way of transforming objects, converting description into presentation

XSLT XSL Transformations, an XML-based language used for transforming XML documents

Z-index Allows the setting of the depth of an element in relation to the overlapping of other elements

Zombie computer (abbreviated to Zombie) A computer that has been compromised by a hacker, virus or other source, so that it can perform tasks on behalf of the hacker

Sources

Books for further study:

Atkinson, Leon. *Core PHP Programming*, Prentice Hall, 2004. ISBN 0-13-046346-9

Bates, Chris. *Web Programming: Building Internet Applications*, John Wiley & Sons, Ltd, 2003. ISBN 0-47084-371-3

Castro, Elizabeth. *HTML for the WWW* (5th Edition), Peachpit Press, 2003. ISBN 0-321-13007-3

Dr-K, *A Complete Hacker's Handbook*, Carlton, 2002. ISBN 1-84222-724-6

Flanagan, David. *JavaScript: The Definitive Guide*, O'Reilly, 2002. ISBN 0-59600-048-0

Harold, Elliotte and Means, Scott. *XML in a Nutshell*, O'Reilly, 2004. ISBN 0-59600-764-7

Laurie, Ben and Laurie, Peter. *Apache: The Definitive Guide*, O'Reilly, 2003. ISBN 0-59600-203-3

McGrath, Mike. *PHP 5 in Easy Steps*, Computer Step, 2004. ISBN 1-84078-282-X

McGrath, Mike. *XHTML in Easy Steps*, Computer Step, 2003. ISBN 1-84078-125-4

Meloni, Julie. *Teach Yourself PHP, MySQL and Apache in 24 Hours*, Sams, 2003. ISBN 0-6723-2489-X

Meyer, Eric. *Cascading Style Sheets: The Definitive Guide*, O'Reilly, 2004. ISBN 0-59600-525-3

Mobily, Tony. *Hardening Apache*, Apress, 2004. ISBN 1-59059-378-2

Sharp, John and Jagger, Jon. *Microsoft Visual C# .NET Step by Step*, Microsoft Press, 2003. ISBN 0-7356-1289-7

Sherry, Phil. *Mac OS X Web Development*, Friends of Ed., 2004. ISBN 1-59059-336-7

Wang, Wallace. *Steal this Computer Book 3*, No Starch Press, 2003. ISBN 1-59327-000-3

Williams, Hugh and Lane, David. *Web Database Applications with PHP and MySQL*, O'Reilly, 2004. ISBN 0-59600-543-1

Index